With the poignant accuracy of a scholar and the  Preston challenges Christians to look at the LGB level. Specifically, he drives home the point tha aren't nameless faces, but real individuals that G voice, deserves to be listened to, and needs to be valued. I'm thankful Preston has pushed us further into the tension of grace and truth.

CALEB KALTENBACH, lead pastor, Discovery Church; author, *Messy Grace*

This is a remarkable book. The tone overflows with love, compassion, and grace. Preston is an exceptional biblical scholar, and as such, his exegesis of Scripture is excellent. As I read, I kept thinking, "Preston really loves the LGBTIQ Community." This book will be a resource at Transformation Church.

DERWIN L. GRAY, lead pastor, Transformation Church; author, *The High Definition Leader; Building Multiethnic Churches in a Multiethnic World*

In his new book, *People to Be Loved*, Preston Sprinkle serves as a trustworthy guide through the debated passages of Scripture that relate to homosexuality. His thoughtful, balanced reflection on the arguments on both sides, as well as his willingness to share with the reader what he has concluded, reflect the kind of "convicted civility" that is often lacking in any discussion of the topic. Sprinkle's approach also models for the Christian a commitment to respectful engagement with others with whom you may disagree.

MARK A. YARHOUSE, PsyD, Professor of Psychology and Rosemarie S. Hughes Endowed Chair, Regent University; author, *Understanding Gender Dysphoria: Navigating Transgender Issues in a Changing Culture*

In a conversation polarized by hate, fear, and misunderstanding, Preston Sprinkle steps into the fray with a thoughtful, articulate, nuanced, humble, and courageous take on the current debate over sexuality and the Bible. His particular cocktail of professor, pastor, and down-to-earth regular Joe is an intoxicating blend that makes for good reading and even better learning. I'm thankful for Preston and this book.

JOHN MARK COMER, pastor for teaching and vision, Bridgetown: A Jesus Church in Portland

Preston Sprinkle has a deep reverence for Scripture and a great love for people, meaning this book is not just accessible and lively, but rewarding and compassionate. It deserves to be widely read.

SAM ALLBERRY, associate pastor, St. Mary's Church, Maidenhead, UK; author, *Is God Anti-Gay?* and *James For You*

Preston Sprinkle does conservative Christians a needed service by guiding them into the complexity of biblical interpretation, sexual ethics, and compassionate listening. His meticulous research is applied with an even hand as he affirms and critiques arguments coming from both affirming and nonaffirming Christians, all the while offering wise pastoral counsel to straight and gay alike.

MEGAN K. DEFRANZA, author, *Sex Difference in Christian Theology: Male, Female and Intersex in the Image of God*; visiting researcher, Boston University School of Theology and the Institute for the Bio-Cultural Study of Religion

With honesty, empathy and all-too-uncommon grace, Preston Sprinkle contributes brilliantly to the ongoing conversation our culture is having regarding Christianity and sexuality. Preston has done a rare thing: addressing controversial issues and dealing with perplexing questions in a way that is fair and gracious to all participants. This is a refreshing and immensely helpful book in navigating the deep waters of sexual ethics. I highly recommend it!

MIKE ERRE, pastor, First Evangelical Free Church of Fullerton

Amidst the arguing at fever-pitch comes Preston Sprinkle and *People to Be Loved*. I am grateful for his thoughtful perspective and great desire to love at the risk of being both criticized and marginalized. I pray more people will opt into relationship and conversation with one another in the way Preston has and find deeper friendship and understanding.

ALAN CHAMBERS, author, *My Exodus: From FEAR to Grace*; www.AlanChambers.org

Powerful and accessible, *People to Be Loved* engages top scholarship from all sides of this conversation in a way that's easy to read and down-to-earth, respectfully avoiding straw men while exploring Scripture with conviction and grace. Moreover, Preston models a posture for straight Christians to allow the abuse and mistreatment gay people have experienced to break and reshape us, to let their beauty and dignity draw our eyes to Jesus, and to "front love" as we seek to embody the sacrificial love of our King for his world.

JOSHUA RYAN BUTLER, pastor, Imago Dei Community (Portland); author, *The Skeletons in God's Closet*

People to Be Loved brings the right posture to one of the most culturally polarized issues of our time. Navigating this topic with grace and conviction, Preston Sprinkle handles a complex topic in a very helpful way.

GABE LYONS, *Q, Founder*

PEOPLE TO BE LOVED

WHY HOMOSEXUALITY IS NOT JUST AN ISSUE

PRESTON SPRINKLE

ZONDERVAN
REFLECTIVE

ZONDERVAN REFLECTIVE

People to Be Loved
Copyright © 2015 by Preston M. Sprinkle

ISBN 978-0-310-51966-9 (ebook)

Requests for information should be addressed to:
Zondervan, 3900 *Sparks Dr. SE, Grand Rapids, Michigan 49546*

Library of Congress Cataloging-in-Publication Data

Sprinkle, Preston M., 1976-
    People to be loved : why homosexuality is not just an issue / Preston M. Sprinkle.
        pages   cm.
    Includes bibliographical references.
    ISBN 978-0-310-51965-2 (softcover)
        1. Homosexuality—Biblical teaching. 2. Homosexuality—Religious aspects—
    Christianity. I. Title.
    BS680.H67S674   2015
    261.8'35766—dc23   2015031812

Published in association with the literary agency of Wolgemuth & Associates, Inc.

Cover design: *Dual Identity*
Cover photo: © *Anton Zabielskyi, Glebstock/premier.shutterstoc.com*
Interior design: *Kait Lamphere*

Printed in the United States of America

22 23 24 25 26 27 28 29 30 31 32 /TRM/ 50 49 48 47 46 45 44 43 42 41

CONTENTS

Foreword by Wesley Hill. 7

Preface. 9

1: "MY NAME WAS FAGGOT" 13

2: HOLY OTHERNESS: *Is Male and Female Sexual*
Difference Necessary for Marriage?. 27

3: FROM *SEX IN THE CITY* TO *LAW & ORDER*:
Homosexuality in the Old Testament. 41

4: RATED R:
Homosexuality in Judaism and Greco-Roman Culture. . . . 55

5: WHOM WOULD JESUS LOVE? *Homosexuality and the Savior* . 69

6: FALL SHORT OF GOD'S GLORY: *Homosexual and*
Heterosexual Sins in Romans 1. 87

7: LOST IN TRANSLATION:
Homosexuality in 1 Corinthians 6:9 and 1 Timothy 1:10 . . 103

INTERLUDE: A SUMMARY. 121

8: "BORN THIS WAY": *Does God Make People Gay?*. 127

9: GAY AND CHRISTIAN: *Can Someone Be Both?* 141

10: ON THE SIDE OF THE ANGELS:
What Does Christian Faithfulness Look Like? 157

Afterword: The Challenge 177

Appendix: Five Affirming Interpretations of Romans 1 . . . 187

Notes 193

For Matt, Brian, Nick, Julie, Nate, Wesley, Lesli,
and the millions of other Christians
who daily wrestle with their Christian faith
and same-sex sexuality.

FOREWORD

WESLEY HILL

I know a Christian scholar who for many years has participated in a weekly meeting with two rabbis. The three men's purpose is to study Scripture together. Initially their meetings focused on the Hebrew Bible, a text that both Jews and Christians treat as inspired and trustworthy. Later, as they went on, they moved to the New Testament.

Hearing about their times together, you might be tempted to focus on all the ways the Scriptural study could go badly. Convinced of the rightness of their own positions, each man might have assumed he had nothing to learn from the others. Or, if he kept an open mind, each man might have treated the others' views as historical or sociological curiosities, much in the way one might catalog a new animal species, without being willing to have his own views challenged and expanded in the process. But, it seems, none of these things has happened. At least for these three men, studying Scripture together in the face of deep division has proved, again and again, to be worth continuing.

I found myself thinking about these weekly meetings as I read Preston Sprinkle's book on homosexuality and Christian faith. I made this connection, first, because of the book's down-to-earth, conversational style. In the pages to come, you'll encounter a voice that is warm, self-effacing, and poignantly honest about ongoing uncertainty and open questions. Reading the book feels like sitting down and sharing coffee with the author.

But second, I also thought of those meetings because of their apparent futility. If Jewish-Christian dialogue seems, at times, too fraught to be viable in the long term, how much more might we be tempted to think something similar about the debates among

Christians over the Bible and homosexuality! If ever there were a futile conversation, we may say to ourselves, this is it. And yet, like the rabbis meeting with the Christian scholar to read the Bible, Preston's book persists in believing that there is value in opening the Scriptures—yet again—and reading them for insight and instruction. In the face of persistent, apparently intractable disagreement, Preston returns to the Bible and interprets it afresh and invites us to join him.

But there's a third reason I think of those weekly meetings when I read this book, and that's because they were meetings *with* others who see matters differently. Rather than a Christian meeting with other Christians, or rabbis meeting with other rabbis, the weekly Bible study between the Christian scholar and the two rabbis is a time for those who disagree to sit around a table together. And that, I think, is the model for what Preston attempts here. On almost every page that follows, you'll see Preston trying to interact fairly, charitably, and deeply with his fellow scholars and authors. He not only quotes their words, he seeks to uncover their passions and worries. He tries to respect their positions but also read between the lines to address their larger, underlying concerns. He admits when they seem to have stumped him, and he freely gives credit when his own points of view depend on their ground-clearing efforts.

As a gay Christian myself, I'm intensely interested in what Preston's written here. I don't agree with him on everything (as a catholic-minded Anglican, I would have liked to see him, for instance, putting Augustine's teaching on the three goods of marriage—including procreation—and the New Testament texts into more conversation with each other), and I'd say several things differently.

But more than anything, I admire the *posture* of this book. It models how to have a fruitful discussion of homosexuality, the Bible, and pastoral care in the church today. If more of our conversations with our fellow believers took their cues from what Preston has written here, the church would be a healthier, holier place.

I hope you will read on. And, perhaps like the rabbis who meet weekly with the Christian scholar, I hope you'll read this book with others with whom you disagree. Preston's book sets the table for us, and I hope you'll take your seats and open your Bibles with him.

PREFACE

I used to sleep like a baby. If a dump truck blew through my living room, I wouldn't wake up. But I don't sleep as well as I used to. I frequently wake up way before my alarm, haunted by the pain that Christians have caused gay people. Sometimes I hit the pillow exhausted but am instantly stirred up by a rush of fear that I have interpreted the Bible incorrectly—and hurt people by doing so. I can no longer read what the Bible says about homosexuality from a distance. I now see real names, beautiful faces, and complex stories splashed across its pages.

This book is by far the most difficult one I've written. If all I did was to study a bunch of Bible verses, it would have been much easier. But as I began researching for this project, I made it a point to spend half my time in books and the other half in the lives of gay people. And my life will never be the same. I have made many unexpected friends whose stories have seeped down into my bones.

I guess that some of you may already be agitated. All this talk about listening to gay people makes you wonder where I "stand." So let me tell you up front: I stand on truth and I stand on love. Figuring out how to stand on both is hard work. The question of homosexuality defies simple answers, so I refuse to give thin answers to thick questions in the pages that follow. If you want quick, easy answers, or if you just want me to affirm all of your assumptions— whatever they may be—then this book isn't for you. There are plenty of books out there that will reaffirm your presuppositions. In this book, we're going to think. We're going to study. We're going to listen to the pain and joy of real people who are gay. We're going to hold our views with a humble heart and an open hand—inviting God to correct us where we have been wrong. We are going to do our best to lay aside our assumptions and genuinely seek to know what the Bible, not our tradition, says about homosexuality.

Some of you may affirm same-sex relations while others may not. I am writing this book for both of you—for all of us—for anyone who cares to know what the Bible says (and doesn't say) about homosexuality. This book is written for Christians, those who consider the Bible to be authoritative. Although I am a biblical scholar by profession, I am also a pastor who cares about people, and an ordinary dude who likes to surf, play baseball, and watch action-packed movies that get bad reviews. I have a PhD in New Testament and Judaism, and yet I didn't read a book from cover to cover until I was seventeen. I am not a natural-born geek. I happened to have become one because I fell in love with learning.

All that is to say, I sought to make the tone of this book more conversational so that anyone interested in the topic will understand it. The professor side of me cringes at books that are built on thin or sloppy research, so I've included many endnotes and an appendix for those of you who wish to go deeper into the subject.

The first two thirds of this book wrestle with what the Bible says about homosexuality, while the last third addresses other questions that come up in the discussion. I am well aware that some people are tired of bantering around about the so-called "clobber passages" in the Bible that mention homosexuality. I can see why people feel this way, but as I've read many books on the subject, I still see a great need for a clear, thorough, and fair-minded study of Scripture. Some books I've read seem like they are using the Bible to justify their previously held beliefs about homosexuality. They feel more like a defense of a particular view rather than an exploration of what the Bible actually says—being willing to go where the text leads, even if it leads them to change their view. There is no such thing as an unbiased reading of the Bible. We all bring assumptions and presuppositions to the text. But as my philosopher friend Jamie Smith recently put it, it is possible to give the text a "fair reading"—a reading that recognizes one's assumptions and invites others to point them out.

I have tried to read the Bible as fairly as I know how with regard to homosexuality. I have listened to people on both sides of the debate, those who affirm same-sex relations and those who do not. To my surprise, I have made many friends with people who hold very different views of homosexuality. Perhaps it's because, as you'll see, I have discovered that the Bible challenges people on *both* sides of the question. It has certainly challenged me.

Whenever I write a book, I seek to do it in the context of a diverse community. I invite feedback and pushback on every sentence, and with this book, I cast the net broadly. There are dozens of people whose voices can be found hidden behind every word, and this book would have been different if I just sat in a room and wrote it by myself. I didn't. This book reflects an ongoing conversation with many people about the Bible, the church, and homosexuality.

The word *ongoing* is important. This book is not my last word on homosexuality, but my first word (in print, at least). It doesn't represent my codified, unchangeable, etched-in-stone declaration of what I have and always will believe about homosexuality. This book is a contribution to a complex conversation about a difficult topic. I would be in sin if I had the audacity to declare that I have it all figured out. But before God and before you, I pray that the pages that follow give honor to my Lord and King who does have it all figured out.

Since this book is the fruit of communal discussion, I have many people to thank. Several people read through all, or portions of, this book: Joey Dodson, Roy Ciampa, Sam Roberto, Mark Yarhouse, Jeff Cook, and I am especially thankful for the many gay and lesbian readers who have offered incisive feedback, especially on my language, tone, and ignorant assumptions: Matt Jones, Nathan Collins, Julie Rodgers, Bill Henson, Brian Gee, Wesley Hill, Bill

Henson, and Nick Roen. Several others, who didn't read the manuscript but whose stories had a significant impact on my thinking, include Lesli Hudson-Reynolds, Justin Lee, Eve Tushnet, and many others whose testimonies have forever shaped my life. I don't know if I would have been able to finish this book were it not for the constant encouragement of my pastor and friend Bren Angelos and my friend Brad Heinrichs, who let me use his mountain cabin to finish writing this book. Most of all, thanks to my wife, Christine, and my four kids who have seen this book take a toll on my life.

Many thanks also to the ninety students in my class: "Homosexuality, the Bible, and the Church" (Spring 2014), as you listened to me test-drive an earlier version of this book. Also, there were many people who interacted deeply with my ongoing series of blogs on the topic. There are too many names to remember, but Julie Perez, Joe Tobias, and David "Ford" Sinclair stand out. None of you would let me get away with any unthoughtful remark—and I am a better person for it. I am sorry for some of the offensive things I have said, and I am very grateful for your critical feedback.

I've given several talks on homosexuality to diverse audiences, and, by God's grace, I'm still alive. In particular, the AudioFeed Music Festival in Champaign, Illinois (July 2014), the Young Adults Conference at First Baptist Church in Arkadelphia, Arkansas (March 2014), and the Clydehurst Family Camp somewhere in the boonies of Montana (August 2014) proved to be incredibly helpful in shaping my thinking. Thanks are also due to Denny Burk, Wesley Hill (again), and Owen Strachan for your stimulating interaction in our seminar on sexual orientation at the Evangelical Theological Society's Annual Meeting in San Diego (November 2014).

CHAPTER ONE

"MY NAME WAS FAGGOT"

Eric Borges was raised in a conservative Christian home. At a young age, Eric realized he was different, and other kids at school let him know it. He endured relentless and ongoing bullying throughout kindergarten, and the rest of his elementary school years were tarnished with horror. "I was physically, mentally, verbally, and emotionally assaulted on a daily basis," recalls Eric. This led to chronic migraines, debilitating depression, suicidal thoughts, and a whole host of other mental and physical problems. "My name was not Eric, but Faggot. I was stalked, spit on, and ostracized." On one occasion, he was assaulted in a full classroom, and nobody intervened, not even the teacher who was present. Throughout school, Eric was treated like a monster, a sub-species of the human race. "I was told that the very essence of my being was unacceptable. I had nowhere safe to go"—not even church.

In his sophomore year of college, Eric came out to his parents; he told them he was gay. After performing an exorcism on their son, they told him, among other things, that he was "disgusting, perverted, unnatural, and damned to hell." Later that year, they kicked him out of the house. Eric shared his story on YouTube in 2011. In the video, he encouraged other youth who have had similar experiences that "it gets better."[1] Having suffered in a hissing cauldron of ridicule and torment, Eric wanted to help others to find comfort and hope to pull them through the pain.

One month later, Eric killed himself.

I wish Eric's story was an anomaly, but it's not.[2] Having listened to countless testimonies and looking at startling statistics, I am disheartened to say that the Christian church has often played an unintended yet active role in pushing gay people away from Christ. Sometimes away from Christ and into the grave.

The ones who don't kill themselves often end up leaving the church. But here's the thing: most people who are attracted to the same sex don't end up leaving the church because they were told that same-sex behavior is wrong. They leave because they were dehumanized, ridiculed, and treated like an "other."

An old Baptist pastor recently told me, "People will always gravitate to where they are loved. And if they don't find love in the church, they'll go elsewhere." He is right. Most of my gay and lesbian friends have diverse stories, but they are all held together by a common thread that looks a lot like Eric's:

I was raised in the church, but everyone knew I was different.
I was made fun of, mocked, and made to feel like a monster.
When I came out, I was rejected, so I found another community where I was accepted.

A gay friend of mine leads a Bible study for gay and lesbian people at his college campus. He recently told me that all the participants of his study are hungry to know God's Word but they are too scared to go to church. My friend didn't say "uninterested" or "turned off" or "too busy." He said "scared," as in *frightened*. They feared they would be harassed or harmed, beat up or bullied—verbally or physically—if they stepped across the holy threshold on Sunday. Another thing they all had in common is that they had all tried to kill themselves at one point. The last place they think they would find good news worthy of life is inside the church. So they remain outside—hungry to know God's Word yet terrified of people inside the church.

Learning about Eric's story and many others like it has caused me to revisit the question of homosexuality. Like many of you, I grew up inheriting a Christian tradition that told me homosexuality is a sin. And for many years, I never questioned this assumption. But after hearing innumerable stories that reflect Eric's, I began to ask myself, *Am I sure we've got this one right?* If the gospel is good news, and the church is to be the light that warms the world with this good news, then why are gay people leaving the church in search of better news? If the gospel is not good news for gay people, then it's not good news.

As I read the Gospels, I see people drawing near to Jesus (Luke 15:1). All kinds of people. Broken people, sinful people, marginalized people, people who are clean and unclean, pure and impure. Some are befriended. Others are confronted. All of them are loved. And none walk away wanting to kill themselves. The people who are most repelled by Jesus are the religious hypocrites. As I think about the question of homosexuality, I see many gay and lesbian people repelled by the church. And so I am asking myself, *Why?*

Has the church handled the question of homosexuality with Christlike love? Are we sure we've understood what the Bible *really* says about same-sex relations? As you read on, you'll see that the answer is both yes and no.

"THE BIBLE IS *VERY* CLEAR"

I was sitting next to a couple on a plane and quickly found out that they were Christians. When I told them I was a writer, they asked me what I was currently working on. "Well ..."—I'm always nervous about dropping the homosexuality bomb with people I don't know—"I am actually writing a book about homosexuality."

The husband immediately looked down and shook his head back and forth slowly while confidently asserting, "The Bible is *very* clear. It's *very* clear. There's no debate. Homosexuality is *wrong*." I didn't know what to say, so I cowardly nodded with apathetic agreement, "Hmmm ... uh ... ya ..." I didn't want to get into the whole debate, but he kept on preaching, "It's *very* clear ... there is no debate."

I found the statement odd since there actually is a debate, a *massive* debate, regardless of how clear he thinks the Bible is. In any case, I couldn't help myself. The opportunity was ripe to gather some evidence. I've often wondered whether Christians who "know for a fact" that homosexuality is wrong could name the passages where the Bible says so. In most cases, they can't. But I wanted to see if this person was different. For him, the Bible's condemnation of homosexuality seemed about as clear as the deity of Christ or the existence of God. "It's *very* clear."

So I asked, "Umm ... which passages are you talking about?"

"Huh?" He was taken aback.

"Which passages are you talking about?" I repeated. "You know, the ones that you say are very clear about condemning homosexuality?"

Silence. Frustration.

"It's *very* clear!" he proclaimed.

"Yes, I know," I cordially agreed. "But which passages are *very* clear?"

"Well ... umm ... uh ... I don't know. But I've studied them. I have. They are there. And they are *very* clear."

And maybe they are. Maybe he had a memory lapse. Maybe he had studied those passages in great detail but through the rest of life's worries, those passages were pressed down in the far reaches of his memory. I get it. I've been there. I still find it odd, however, that most Christians know "for a fact" that homosexuality is wrong—there's no debate, no discussion, the Bible is *very* clear. But those same Christians oftentimes can't name the passages where the Bible refers to homosexual relations.

You may think, "Well, that's because there are too many passages to remember! The Bible says it's wrong in so many places that there's no way anyone could possibly keep track of them all."

Actually, there are only six.[3]

Six passages.

Six passages in the Bible that seem to say that homosexual behavior is wrong.

And even with those six, there is a massive debate about whether those passages can apply to monogamous, consensual, loving gay relations.

Because that's the real question Christians are asking. The question is not about whether gay sex outside marriage is wrong. It's not about whether soliciting a same-sex prostitute or sleeping around with several partners is wrong. All genuine Christians believe these are sin. The question is whether two men or two women can date, fall in love, remain sexually pure before their wedding day, and commit to a life-long, consensual, Christ-centered, self-giving, monogamous union.

So the question is: Does the Bible really address—and prohibit—these types of relations?

MY JOURNEY

For much of my life, I was that guy on the plane. I believed that homosexuality was wrong; I just didn't know why it was wrong and where it said so. My beliefs stood firmly in midair with no reasoning, no rationale, no biblical foundation. So I began to study.

At the beginning of my journey, I set out to study what the Bible says about homosexuality. And to be honest, I thought this part of my study would take a few weeks. After all, my tradition had already concluded that same-sex relations are wrong, and so I only needed to find the verses that supported this tradition. But as I started to study those verses, I quickly found that the discussion is not so simple. You may find it shocking, but most scholars who have written books about homosexuality in the last forty years have concluded that the Bible does not condemn consensual, monogamous, same-sex relations.[4] The debate is not about what the Bible says. That much is clear. The debate is over what the Bible means.

I've always been eager to test my traditional beliefs by Scripture. After all, I'm a product of the Protestant Reformation, which upholds Scripture—not tradition—as our ultimate authority. Sometimes the church's tradition needs to be corrected and reformed by Scripture. For many years, the church stood on the wrong side of the question of slavery. Many Christians held the Bible in one hand while they whipped their slaves with the other. Christians have also stood on the wrong side of science. The famous Christian astronomer Galileo was excommunicated and imprisoned for trying to overturn the church's traditional belief that the sun revolves around the earth. Yet we are all thankful that Galileo had the nerve to question tradition—even one that was written in stone.

I underwent a similar shift in my own thinking a few years ago when I set out to study what the Bible says about warfare and violence. As a reformed evangelical and son of a Marine, I always assumed that it's perfectly okay for Christians to kill if it was during a war or to save an innocent person. It seemed like a no-brainer, and my tradition had all but unanimously affirmed it. But when I studied what the Bible actually says about violence and warfare, I ended up advocating—to my own surprise—absolute nonviolence, even though this goes against the tradition I grew up with.[5]

All that to say, I am quite eager to let the Bible challenge tradition. It's not that tradition is bad or doesn't carry any authority. I think it does. But all evangelical Christians agree that the Bible stands over tradition as our ultimate authority.[6]

So when I began my study a few years ago, I came before God and said, "If my tradition has been wrong about homosexuality, then please show me through your Word and give me the courage to proclaim the truth." I have prayed that prayer several times throughout this study, and I encourage you to do the same. If the Bible is our ultimate authority, and if tradition is subject to error, then we all should eagerly drag our traditions to the foot of Scripture and mandate a re-evaluation. That's what "reformation" means. It means that we submit our traditions to the authoritative Word, even if it compels us to reconfigure long-held beliefs.[7]

I'm not trying to create a spiritual force field around my interpretation, as if to say, "Since I prayed about it, I must be right." I only share this with you to say that I have genuinely tried to approach this discussion as fairly and honestly as I know how. Yes, of course, we all have biases and presuppositions that we bring to the text. I'm well aware of that, and you should be too! But I also believe we have the ability to identify our assumptions, invite people to challenge those assumptions, consider the strengths and weaknesses of alternative interpretations, and prayerfully and communally interpret the text of Scripture in a responsible and humble manner—always being open to the possibility that we could be wrong. Before God and before you, I can say that I've tried to do that with the question of homosexuality.

Over the last few years, I have devoted countless hours to studying the Scriptures with an open mind. I have read piles of books and articles on the topic from both sides of the debate. I have researched the ancient Near Eastern and Greco-Roman context in which the Bible was written. I have looked at the ever-evolving conclusions of psychologists, counselors, and medical researchers. But studying the issue of homosexuality is not enough. Like flying an airplane with only one wing, reading about homosexuality is necessary—but dangerously insufficient.

We need to listen to gay and lesbian people.

I have enjoyed countless hours of conversations with gay and lesbian people, some who share my Christian faith and others who don't. I have invited their input and pushback through blogs, emails, Facebook conversations, and over many meals, which usually involve spicy food and good beer. Throughout my study, I have made many gay friends who have solidified my belief that homosexuality is not about an issue. It is about people.

With some topics, it's easy to keep the Bible at arm's length from real people. Plenty of writers have done this with homosexuality. But I can't, and I won't. When I read Leviticus 18, Romans 1, and other passages that talk about same-sex relations, I no longer see words on a page but people with a story—people whom I know and love.

I see Jeremy, Matt, David, and Andrew. I see Laura, Julie, and my friend Caleb, whose parents both came out as gay when he was two years old. I love the Bible and I cherish its life-giving words. But like a gladiator's sword, some of its passages are dripping with blood. They have been wielded with reckless ignorance to slash open old wounds and carve out new ones. Razor-sharp verses are thrust between the ribs of people like Maddie, whose dad chained her to a toilet in the basement for three months when she was nine. He gave her scraps of food to keep her alive and then raped her repeatedly for the next four years. Now Maddie chooses to have relationships only with other women. "I'm not attracted to girls, but no man will ever touch me again," she says.[8] When I read what Paul says about female same-sex behavior in Romans 1, my heart breaks for Maddie, and it's tough to read that passage without tears.

If the church is ever going to solve this issue, it needs to stop seeing it as an "issue." Homosexuality is not an issue to be solved; it's about people who need to love and be loved.

People like Tim Otto.

SEX IN SEARCH OF LOVE

Tim realized at a young age that he was attracted to other boys. But as a missionary kid and devout follower of Jesus, he believed he shouldn't act on his attractions. Tim suppressed his sexual desires for years until one day his passions overcame him. He entered an adult bookstore in downtown San Francisco and was scanning the magazines when another guy propositioned him. They went to a back room and had sex. Tim got dressed, left the store, sprawled out on the urine-stained sidewalk in the middle of the night, and contemplated suicide. "[A]s I lay on the sidewalk in front of an adult bookstore, the fact that the Mission Street pawn shops sold guns began to seem like a solution."[9]

By God's grace, Tim didn't kill himself that night. But his reflections on what happened are remarkable: "I wish that somehow, rather than ending up in the arms of that anonymous man, I could have found myself in the arms of the church … I wish in the church I had found myself loved."[10]

That last phrase should be branded on our hearts with glowing iron: "I wish in the church I had found myself loved." Tim is a person, not an issue. A person who had sex with an anonymous man because he didn't experience the rich, satisfying, intimate love of Christ mediated through Christ-followers in the church.

What would happen if Christians were known more by their radical, otherworldly love for gay people than their stance against gay sex? Just maybe there would be fewer people seeking anonymous sex to satisfy a craving to be loved.

In the pages that follow, you will be looking over my shoulder as I pore over the text of Scripture to see what it says about homosexuality. But I never want us to forget about Tim, Jeremy, Julie, Wes, or my beautiful friend Lesli who was born into a Christian home and grew up transgender. She too was mocked, spat upon, and pushed down the stairs at school more times than she can remember. Homosexuality is about people. At the same time, I want to be ruthlessly biblical in how we formulate our thoughts about homosexuality. It's not an either the Bible or people question; it's both the Bible *and* people. Homosexuality is not about either truth or love; it's about both truth and love, since truth is loving and love is truthful. Our God is both. There's no room for false dichotomies here. We need to be thoroughly biblical because we desire to thoroughly love people.

WORDS MATTER

Before we dive into the text, let's talk about some words. An old saying goes "Sticks and stones may break my bones but words will never hurt me." This is a terrible lie. Words have the power to heal and to hurt, to comfort and to kill, to push someone off the edge of a twenty-story building. Or in the words of Albus Dumbledore: "Words are, in my not-so-humble opinion, our most inexhaustible source of magic. Capable of both inflicting injury, and remedying it."[11] Just ask your gay or lesbian friend if they've ever been hurt by words hurled at them by other people. And then ask them if those people were Christians.

Obviously, gay jokes, which are neither funny nor Christian, and words like *fag* and *homo* do not belong in the mouths of people who sing to Jesus on Sundays. James says that dehumanizing speech stokes the fires of hell (James 3:6), and I assume that we all want to avoid that place. But there are other words and phrases that we need either to ditch or to use with precision and care.

I would recommend not using the word *homosexual* as a noun to refer to a person who is gay. (It is okay to use *homosexual* as an adjective: homosexual relations, homosexual unions, etc.) The noun *homosexual* gained currency back in the day when psychologists thought gay people were pathologically nuts, and it sometimes still carries this nuance. Plus, *homosexual* feels clinical and impersonal; most gay people do not use this term to describe themselves. Most gay people I know prefer the term *gay*, which works for both men and women, or *lesbian*, which applies exclusively to women. When in doubt, you can use the popular and ever-growing acronym LGBT (Lesbian, Gay, Bisexual, Transgender), although you have to practice saying it thirty times in the mirror to make sure you put the L before the G and don't mistake the T for a D. Many people add a Q ("Queer" or "Questioning") at the end, which is sort of a catchall for all sexual minorities. And if you want to show off the fact that you took a human sexuality class in college, you can roll out the ever-growing acronym LGBTTQAIA: Lesbian, Gay, Bisexual, Transgender, Transsexual, Queer/Questioning, Asexual, Intersex, Ally. For this book, I'll just stick with LGBT to save some ink.[12]

I would also recommend using the term *homosexuality* with care. When we say "homosexuality," what exactly do we mean? Again, we're talking about a diverse group of people, so which person or people are you referring to? Those who are married to someone of the same sex? Someone who is having same-sex intercourse?

Someone who is attracted to the same sex? If so, how much attraction on a scale of 1–10 qualifies one to be included in your concept of homosexuality? A four? A six? An eight?

Homosexuality, as you can see, is a broad term that has the potential of erasing the faces of real people with different stories. When I get asked, "Do you think homosexuality is a sin?" I immediately ask, "What do you mean by *homosexuality*?" and "Which person are you talking about?" Many Christians view "homosexuality" through the lens of what they see and read in the media and don't think about the fourteen-year-old Awana champ who is isolated, depressed, and contemplating suicide because he experiences same-sex attraction and has no one at home or at church to talk to—no one who would listen, anyway.

I would also recommend ditching the term *lifestyle*, as in "the gay lifestyle." It's one of those one-size-fits-all phrases that ignores the vast diversity of actual LGBT people. Do you really know the style of life every gay person is living? Their jobs, their friends, their favorite food? Usually when people say "gay lifestyle" they mean "gay sex." But this singles out one aspect of an entire person's life. How do you know that all gay and lesbian people are having sex? Are you peeking through the window? Should someone call the cops? If there is a "gay lifestyle," then there must also be a "straight lifestyle": a pre-packaged stereotype that accurately describes every heterosexual on the planet. If you are straight, would you want to be associated with the lifestyle of all other straight people?

As you can see, the phrase *gay lifestyle* can be unnecessarily offensive and impersonal to the ears of LGBT people.

I've also gone back and forth on what to call people who hold different views on what the Bible says about same-sex relations. Some of the options for those who believe that the Bible allows for same-sex relations are *pro-homosex, revisionist, Side A*, or *affirming*. Those who believe that the Bible prohibits same-sex relations are called *traditionalists, conservative, Side B*, or *nonaffirming*. Quite honestly, I think all of these terms have problems. The terms that carry the least amount of baggage and misunderstanding to my mind are *affirming* and *nonaffirming*. The one thing I don't like about *nonaffirming* is that it feels too negative. There are many things that nonaffirming people may *affirm* about gay people: their humanity, their love, their desire and need for relationships. The term *nonaffirming* could sound dehumanizing, and this is what I don't like about the term. Still, until I find a better pair of terms, I think *affirming* and *nonaffirming* are the best we've got.

To be clear: I'm using the word *nonaffirming* to describe those who don't believe that the God sanctions same-sex sexual relations and the word *affirming* to describe those who believe that consensual, monogamous, same-sex sexual relations can be sanctioned by God.

OUR APPROACH

There are other terms and phrases that I'll try to explain as I go (for example, the difference between sex and gender, the different meanings of *gay*). But let's go ahead and jump into our discussion. We will spend a good two-thirds of our time looking at the Bible, and at times it will get deep. But I assume you picked up this book because you don't want quick and easy Tweetable answers. You want to know what the Bible actually says. And to do that, we have to work hard and think deeply. Shallow answers to complex questions are offensive to our God-given minds and they fail to shape our hearts into being more like Jesus'.

After looking at the Bible, we will wrestle with pastoral questions that surround this discussion. Are people born gay or do they choose it? Can gay people become straight? Should gay people become straight? Is it right to force someone to be celibate if they are attracted to the same sex? Can a nonaffirming church truly love gay people without affirming same-sex behavior? Is same-sex attraction itself sinful? And should same-sex attracted Christians refer to themselves as "gay"? We will wrestle with these and many other questions.

But we can't responsibly address them unless we have a clear understanding of what the Bible actually says about same-sex relations.

So let's take a journey through Scripture. But before jumping to those six passages that mention homosexual behavior, I want to look first at what the Bible says about marriage; specifically, Does the Bible require biological sexual difference (male and female) in marriage?

Let's jump into Genesis 1–2.

CHAPTER TWO

HOLY OTHERNESS

*Is Male and Female Sexual Difference
Necessary for Marriage?*

The Bible talks a lot about marriage. Good marriages, bad marriages, and marriages that should never have happened—like Solomon's herculean effort of leaving and cleaving with seven hundred women. But what relevance do biblical marriages have for our discussion of homosexuality? As expected, there are two very different views.

Many nonaffirming Christians consider the ubiquitous heterosexual marriages in the Bible to be clear evidence that homosexual marriages are ruled out. After all, "God made Adam and Eve, not Adam and Steve," and that about settles it.

This is not only bad humor, but it's also terrible logic. Yes, it's true, God created a man and woman in the garden, and they got married and had kids. But it doesn't logically follow that since the first human marriage was between man and woman that therefore all other marriages of all time must be between a man and woman. I like the Dodgers, but this doesn't rule out the possibility that I also like the Giants, unless I explicitly say, "I don't like the Giants." (I actually can't stand the Giants, but you know this because I just said it; you shouldn't deduce it from the fact that I'm a Dodgers fan.) Likewise, if I said I was married to Christine, most of you would assume that she is my only wife. But saying that I'm married to Christine doesn't in itself rule out the possibility that I'm also married to Bertha, Gertrude, and Hilda. Improbable, but not impossible.

The other view, held by affirming Christians, agrees that opposite-sex marriages in the Bible don't in themselves rule out homosexual marriages. Some go on to argue that there was no such thing as homosexual marriages in the ancient world. The same-sex behavior that existed had to do with power rape, prostitution, or men who had sex with boys. Therefore, the reason the Bible only talks about heterosexual marriages is because homosexual marriages weren't a live option back then. But since they are an option now, our situation is much different than what's going on in the biblical world. Heterosexual marriages in the Bible, therefore, do not nullify the possibility of God-sanctioned consensual, monogamous, loving gay marriages today.

So here's the question: Does the presence of opposite-sex marriages in the Bible contribute anything to the discussion of homosexuality?

I actually think they do, although I believe both views have misread certain passages. What we need to figure out is whether male and female sexual difference is necessary for marriage. That's our leading question. It's not enough just to identify positive statements about heterosexual marriages. What we need to see is if the Bible highlights sexual difference—male and female—as a universal requirement for marriage.[1]

We'll begin by looking at Genesis 1–2, which is a foundational passage on marriage. Then we'll look at other marriage passages in the New Testament that might carry relevance for our discussion.

MARRIAGE IN GENESIS 1–2

Genesis 1 doesn't actually mention marriage. God creates humanity and stamps them both with the divine imprint: "In the image of God he created mankind, male and female he created them" (1:27). Single or married, widowed or divorced, fertile or infertile, every single person bears God's image. Marriage is probably implied, however, when

God then tells the man and woman to be fruitful and multiply and to have dominion over the earth. In other words, have lots of sex and rule the world. Whoever said God is a cosmic killjoy?

Genesis 2 is not primarily about marriage, but it does contain some important statements about marriage. Both Jesus and Paul, in fact, refer to Genesis 2 when they face questions about marriage or related issues.

The most relevant passage for marriage in Genesis 2 comes in verses 18–25. More specifically, two statements bear the most significance for our discussion. First, Eve is created to be Adam's "suitable helper" (2:18, 20), which says something about why Eve was a good fit for Adam. Second, Adam and Eve's marriage is given universal application in 2:24 where it is said: "a man leaves his father and mother and is united to his wife, and they become one flesh."

This raises an important question for our topic: Do the phrases "suitable helper" and "become one flesh" require sexual distinctions in marriage? Let's begin with the second one first: "become one flesh."

ONE FLESH

I used to think that "one flesh" simply meant the joining of opposite sex people in sexual intercourse. After all, men and women exhibit "anatomical complementarity," as some scholars call it.[2] Or as my mother used to say, the different parts just fit together like a plug in a socket. The two become—quite explicitly—one flesh when they are plugged in.

I'm not sure if Genesis is thinking about how the parts fit together with the phrase "one flesh," but some sexual connotation seems to be implied in the phrase. In fact, when Paul confronts the Corinthians for having sex with prostitutes, he points them back to Genesis 2:24: "Do you not know that he who unites himself with a prostitute is one with her in body? For it is said, 'The two will become one flesh'" (1 Cor. 6:16). Paul here refers to sex with a prostitute as becoming "one flesh" with her. Sexual union between two people does seem to capture at least one aspect of becoming "one flesh."

I don't think, however, that the phrase in itself necessitates sexual difference. For instance, if the people Paul confronted had sex with male prostitutes, would the "one flesh" statement not apply? Wouldn't they have still violated Genesis 2:24 by having a sexual encounter with another person? I think they would have.

As I studied the phrase *one flesh* a bit more, I realized that the primary meaning of two becoming one flesh is not male-female sexual union, but two people forming a new family.[3] This may include sexual union—yes, sex usually comes with marriage—but I don't think the primary emphasis in the phrase *one flesh* has to do with sex. In fact, when you look at other uses of the word *flesh* in the Bible, it almost always refers to a kinship bond, not a male-female sexual encounter.

For instance, Laban declares that Jacob, his cousin, is "my bone and my flesh" (Gen. 29:14). Abimelek affirms his family ties with the people of Shechem by saying, "Remember, I am your flesh and blood" (Judg. 9:2). David tells the elders of Judah (David's tribe), "You are my relatives, my own flesh and blood" (2 Sam. 19:12). In all of these passages, *flesh* refers to a family bond, not a male-female sexual act. When two people of different families become "one flesh," this means that they are leaving their old families and forming a new one.

Becoming "one flesh" may include sexual union in Genesis 2:24, but "one flesh" does not mean sexual union, and it doesn't seem to rule out same-sex unions.

The same is true of the word *united* (NIV) in 2:24: "a man leaves his father and mother and is united to his wife." While the word *united* (Hebrew *dabaq*) here refers to two humans getting married, the word itself does not demand a male and female pairing. Like the word *flesh*, *united* is often used of a kinship bond or a close friendship, and rarely, if ever, is it used elsewhere of sexual union. Ruth, for instance, "clung" (*dabaq*) to Naomi, her mother-in-law

(Ruth 1:14), and this doesn't mean she had sex with her. Ruth and Naomi were forming a new kinship bond, and this seems to be the basic point of Genesis 2:24: the man shall leave his old kinship bond of mother and father and form his own family with his spouse.

In sum, I don't think that the phrase *one flesh* (or *united*) in itself demands that marital partners must be opposite sexes. The only clear demand is that two people leave their former families and create their own new family. Genesis 2:24 doesn't inherently rule out homosexual marriages.

But what about the phrase *suitable helper*?

SUITABLE HELPER

The importance of Genesis 2:18 far outweighs its brevity. Though only one verse, it gives us a quick peek into God's motivation for creating the first woman:

> The LORD God said, "It is not good for the man to be alone.
> I will make a helper suitable for him."

The phrase *suitable helper* certainly sounds sexist, as if women were created to serve men in all of their wants and needs. But the word translated "helper" (Hebrew *ezer*) is almost always used of military help and it's most often applied to God's actions toward Israel throughout the Old Testament.[4] Since God is called Israel's "helper," the word certainly doesn't imply inferiority or weakness.

With regard to homosexuality, some say that Eve was the perfect "helper" for Adam, not because she was a female, but because she was a human.[5] If this were true, then sexual difference would not be relevant. As long as a human becomes a suitable helper to another human (and not an animal), then the two can become one flesh.

And there is some truth to this argument. Just look at the next three verses, where Adam seeks to find a suitable helper among the animals and comes up short:

Now the LORD God had formed out of the ground all the wild animals and all the birds in the sky. He brought them to the man to see what he would name them; and whatever the man called each living creature, that was its name. So the man gave names to all the livestock, the birds in the sky and all the wild animals. But for Adam no suitable helper was found. (Gen. 2:19–21)

Adam needed a helper, but when he looked around at all the animals, he must have thought: *Umm ... I don't think these are going to work.* So God created not just any helper, but a suitable helper. And this is why God created Eve. Eve was suitably helpful because she was human.

But is Eve's humanness the only thing that qualified her as a suitable helper? I think her femaleness actually played a role as well.

The Hebrew word translated "suitable" by the NIV is *kenegdo* and it is only used here in the Old Testament (2:18 and 2:20). *Kenegdo* is somewhat difficult to translate into English, since it is a compound word made up of *ke*, which means "as" or "like," and *neged*, which means "opposite," "against," or "in front of."[6] Together, the word means something like "as opposite him" or "like against him." It's a complex word that captures how it is that Eve can qualify as the perfect partner for Adam.

So here's the relevant point. If it were simply Eve's humanness that made her a helper, then the word *ke* ("like") would have been just fine. The verse would then read: "I will make a helper *like (ke)* him." But to make the point that Adam needed not just another human, but a different sort of human—a female—God used the word *kenegdo*. This word potentially conveys both similarity (*ke*) and dissimilarity (*neged*).[7] Eve is a human and not an animal, which is why she is *ke* ("like") Adam. But she's also a female and not a male, which is why she is different than Adam, or *neged* ("opposite him").

Now, every good interpreter knows that it's dangerous to squeeze too much out of one word. So I don't want to just end the book here and say, "Well, that settles it. Homosexual unions are prohibited by *kenegdo.*" That would be irresponsible. I am surprised, though, at how little attention is given to this word in the discussion.[8] Some people say that Eve's dissimilarity doesn't refer to her femaleness, but to other differences like Eve's personality. Quite frankly, I think this is a stretch. Certainly two people of the same sex will display differences. One may be shy, while the other is outgoing; one may be Type A, while the other may be Type B. But it seems clear from Genesis 1–2 that the otherness of Eve is precisely her sexual difference and not her different Strengths Finders evaluation (Gen. 1:27; 2:18).

It doesn't seem convincing that Eve's dissimilarity wrapped up in *kenegdo* is something other than her biological sex. At the very least, we would need to see a good argument from other marriage passages in Scripture to overturn the apparent significance that *kenegdo* seems to have in Genesis 2. And remember: Adam and Eve's relationship in 2:18–23 becomes the foundation for marriage in 2:24: "That is why a man leaves his father and mother and is united to his wife, and they become one flesh." No longer are we just talking about Adam and Eve in Genesis 2:24. We're talking about God's basic design for marriage, which is why this verse is quoted so often in the New Testament when the question of marriage comes up.[9]

Three things seem to be necessary for marriage according to Genesis 2: (1) both partners need to be human, (2) both partners come from different families (2:24), and—if I'm right about *kenegdo*—(3) both partners display sexual difference.

It's striking too that the sexual difference of man and woman in Genesis 1–2 appears to reflect many other differing pairs embedded in creation. Notice that Genesis 1 ripples with a creative display of diversity that complements each other: God and creation, light and darkness, earth and sky, sun and moon, land and sea, humans and animals. And at the pinnacle of God's creation stands the masterpiece of male and female: "God created mankind, male and female he created them" (Gen. 1:27).

Creation is not uniform, but a beautiful display of differences interacting with each other.[10] The coming together of male and female in marital and sexual union is the height of creation's astonishing union of otherness.

In no way am I saying that this interaction of otherness settles the matter.[11] What it does is situate the different male and female sexes in the larger creational design of God. Adam and Eve's sexual difference seems to be a beautiful and intentional necessity for marriage. But we want to hold this observation with an open hand in case other passages and themes correct our tentative view.

So here's what we've seen in Genesis 1–2 thus far. First, while it's obvious that the first marriage was between a man and a woman, this does not *in itself* mean that *all* subsequent marriages must be heterosexual. Second, the idea of becoming "one flesh" does not demand an opposite-sex couple. It simply emphasizes two people forming a new kinship bond in marriage. Third, the repeated statement that Eve was created as a "suitable" or "like opposite" (*kenegdo*) "helper" for Adam seems to emphasize both similarity (human, not an animal) and dissimilarity (female, not a male). Such sexual difference appears to grow out of a larger fabric of unity within otherness in creation.

Genesis 1–2 does seem to suggest that sexual difference is necessary for marriage. But let's not make a hasty conclusion just yet. We need to see if there are any other passages in Scripture where male-female pairing is necessary for marriage.

GOD CREATED THEM MALE AND FEMALE

Mark 10:2–9 might be such a passage (see the parallel in Matt. 19:3–11):

Some Pharisees came and tested him by asking, "Is it lawful for a man to divorce his wife?" "What did Moses command you?" he replied. They said, "Moses permitted a man to write a certificate of divorce and send her away." "It was because your hearts were hard that Moses wrote you this law," Jesus replied. "But at the beginning of creation God 'made them male and female.' 'For this reason a man will leave his father and mother and be united to his wife, and the two will become one flesh.' So they are no longer two, but one flesh. Therefore, what God has joined together, let no one separate." The context is about divorce and not homosexuality, which is important to keep in mind. It's not as if the Pharisees were wondering if two men could get married and Jesus shuts them down with an argument from Genesis about Adam and Eve not Adam and Steve. We must honor the context when we look at this passage. It's about divorce.

On that note, it would be freakishly hypocritical if straight Christians who divorced their spouses for reasons other than fornication used this passage to condemn gay marriages. How pretentious would that be—using a passage that's directed at you to sling it at someone else? There are few things that stoke the fires of hell hotter than moral hypocrisy. So let's be careful how we use God's Word. Let's make sure our eyes are log-free before we preach it at others.

For our study of same-sex marriages, notice that Jesus goes back to Genesis 1–2 to argue for the permanency of marriage. Jesus quotes Genesis 2:24 about becoming "one flesh" to argue that marriage is an indissoluble kinship bond that shouldn't be torn apart by divorce. So far, Jesus' words don't rule out same-sex marriages.

But look at what else Jesus does. He actually starts in Genesis 1:27: "At the beginning of creation God 'made them male and female'" (Mark 10:6). Then, in the very next phrase, Jesus fast-forwards to Genesis 2:24: "For this reason a man will leave his father and mother and be united to his wife, and the two will become one flesh" (Mark 10:7–8).

The significance of Genesis 1:27 here should not be missed.

Yes, of course, Jesus is talking about divorce. But think about it. He only needed to quote Genesis 2:24 to make his point about divorce— married people have become "one flesh" and therefore shouldn't get divorced. Why, then, does Jesus start in Genesis 1:27—"God made them male and female"—which explicitly highlights sexual difference? Such difference is, in itself, irrelevant to the question of divorce.

That is, it's irrelevant if one's sex makes no difference in marriage. If Jesus didn't think that sexual difference is essential for marriage, then his quotation of Genesis 1:27, which talks about sexual difference, is unnecessary and superfluous. But Jesus does quote it, so it would seem that male-female pairing is part of what marriage is according to Jesus.

I've heard some people say that Jesus quoted Genesis 1:27 not to highlight sexual difference, but to underscore a female's equal worth as a bearer of God's image.[12] This actually makes some sense in light of Jesus' context. After all, the Jews who wanted to divorce their wives probably thought that they were superior to women. It would therefore make sense for Jesus to bring in a passage that highlights the equality of women (1:27) in order to show that divorce is a degrading way to treat one's wife.

But one problem makes this view unlikely: Jesus leaves out the bit about women possessing the image of God.

Genesis 1:27 reads: "So God created mankind in his own image, in the image of God he created them; male and female he created them." But Jesus only quotes the last part about "male and female" and doesn't mention the part about women possessing the image of God. If Jesus only wanted to show that women are equal to men, then why did he leave out the part about women being equal to men? Needless to say, this doesn't seem to be a very convincing argument.

I really don't think it's much of a stretch to say that Jesus cites the portion of Genesis 1:27 that highlights sexual difference because Jesus wanted to highlight sexual difference.

MAN, WOMAN, AND THE TRIUNE GOD

There are two other passages that might highlight sexual difference in marriage, although I don't think they are as clear as Mark 10. The first passage is Ephesians 5:21–32, where Paul compares human marriage to Christ's spiritual marriage to the church. Paul maps the roles of husband and wife onto Christ's relationship with the church. The analogy should not be pressed too far, which is why I'm cautious about applying this passage to the homosexuality debate. After all, Christ is God and the church is human: Does this mean that husbands are the divine partner in marriage? I don't think my wife would buy this. She knows me too well. And what about the singularity of Christ and the multiplicity of people in the church? Does the analogy support polygamy? And half of the members of the church are men. Could their marriage to Christ be taken as support for same-sex unions?

You can see why we need to think hard about how—if at all—this passage applies to sexual difference in marriage. In any case, if we see the church as a singular entity—a bride and not a harem—then there might be some relevance for our discussion. Clearly, Jesus' love toward the church is mirrored in a husband's love for his wife, and the wife's submission to her husband is mirrored in the church's submission to Christ. Since Paul roots marital role distinctions in sexual distinctions, I'm not sure what this would look like in same-sex marriages. The relationship between Christ and the church requires a fundamental difference; a man marrying a man would seem to reflect the church marrying the church or Christ marrying Christ.[13] The analogy demands some sort of difference, and it appears that Paul has sexual difference in mind.

While Paul is not arguing against homosexual relations, I think such relations would have a hard time reflecting Paul's words. The marriage between Christ and the church assumes unity among otherness and celebrates sexual difference.[14]

Some people say that this passage assumes a patriarchal "gender hierarchy," where men are considered superior to women. Therefore, they say, we should move beyond such sexist assumptions and advocate for equality in marriage.[15] But I don't think this passage is as chauvinistic as some people think. Yes, Paul says that wives should submit to their husbands. But he also says that all Christians should submit to each other in Ephesians 5:21.[16] If submission means inequality, then are we all unequal since we are to submit to one another? Plus, compared to other marriage manuals of Paul's day, this passage is radically egalitarian.[17] Paul never says that wives are inferior to their husbands, and the overwhelming emphasis in the passage is on the husband's self-giving, self-sacrificial, unconditional service toward his wife. No one in Paul's day would have read this passage and thought he was demeaning women. They would have been shocked, actually, at his excessive demands of the husband.

The Christian view of submission assumes equality, not hierarchy. That is, the one doing the submitting is not considered inferior.[18] This is seen in other passages where Christ submits to the Father, which certainly doesn't mean that Jesus is inferior to God the Father. This brings us to our second passage, 1 Corinthians 11:2–16, where Paul discusses the roles of men and women in the church.

If you read this passage, you'll see that it's filled with many interpretive questions: What's with the head coverings, and do men really have to have short hair? But we don't need to answer all of these questions in order to identify some relevance for our topic. We only need to notice that Paul roots the sexual difference between man and woman in divine difference within the Triune God. Look at 1 Corinthians 11:3:

But I want you to realize that the head of every man is Christ, and the head of the woman is man, and the head of Christ is God. (1 Cor. 11:3)

Unlike Ephesians 5, this passage is not clearly talking about marriage, although some translations have "husband" and "wife" instead of "man" and "woman" (for instance, the NRSV). What is clear, and the only point I want to make, is that the equal-yet-different relationship between God the Father and God the Son parallels in some way the equal-yet-different relationship between men and women. Paul urges the Corinthians to celebrate and not erase the differences between male and female, since differences exist within the Trinity. It would make sense, therefore, that Paul believes that these same differences are necessary when he explores the male/female–Christ/church analogy in Ephesians 5.

Again, I don't want to make Paul say more than he is saying, and we need always to keep in mind that he's not directly addressing same-sex relations. Whatever relevance we think Ephesians 5 and 1 Corinthians 11 have on our discussion of homosexuality, we need to hold it loosely.

I don't think it's sufficient, however, to say that Paul assumed that marriage was between a man and a woman simply because that's what was common in his day. What Paul says about marriage transcends culture as it finds its shape and identity in the diversity of the Triune God. Sexual difference seems to be an essential ingredient in showcasing the unity and diversity of the Triune God in marriage. It doesn't appear to be irrelevant.[19]

MARRIAGE: MALE AND FEMALE?

Does the Bible demand that marriage is only between a man and a woman? Let's sum up what we've seen thus far.

Several statements in Genesis 1–2 do not appear to exclude same-sex marriages. Becoming one flesh, being united, or even the mere creation of Adam and Eve do not rule out the possibility of same-sex relations. However, the use of *kenegdo* ("suitable," Gen. 2:18, 20) in light of the unity among diversity in Genesis 1–2, probably highlights sexual difference in marriage. This is reflected in several passages in the New Testament that pick up on sexual difference and consider it to be essential for marriage.

Again, I have no interest in simply defending some traditional view for the sake of maintaining tradition. This is why I want to keep challenging myself and trying to see things from both perspectives so that I fill in any gaps in my thinking.

When I look at the evidence, however, the weight seems to support the nonaffirming view thus far. The key biblical passages on marriage don't just assume opposite-sex marriages because that's what was known in the culture of the day. Rather, the authors go out of their way to ground sexual difference in something, or Someone, outside of culture. For Jesus, it was the creation of "male and female" oddly fronted to his argument about divorce (Mark 10:6–7). For Paul, diversity within the Trinity and the different roles of Christ and the church parallel sexual difference in marriage (Eph. 5:22–33; cf. 1 Cor. 11:3).

In any case, what would be the best affirming pushback to this tentative conclusion? We need to ask this question if we are going to interpret the text fairly.

I think the best counterargument is that none of the texts we've looked at were written to refute same-sex relationships. Gay marriages were probably not an issue when Genesis 1–2 was written. Jesus was faced with the question of divorce and not gay marriage in Mark 10. Paul's statements on marriage did not arise out of a debate about same-sex relations.

Nonaffirming Christians need to keep this in mind. This is why I don't think this chapter settles the debate. I do think it offers strong evidence for the nonaffirming view, but I don't think the case is closed. We need to look not only at what the Bible says about sexual difference in marriage, but also what the Bible explicitly says about same-sex relations.

So let's turn to Genesis 19 where a bunch of Sodomites try to gang rape a couple of angels.

CHAPTER THREE

FROM *SEX IN THE CITY* TO *LAW & ORDER*

Homosexuality in the Old Testament

So far we've seen evidence that sexual difference is necessary for marriage. As stated in the last chapter, however, these marriage passages were not directly addressing questions about homosexuality, so we want to hold our working conclusion with an open hand. There are many other passages we need to consider before we arrive at a biblical understanding of homosexuality.

THE "CLOBBER" PASSAGES

The most natural place to go next would be to those passages in Scripture that do directly address same-sex relations. As stated in the preface, there are six passages that mention same-sex intercourse (Gen. 19:1–9; Lev. 18:22; 20:13; Rom. 1:26–27; 1 Cor. 6:9; 1 Tim. 1:10). Before we venture to study these passages, let's remember that we are talking about people, not some issue or text. We can never leave that important truth behind.

The passages we're going to look at have been called the "clobber passages," since Christians throughout history have ripped them out of their life-giving context and used them to club gay people. Genesis 19, Leviticus 18, Romans 1, and others have been wielded to slap, kick, abuse, curse, and stab many—if not most—gay people today. These texts are dripping with blood. When gay people hear them, they immediately think of hate, not love; abuse, not embrace; ignorance, not understanding. They think of being tossed down the stairs by Christian kids at youth group, or the red-faced preacher calling down fire from heaven on "disgusting abominations."

But people are not abominations.[1] We are image bearers of Creator God. Sometimes we do things that are abominable—like slander and hording wealth—but this does not make us abominations.

We need to be sensitive to the painful misuse of these texts before we try to interpret them. After all, we are not just studying a text, we are trying to love real people with real pain. And perhaps no passage is more bloodstained than Genesis 19—the story of Sodom.

THE FIRST ALL-GAY CITY?

For centuries, Sodom has been synonymous with God's hatred of gay people. Genesis 19 has been preached from pulpits and plastered to many "God hates fags" protest signs, as one sign publicized: "Gay pride is why Sodom fried." Like Jonah, some people are more addicted to judgment than they are to grace. The very term *sodomy*, which was derived from Genesis 19, has come to refer to a person who engages in homosexual sex. In fact, the New King James Version even uses the term *sodomite* to refer to men who have sexual intercourse with other males (1 Cor. 6:9).

It's fascinating how bad interpretations are solidified by repetition. Let me be frank: I don't think the story of Sodom contributes to the discussion about homosexuality. Here's why.

According to Genesis 19, two men visit Lot and attract the attention of the men of the city—every single one, even the kids:

All the men from every part of the city of Sodom—both young and old—surrounded the house. They called to Lot, "Where are the men who came to you tonight? Bring them out to us so that we can have sex with them." (Gen. 19:4–5)

It seems odd that "all" the people, "both young and old," were seeking to have sex with Lot's guests. This raises the question: Was Sodom the first all-gay city? And if so, how did it get this way? Did someone spike the punch with gay tonic?

It turns out that Lot's guests weren't actually men. They were angels who appeared as men. As the story unfolds, the men of the city never have sex with Lot's visitors. Lot offers his virgin daughters instead, but the Sodomites decline and try to attack Lot for refusing to give up his guests. Then the angels intervene and strike the men and boys of Sodom with blindness (Gen. 19:4–11).

What are we to make of this story? And does it have anything to say about consensual, loving, monogamous same-sex relations today?

Some scholars say that the passage isn't talking about sex at all. The Hebrew word translated "sex" actually means "to know." Some interpreters therefore say that the men of Sodom only wanted to "know" more about Lot's guests. Where are you from? Why are you here? Would you like a falafel or perhaps a shawarma? This is the view of the late John Boswell—a world renowned Yale theologian—who said:

When the men of Sodom gathered around to demand that the strangers be brought out to them, "that they might know them," they meant no more than to "know" who they were, and the city was consequently destroyed not for sexual immorality but for the sin of inhospitality to strangers.[2]

Others agree with Boswell, but this is a minority view.[3] The Hebrew word for "know" (*yadah*) almost certainly refers to sexual intercourse here. In the same passage, Lot describes his daughters as never having "known any man" (19:8), which clearly means that they were virgins, not just socially awkward. Since "know" refers to sex in 19:8, it probably means the same thing in 19:5. Therefore, the men of Sodom were most likely trying to have sex with God's angels.

But does Genesis 19 condemn loving, consensual, monogamous gay sex?

No, I don't think it does. The men of Sodom were not courting Lot's guests. They were not flirting with them or bringing them chocolate and flowers. They weren't pursuing consensual, monogamous, sexual relations with these men. They were trying to gang rape them. Such an atrocity would have pulled down fire from heaven even if Lot's guests were women. There's no debate today about whether it's okay for a bunch of men to gang rape another man. No one I know is arguing for this. The question is whether two people of the same sex, who are in love and committed to each other, can get married. Sodom was not fried because of gay pride. They were fried for many other sins, including attempted gang rape.[4]

In fact, whenever the Old Testament refers to Sodom, homosexual sex is never mentioned.[5] Just look at Ezekiel's reference to the sin of Sodom: "This was the guilt of ... Sodom," writes the prophet: they had "pride, excess of food, and prosperous ease, but did not aid the poor and needy" (Ezek. 16:49 ESV). Sodomy—biblical sodomy—is not gay sex but being stuffed full of food and comfort with no concern for the two billion people on earth today living in grinding poverty.[6]

That should be convicting if you're living in North America and therefore among the richest humans ever to walk the earth.

What chilling hypocrisy: some Christians who have "excess of food, and prosperous ease" and fail to "aid the poor and needy"— the sins that caused heaven to rumble—have the audacity to condemn gay people when, according to the Bible, they are the real Sodomites. Six thousand children die daily from hunger and preventable diseases. Still, some Christians shed more tears over the repeal of DOMA and Prop 8.

Whenever Sodom is mentioned in the Bible, homosexual sex is never clearly singled out. Isaiah 1:10–17 mentions Sodom; no mention of gay sex. Isaiah 3:9 mentions Sodom; still, no trace of homosexuality. Jeremiah 23:14, Lamentations 4:6, and even Jesus in Matthew 10:5–10 refer to Sodom, but they never gave the slightest hint of anything related to same-sex relations. Did the biblical prophets and Jesus misread Genesis 19? Or have we?

If the Bible condemns all forms of homosexual relations, we need to look elsewhere.[7]

LEVITICUS 18 AND 20

The next two verses that mention some sort of homosexual act come from Leviticus:

Do not have sexual relations with a man as one does with a woman; that is detestable. (Lev. 18:22)

If a man has sexual relations with a man as one does with a woman, both of them have done what is detestable. They are to be put to death; their blood will be on their own heads. (Lev. 20:13)

As we read these verses, we're faced with two questions: First, do these verses prohibit all forms of homosexual acts or just certain exploitative forms of it (rape, prostitution, etc.)? That is, do these prohibitions apply to consensual, monogamous, loving gay couples? And second, do these verses still carry authority for Christians today? Let's tackle the first question.

ALL TYPES OF SAME-SEX RELATIONS?

Some people argue that these two verses are only talking about certain types of exploitative sex: rape, temple prostitution, or a man forcing himself on a boy.[8] Certainly all of these acts are wrong. But the question is: Should Leviticus 18 and 20 be limited to these particular forms of same-sex intercourse? A close reading of the texts suggests not.

For example, notice that the commands in these two verses don't come with any qualifications, comments, or specifications that could limit the commands to a particular type of same-sex behavior.[9] That is, there's no mention of rape, coercion, age difference, or anything else that we saw in the Sodom story. No one is trying to force another person into having sex. And if two men do sleep with each other, they are both condemned: "They are to be put to death; their blood will be on their own head" (20:13). The commands appear to include same-sex acts that are mutual and consensual; both partners are deemed guilty. If the verses were talking about some sort of ancient "prison rape," then only the one doing the violence would be condemned.[10]

Other interpreters say that Leviticus 18 and 20 only prohibit male cult prostitutes—men who would service other men in devotion to a pagan god. If this were what Leviticus is talking about, then of course it would not have much relevance for today. None of my gay friends are trying to reinstitute cultic prostitution.

But this interpretation is supported by little (if any) evidence. Several scholars have recently shown that cultic prostitution probably didn't exist in the world at this time, let alone in Israel. At least, there's meager evidence to support it.[11] I know a lot of people who assume that the ancient world was filled with cultic prostitution. But there's more evidence that this is a myth and not a reality, as shown in Stephanie Budin's aptly titled book, *The Myth of Sacred Prostitution in Antiquity*.[12] Now most English translations of the Old Testament refer to "male cult prostitutes" throughout the Old Testament (for instance, 1 Kings 14:24), but they wrongly translate the Hebrew term *qadeshim*—a word that simply means "holy ones."[13] Although *qadeshim* probably refers to some sort of service at pagan shrines, there's no evidence that such service was sexual. In any case, the Hebrew term *qadeshim* isn't used in Leviticus 18:22 and 20:13. Leviticus simply prohibits men from having sex with other males, and there's nothing in the context suggesting that prostitution is in view.

Now, everything I've said about male cult prostitution is well known to most Old Testament scholars. It's unfortunate that some popular writers and even some New Testament scholars continue to assume that cultic prostitution was alive and well in Israel and that this is probably what Leviticus has in mind.

For instance, Justin Lee in his popular book *Torn* makes a case that the Bible is rather unclear about homosexual relations.[14] When he looks at Leviticus 18, he argues that it's probably talking about cultic prostitution. Later on he says that Romans 1 is similar to Leviticus: "In Paul's day, as in the time of Leviticus, some idol-worshiping cultures included sex as part of their worship rituals."[15]

I actually really like Justin's book. I liked it so much that I assigned it for a class I taught on homosexuality at Eternity Bible College where I teach. But Justin's understanding of Leviticus is, I believe, inaccurate. Even some nonaffirming New Testament scholars, like Robert Gagnon (who does not think that Leviticus 18 and 20 should be limited to male prostitution), still assume that male cult prostitution was alive and well in Israel during this time.[16] But this view has very little evidence to support it. Some scholars may have argued this in the past, but such a myth has been more or less put to death by recent Old Testament scholarship.

So if Leviticus 18 and 20 are not talking about exploitative sex, rape, or temple cult prostitution, are there any other interpretations that we need to consider?

There is another interpretation that agrees that both passages forbid all forms of male-male sex. But this view adds an important caveat: the *reason* homosexual sex is forbidden is because it feminizes the passive partner.[17] This view points out that Israelite culture had a high view of men and a low view of women. So to treat another man like a woman (by having sex with him) would strip him of all male honor and thus treat him like a lowly woman.

Perhaps you can see the implications of this interpretation: the Leviticus prohibition against male-male sex assumes a low view of women. Should we still follow the Leviticus commands with all the chauvinism that shaped them? If we say Leviticus 18 and 20 are for today, then to be consistent, we should also say that the *moral logic* that drives these commands is also for today.[18] But do we really want to maintain such a Neanderthal view of women?

I certainly don't. However, I think this interpretation assumes things that aren't clearly stated in the text.

Notice that Leviticus 18 and 20 both highlight gender distinctions: "You shall not lie with a male as with a woman" (Lev. 18:22).[19] But neither text goes on to say because women are inferior to men. The text hints at maintaining gender distinctions; men should act like men, and women should act like women. But there is nothing in either passage that assumes a low view of women. Men should act like men not because they are superior, but because they were created differently.

Plus, the "low view of women" view assumes a view of the Old Testament that is hardly consistent. For instance, Genesis 1:27 makes a fundamental claim about women that was radical in the ancient world: *women*, and not just men, are created in God's image. Did the same God who breathed out Genesis 1 also breathe out Leviticus 18:22 and 20:13? Was he confused? I'll admit, there are some passages in the Old Testament that seem to demean women, but when we study the cultural context of those passages, it's not clear that the biblical writers considered women to be inferior to men.[20] Granted, if there were something in Leviticus 18 and 20 that degraded women, then this interpretation might have a case. But there is nothing in the actual passage that says that women were inferior to men.[21]

In summary, Leviticus 18 or 20 don't appear to have a specific form of male-male sex in view. The verses use general language, which includes all forms of homosexual sex. There's no concern over the status of the male partners. There's nothing about prostitution, rape, or men having sex with boys. The commands most naturally include all forms of male same-sex intercourse—thus including consensual sex between two men in love.

ARE LEVITICUS 18:22 AND 20:13 STILL AUTHORITATIVE TODAY?

Some people write off these same-sex commands since there are a lot of weird laws in Leviticus that no one follows anymore. Few Christians obey the laws about not eating catfish and sowing your fields with one type of seed. Therefore, whatever it says about gay sex shouldn't be followed either.

For instance, affirming writer John Shore points out:

In practice, Christians do not follow the dictates of the Old Testament. If they did, polygamy would be legal, and forbidden would be things like tattoos, wearing mixed fabrics, eating pork and seeding lawns with a variety of grasses—and the Christian day of worship would be Saturday, not Sunday.[22]

When I first studied these two verses in Leviticus my first reaction was similar to Shore's. I wanted to toss them aside, grab a bacon sandwich, and move on to the more important verses in the New Testament. After all, I love to eat shellfish and wear poly-cotton blends. So why obey these two verses?

But then I studied the passage in more detail and realized that the question is not so easily answered. There are many commands in Leviticus that Christians *do* obey, even though some laws are fulfilled in Christ (such as animal sacrifices). And yes, it's true, the food laws are no longer binding on Christians, but the New Testament makes this clear.[23] So we need to ask the question: Does the New Testament also say that same-sex intercourse is now okay since Jesus has arrived? Clearly, there's no verse in the New Testament that reverses the same-sex commands of Leviticus as it does with the dietary laws.

The fact is, we shouldn't dismiss Leviticus 18 and 20 just because they are in, well, Leviticus. We must figure out whether these specific laws are still binding on Christians in the new-covenant age.

On the flip side, nonaffirming interpreters shouldn't say that since Leviticus 18:22 and 20:13 are in the Bible they are therefore binding on believers. This also is simplistic and inconsistent; otherwise, you'd better hand over that BLT before you get disciplined out of church. You can't assume that Leviticus 18 and 20 are still authoritative; you must provide evidence—evidence why these laws *are* still binding while others are not.

As we wrestle with whether Leviticus 18 and 20 are authoritative for Christians, here are a few things to consider.

First, we should notice that Leviticus 18–20 is one literary unit. No one disputes this; like the creation account in Genesis 1–2 or the Sermon on the Mount in Matthew 5–7, some sections in the Bible contain one unit of thought and should be interpreted as such. This section in Leviticus (18–20) contains a whole string of commands that deal with various social issues in the life of Israel. And if you read through this section carefully, you will see that almost every law given to Israel is still relevant for Christians. For instance:

incest (18:6–18; 20:11–14, 17, 19–21)
adultery (18:20; 20:10)
child sacrifice (18:21; 20:1–5)
bestiality (18:23; 20:15–16)
theft (19:11)
lying (19:11)
taking the Lord's name in vain (19:20)
oppressing your neighbor (19:13)
cursing the deaf (19:14)
showing partiality in the court of law (19:15)
slander (19:16)
hating your brother (19:17)
making your daughter a prostitute (19:29)
turning to witches or necromancers (19:31)

We could add to this list one of the most central commands for the Christian faith: "You shall love your neighbor as yourself" (19:18). Certainly, there are many laws in Leviticus 18–20 that are clearly for today.

Now, some laws in this section are fulfilled in Christ, like the sacrificial laws (for example, 19:21–22). Others, such as not wearing different types of fabric (19:19) or shaving the edges of your beard (19:27) were probably bound to the specific culture in which Israel lived and are therefore not binding on Christians. At least, we see nothing in the New Testament that repeats these commands.

Then there are a few other laws in Leviticus 18–20 that aren't binding on Christians in all their specificity, but still contain a core principle that's still relevant for today. For instance, Leviticus 19:10 tells Israel not to gather fallen grapes from their vineyards but leave them for the poor. You may wonder: is this still binding? Well, yes and no. The principle of taking care of the poor is certainly still relevant, but the particular application may not be (giving your extra grapes to poor people).

In summary, most of the commands in Leviticus 18–20 are applicable either in their full literal meaning (don't have sex with your neighbor's wife) or in the principle that drives them (use excess income to help the poor). This doesn't in itself answer our question, but it does suggest that it is more likely that 18:22 and 20:13 are still binding on believers. At least, we would need to see a good argument to the contrary, since most other laws in this section *are* still binding.

Second, Leviticus 18–20 contains many different laws about sex, and here's the thing: all of these sex laws are still authoritative for Christians: incest (18:6–18), adultery (18:20), bestiality (18:23), and pimping your daughter (19:29). However, there's another sex law that's not often talked about in Sunday School. Leviticus 18:19 says that a man shouldn't have sex with his wife while she is menstruating, and some people say that this law is no longer binding. I've never actually seen a good argument that shows why it's totally okay for a husband to have sex while his wife is menstruating. Personally, I don't know why people dispute this one, as if to say, "No, I *will* have sex with my wife while she's bleeding!" Really? Let me give you some free marital advice: keeping this law is actually good for the marriage. There's nothing in the Bible that tells Christians that after Jesus' resurrection, they can go ahead and make love to their wives while they're menstruating. But that's for another book.

Even if we grant that the law against having sex during menstruation is not binding on believers (even though there's no evidence for this), the rest of the sex commands in this section are. So again, as with the first point above, it seems more natural to consider the law against male-male intercourse to be authoritative.

The third observation is the most important. The most fail-proof test to see if an Old Testament law is still valid for Christians is if it's repeated in the New. Cheating, lying, stealing—it's all repeated in the New Testament. Adultery, murder, drunkenness. Yup, it's all there. But what about eating pork? Leviticus outlaws it, but the New Testament says that Christians don't need to obey this law. The same goes for animal sacrifices. The Sabbath is tricky, and Christians debate its relevance, but there are several verses that seem to say that it's a matter of conscience and not every believer needs to observe the Sabbath.[24]

So are the commands against same-sex intercourse repeated in the New Testament? Well, that's what this book is all about, so we'll have to suspend judgment until we read further. Just to give a sneak peek, however: not only are Leviticus 18:22 and 20:13 repeated in the New, but Paul uses a Greek word that appears to have been created directly from these two verses. We'll discuss this in chapter 7 when we look at 1 Corinthians 6:9 and 1 Timothy 1:10. In short: yes, the New Testament repeats the prohibitions against same-sex intercourse as it is described in Leviticus 18 and 20.

SUMMARY

Of our three Old Testament passages, we've seen that Genesis 19 (Sodom) is largely irrelevant other than declaring that gang rape and disregard for the poor are abominations before God. The two verses in Leviticus, however, are a bit more difficult. While some people have written them off as relics of Israel's past, we've seen evidence for their abiding authority for three reasons:

Most of the laws in the surrounding context are still authoritative.

Most—I would say, all—of the sexual laws of Leviticus 18 are still binding.

The commands in Leviticus 18:22 and 20:13 are repeated in the New Testament.

Given everything we've seen, it would appear that these laws are still for today. There's no clear reason why these laws should not be obeyed simply because they are in Leviticus. Still, we should be open to the New Testament possibly making a surprising move and doing away with the same-sex commands in Leviticus.

We're going to turn to the New Testament shortly. But first, let's widen our scope and understand the broader world in which the New Testament was written. In the next chapter, we'll look at how Judaism viewed same-sex relations within the context of their Greco-Roman environment. After all, Christianity was born out of Judaism, and despite some theological disagreements between Jews and Christians, they still agreed on a good number of ethical questions.

CHAPTER FOUR

RATED R

*Homosexuality in Judaism
and Greco-Roman Culture*

It's tough to understand what the Bible says about homosexual relations until we first understand the historical context in which it was written. After all, the biblical writers were not writing to a modern Western nation. They were writing to ancient people living in a time and culture much different than ours. The Old Testament writers were interacting with concepts and worldviews trafficked into Israel from Mesopotamia, Egypt, and other surrounding cultures, and the New Testament was written to people steeped in a Jewish or Greco-Roman environment. To understand what the Bible means, we'll need to understand the world in which it was first written and read—especially with a topic as important as homosexuality.

HOMOSEXUAL PRACTICE
IN THE ANCIENT WORLD

In the ancient Near East, homosexual practice was more or less accepted as long as it followed a particular social protocol. As long as the "active" partner was a man of higher social standing, while the "passive" partner was one of a lower social standing, no one would have considered the relationship (or sex act) to be strange. For example, a warrior may penetrate a conquered enemy, or a master may penetrate a household slave, and no one would have considered the active partner to be gay in the modern sense of the term.

If a man penetrated another man of equal status, however, this would have been frowned upon. According to ancient Assyrian law, ruthless punishments were given to men who penetrated a social equal—or for simply spreading a rumor that his social equal had engaged in passive intercourse.[1] People of high social standing were supposed to be the givers not the receivers of sexual intercourse. The gender of the receiver was largely irrelevant.[2]

We do have some evidence of what we would call "peer" same-sex relations, but these seem to be rare.[3] For the most part, same-sex relations followed the dominant versus dominated social paradigm. If you think back to Leviticus 18 and 20, you'll remember that social status doesn't play a role in the same-sex prohibitions. It doesn't matter whether you are the giver or receiver, or a man of high social standing or low. If two men have sex, it violates God's design. And remember: both partners are punished.

HOMOSEXUALITY IN GREECE AND ROME

When we get to the Greco-Roman period (500 BC—AD 400), sexual practices are described much more pervasively—and perversely. If you venture to study this stuff, beware: Greco-Roman writers talk about sex in quite graphic terms. I don't care how promiscuous you think our modern culture is, let me assure you: it is nothing like first-century Rome. What we call pornography, the Romans simply called life. The junk you can find on HBO at 2:00 a.m. was plastered on bathhouse walls and inside homes as decoration.

For instance, it wasn't uncommon to have pictures of men having sex with boys painted on water pitchers served at the dinner table. Imagine that—"And in Caesar's name we pray, Amen ... please pass the water, Mom." If I went into detail about the sexual practices of ancient Rome, and the frankness in which they talked about it, Lifeway wouldn't sell this book in their stores. What I've seen portrayed in the Roman world makes Miley Cyrus appear modest and Lady Gaga look like a nun (or a priest). I can only imagine how weird the early church must have seemed. Like an Amish community planted in downtown Vegas.

While at times I feel like I need to scrub my eyes with soap and dip my Kindle in sanitizer, combing through these ancient sources has helped me understand the historical context of the New Testament. In an effort to preserve your sanctification, I'll sum up the homosexual practices in the Greco-Roman world with a good deal of tact.

First of all, we need to make sure we don't assume a modern understanding of "homosexuality" or "gay" and "lesbian" when describing the same-sex practices of people living during the New Testament times. The term *homosexuality* is a modern sociological construct invented in the nineteenth century, and *gay* and *lesbian* refer to people whose identity is based on their sexual attraction. But ancient people didn't think in terms of sexual identity; they thought in terms of gender identity. There is no ancient term or concept for homosexuality, gay, or lesbian.

That is, they didn't raise questions like "Is Joey gay?" or say things like "If Joey has sex with Frank, then they both must be gay." Having sex with someone of the same sex didn't automatically mean someone was gay. What mattered was masculinity and femininity. "Is Joey manly?" or "Is Joey effeminate?" were the questions they would raise.

Now, there were many different things that would make Joey a man (and I'm terribly sorry if you're reading this and your name is Joey). If Joey fought valiantly in battle, avoided PDA with his wife (which was considered unmanly), and kept his household in submission, then he might be a manly man. Thick chest hair only added to his manliness. But if Joey doused himself in perfume, plucked out his chest hair, and cried on the battlefield, he would probably be called effeminate—or *mollis* ("soft") in Latin. Again, what mattered was how well Joey matched up to the societal standards of gender.

In terms of his sexual activity, if the manly Joey also had sex with his male slaves and, on occasion, hired out "call boys" (teenage male prostitutes), Joey would not lose his man card. That is, as long as he was the active partner in sexual intercourse. These activities may annoy his wife, but such was life in ancient Rome. Joey would not be considered gay or even feminine by his peers.

On the flip side, if we met an effeminate Joey who dripped with perfume and wore soft, elegant clothes, we would consider him to be womanly, even if he had sex exclusively with women. That's because ancient Romans didn't think in terms of sexual identity (gay or straight) but in terms of gender identity (manly or womanly). The biological sex of the person you had sex with didn't matter a whole lot. What mattered was whether you were the active or passive partner in sexual relations. If you were active, then you'd be manly. If passive, then effeminate.

Does this mean gay people (that is, same-sex attracted) didn't exist in the ancient world? No, of course they did. What it means is that they were not classified in terms of their sexual identity. Just because someone may have engaged in homosexual sex does not mean they were "gay" by modern standards.

Now, many books have been written on homosexuality in the ancient world, and we could go on and on describing same-sex behavior in the ancient world.[4] But let's stay focused and look at a couple of aspects of homosexual practice that are most relevant for understanding the Bible.

SAME-SEX ORIENTATION

Some people think that ancient writers didn't know about same-sex orientation. If this were true, then one could say that the New Testament writers didn't know what we know now, that some people are born with same-sex attraction. If they did, then they would have made an exception to their negative talk about same-sex behavior.

For instance, one of the leading affirming scholars, James Brownson, assumes that "writers in the first century, including Paul, did not look at same-sex eroticism with the understanding of sexual orientation that is commonplace today" and that "the notion of sexual orientation was absent."[5] Another affirming Christian, Matthew Vines, says that "same-sex relations in the first century were not thought to be the expression of an exclusive sexual orientation."[6] Even nonaffirming scholars, such as Richard Hays, assume that ancient writers didn't have any awareness of innate same-sex desires.[7]

There is some truth to these claims: our modern conception of same-sex orientation didn't exist back then. As we'll see, however, some Greco-Roman writers did believe in some form of inborn same-sex desires. Their understanding isn't exactly the same as what we call same-sex orientation, but it is a relevant parallel.

Quick word of warning: the following discussion is going to be somewhat technical, but I assure you that it's necessary. We need to dig deeply and study hard to make sure we are rightly understanding the Bible in its historical context. With that in mind, consider the following.

In the fourth century BC, Aristotle said that some homoerotic desires come from habit, but others spring from nature.[8] In other words, some people are born with same-sex desires.[9] Another ancient writer argued that some men desire to play the passive role in same-sex intercourse because of a biological defect. His theory was absurd and medically invalid.[10] But the point is, he believed that a particular form of same-sex erotic desire was biological and inborn.[11]

Parmenides, an early fifth-century BC philosopher, believed that men who desired to be penetrated were "generated in the act of conception."[12] Likewise, a Greek physician from Ephesus named Soranus, who lived around the same time as Paul, believed that homoerotic desires are shaped more by nature rather than nurture. That is, men didn't just freely choose to have sex with men when they could have just as easily desired sex with women. There was something else internally driving them to desire men.[13]

Now it's probably true that some of the men being described here also had intercourse with women. They may have even been married to women. This was common in the ancient world. And actually, there are quite a few gays and lesbians today who either came out of, or are still living in, a heterosexual marriage. Regardless of whether or not they swung from both sides of the plate, the above references show that ancient people recognized that something biological was driving their sexual passions for the same sex.

Now, I want to make it clear that I'm not just promoting some view that's been cooked up by nonaffirming scholars. Bernadette Brooten, for instance, is a lesbian affirming scholar and a renowned expert on female homoeroticism in the ancient world. In her book *Love Between Women*, she examines many ancient astrological, medical, and magical texts and actually argues for the very thing I've seen in the ancient literature: some ancient writers believe that same-sex desires were fixed at birth.

For instance, one text says: "If the Sun and Moon are in masculine signs and Venus is also in a masculine sign in a woman's chart, women will be born who take on a man's character and desire intercourse with women like men."[14] Another text written around the time of Paul says that if the sun and moon are at a particular location when a woman is born, she "will be a Lesbian, desirous of women, and if the native is a male, he will be desirous of males."[15] After looking at many more examples, Brooten concludes: "Contrary to the view that the idea of sexual orientation did not develop until the nineteenth century, the astrological sources demonstrate the existence in the Roman world of the concept of a lifelong erotic orientation."[16]

As I studied more broadly, I've seen many affirming and non-affirming scholars agree with Brooten.[17] I can cite other examples, but the point seems clear: an ancient version of same-sex orientation existed when the New Testament was written. I'm not saying that everyone was aware of this or that Paul and other New Testament authors necessarily held the same perspective. I'm not even saying that Greco-Roman writers understood same-sex orientation in the same way we do today.[18] What I am saying is that it is historically inaccurate to say: "the notion of sexual orientation was absent" in Paul's day and then use this to reinterpret Paul.[19]

The evidence shows that the notion of inborn, biologically driven, same-sex desires existed in Paul's day.

DIVERSITY IN SAME-SEX RELATIONS

Some scholars argue that there was no such thing as loving same-sex relations in Paul's day and therefore he could not have been addressing them in his writings. After all, Paul can't condemn something that didn't exist.

I've spent a good deal of time wrestling with this question, and here's what I've found so far: Most same-sex erotic relations in the Greco-Roman world exhibited some sort of power differential. That is, there was the dominant partner and the dominated partner, the master and the slave, the man and the boy, the guy seeking homosexual sex and the male prostitute who gives it to him for a price. I think we need to be very careful mapping contemporary democratic sexual relations onto the Greco-Roman world where its sexual mores were imbedded in a social fabric of inequality. Emperor Nero, for instance, publicly married two men on different occasions, but this can hardly be taken as evidence for consensual gay marriage in the first century. In fact, Nero turned one of his slaves into a "bride" by castrating him because he reminded the emperor of his former wife. This certainly isn't evidence for a consensual same-sex relation.[20]

I also think it's wrong, however, to paint all same-sex relations with the same brush. There was no one-size-fits-all pattern of same-sex relations. There was a spectrum. Yes, it is true, some men ran around trying to hump anyone and anything that couldn't run fast enough. Such sexual immorality was condemned by biblical writers. But I also think it's wrong to say that *all* same-sex relations in Paul's day were exploitative. On the other side of the spectrum existed consensual, loving, and even marital unions between couples of the same sex. Some of these would be similar to the types of relations that affirming Christians are arguing for today.[21]

To be sure, the most common form of same-sex relations occurred between men and boys; or more specifically, between men and male teenagers between the ages of thirteen and seventeen. Scholars call this "pederasty," which means "the love of boys." Sound creepy? I know. It does to me too. But within the worldview of Greco-Roman writers, pederasty was believed to foster several virtues. It was not the rape of children, though that did happen. Nor was pederasty simply an avenue of sexual release.[22] Pederasty was part of a larger relationship, which involved education, discipleship, friendship, and—according to those who promoted it—love. Some men preferred sexual relations with boys not because they were pedophiles, but because beardless teenagers were considered the purest form of maleness. That is, men who sexually desired teenage boys were attracted to maleness in its purest form.[23]

Pederasty was the most common form of same-sex relations in the Greco-Roman world, but it wasn't the only kind. There is at least some evidence for consensual "peer" same-sex relations as well. That is, there were men and women who engaged in same-sex relations that were mutual, consensual, interdependent, loving, and committed. These were the minority, but they certainly existed.

For instance, Agathon was a famous Greek poet known for his physical beauty. He was also known for dressing up like a woman and for having a life-long, consensual lover named Pausanias.[24] To be sure, the relationship between Agathon and Pausanias began as pederasty—Pausanias fell in love with Agathon when Agathon was a teenager.[25] However, while most pederastic relationships ended when the "beloved" youth grew a beard, Pausanias and Agathon remained committed well into adulthood.

A Greek philosopher named Parmenides (age sixty-five) was in a same-sex relationship with Zenon. Although Parmenides was much older the relationship wasn't mere pederasty. Zenon, his lover, was forty years old.[26] The relationship between the epic Greek heroes Achilles and Patroklos was considered by many ancient authors to be homoerotic and consensual.[27] These two mythical heroes were not real people, of course. But such myths help form, and are formed by, the worldviews and lives of real people.

Some people dismiss these examples since they are from the Greek period, which predates the New Testament by a few hundred years. This is true. Consensual same-sex relations were much more popular during the early Greek period than in the Roman period, which is when the New Testament was written. But this argument is overplayed. There were many aspects of ancient Greek culture that continued to have a massive influence on the way people thought and lived for many years to come—even down to the present day. Just think of the lasting influence of Homer, Plato, Aristotle, or Aesop. Or look at the architectural influences of Greek culture that are still splattered across the Western world today. I think it's wrong to say that since same-sex peer relations existed a few hundred years before Christ they made no difference for understanding the background of the New Testament.

In any case, consensual and loving homosexual relationships can be seen during the Roman period as well. For instance, Xenophon's second-century AD novel *An Ephesian Tale* depicts a young man named Hippothous who falls in love with another man of the same age named Hyperanthes. Hippothous says "our first steps in love-making were kisses and caresses, while I shed floods of tears . . . we were both the same age, and no one was suspicious. For a long time we were together, passionately in love."[28] Another novel by Achilles Tatius written around the same time depicts male lovers who are roughly the same age.[29] Both of these are novels and not histories, but novels only make sense if they mirror the real world. Likewise, the first-century Roman author Petronius wrote a book called the *Satyricon*, which discusses homosexuality at great length. In it, the author portrays two male lovers, Encolpius and Ascyltos, who are equal in age and status. Strikingly, the author doesn't make a big stink about their relationship—as if it's some weird, crazy, abnormal thing. It appears that their consensual, nonexploitative, mutual love-relationship may have been more common than some scholars think.

Consensual, same-sex love—even marriages—can be found among women around the time of Paul. A second-century writer named Iamblichos talks about the marriage between two women named Berenike and Mesopotamia.[30] Lucian of Samosata also mentions the marriage of two wealthy women named Megilla and Demonassa.[31] The early Christian theologian Clement of Alexandria refers to women-women marriage.[32] And Ptolemy of Alexandria, a famous second-century scholar of many trades, refers to women taking other women as "lawful wives."[33] Two Jewish documents that were written shortly after the New Testament refer to (and forbid) female marriages that were happening in their day.[34] Several archaeological discoveries depict mutual love between women, including a funeral relief that dates back to the time of Caesar Augustus, where two women are holding hands in a way that resembles "the classic gesture of ancient Roman married couples."[35]

I don't think these examples of consensual love should be overplayed. Again, the most dominant forms of same-sex relations were pederastic or driven by unhealthy power structures (masters and slaves, etc.).[36] However, it does seem that there was a spectrum of same-sex relations and even some examples of consensual same-sex relations—especially among women. Female same-sex relations did not follow the dominator/dominated, master-slave, or pederastic paradigm. Tuck this last point in your back pocket since it will be important when we interpret Romans 1.

We cannot assume therefore that Paul only had nonconsensual, unhealthy, exploitative same-sex relations in view when he wrote about same-sex relations.

JUDAISM ON SAME-SEX RELATIONS

What did Judaism think about same-sex relations?

This is one of the most important questions in the current debate. It's important because Christianity was birthed out of Judaism and still maintained a very Jewish perspective on most ethical questions. Therefore, understanding the Jewish context of Christianity will give us the broad brushstrokes of early Christian morality. After all,

Christianity wasn't a separate religion, but was considered a sect of Judaism when it began.

What then did Jewish people believe about same-sex relations?

The two most prolific Jewish writers in the first century were Josephus and Philo. Both were Jewish to the core, and yet both were steeped in the Greco-Roman culture. When it comes to same-sex relations, Josephus and Philo had much to say and all of it was negative. When they mentioned same-sex relations, they were usually thinking of pederasty—the most common form known to them.[37] But there are at least a few places where they seem to condemn all forms of homosexual unions.

Josephus, for instance, raises the question, "What are our laws about marriage?" His answer is: "The law owns no other mixture of sexes but that which [is] according to nature [*kata physin*]."[38] Notice that Josephus is not talking about rape, prostitution, or men having sex with boys. He's talking about marriage. Josephus believes that all forms of same-sex relations are wrong because the Law—specifically Leviticus 18:22 and 20:13—say they are wrong. Likewise, Philo interprets the Sodom story through the lens of his Greco-Roman culture and condemns the "unnatural desire" of men who lust after one another. It's clear that Philo is not just talking about the attempted gang rape of Lot's angelic visitors but is reading the passage in light of his own environment.[39]

There were many other ancient Jewish writers living around the time of the New Testament who mentioned same-sex relations. A Greek-speaking Jew living in Alexandria one hundred years before Christ observed that many men "defile themselves in their relationships" by "having sex with the males," and he goes on to say, "We [Jews] are quite separated from these practices."[40] Another Jewish writer, who lived right around the time of Christ, spoke out against same-sex practices on a number of occasions. In the context of discussing the Ten Commandments, he writes: "Neither commit adultery nor rouse homosexual passion."[41] And again: "Do not transgress with unlawful sex the limits set by nature. For even animals are not pleased by intercourse of male with male."[42]

Later on, after the time of Jesus, Jewish rabbis continued to interpret Leviticus 18 and 20 in a straightforward manner: all forms of same-sex relations were outside of God's will.[43] In some instances, the rabbis were a little more lenient on same-sex female relations, although they still believed they were sin.[44] In any case, whenever same-sex relations are mentioned, they are condemned as violations of God's will. No exceptions, no caveats, no debates or footnotes.

WHY WERE SAME-SEX RELATIONS WRONG?

We could go on to cite many other Jewish writers, but the point is not a matter of debate among scholars. I've never heard of anyone who has tried to argue that some ancient Jews affirmed same-sex relations. There's just no evidence to support this. The Jewish view was unanimous. Homosexual relations were considered sin.

But there are two other questions that come up in this discussion. First, didn't Jews only condemn pederasty? And if so, then what relevance does this have for today's discussion?

Second, didn't Jews say that same-sex intercourse was wrong because it couldn't procreate? That is, it wasn't the same-sex nature of the act that was wrong, but the fact that same-sex intercourse (like masturbation and sex during menstruation) was a waste of life-giving semen.

These are both very good questions. Let's wrestle with the first one.

DIDN'T JEWS ONLY CONDEMN PEDERASTY?

It is true that Jews most often condemned pederasty. But this does not mean that the same writer would have been fine with two adult males getting married and having sex. Pederasty was simply the main form of same-sex relations available to the ancient writers, so of course they would speak out against it the most. This doesn't mean that these writers only had a problem with the age difference and not the biological sex. After all, most boys that attracted older men were teenagers between the ages of thirteen and seventeen. For a Jew, that's roughly the same age of women who got married. So the problem for Philo, Josephus, and other Jewish writers could not have simply been that these "boys" were too young; the problem is that these boys were males.

Plus, pederasty was not the only form of same-sex relations that was condemned. As we just saw above, some Jewish writers condemned same-sex relations without any clear reference to pederasty.[45]

DIDN'T JEWS CONDEMN SAME-SEX INTERCOURSE BECAUSE IT COULDN'T PROCREATE?

The second question can be answered in much the same way. It is true that for many Jewish writers, sex was designed for pro-creation and not for pleasure.[46] Therefore, homosexual unions are struck down right out of the gate. But again, the lack of procreative potential did not replace the same-sex nature of the act as the reason why it was wrong. The two go hand-in-hand. Lack of procreation was one of several reasons why same-sex intercourse was considered sin. Blurring gender distinctions, using your body in a way it wasn't designed, and forcing another man to act like a woman, were among other reasons.[47] Or in some cases, there was no reason other than "God said so."[48] Ancient Jews were much more reluctant than we are to question God's commands.

A NON-JEWISH NEW TESTAMENT?

Jewish people disagreed amongst themselves on many different issues. We see this in the New Testament, where Pharisees and Sadducees disagreed over the resurrection. Other Jews disagreed on whether they should follow a lunar calendar or a solar calendar, which makes a huge difference when you're trying to set the table for Passover. Despite their many differences, every Jew who wrote on the subject five hundred years before and five hundred years after

Christ agreed on one thing: same-sex relations were against the will of God.

So here's the million-dollar question: Did Christianity depart from Judaism with regard to same-sex relations?

We're only halfway through our study, so we don't want to make any firm judgments just yet. Much more Bible to go! But the point is still an important one to keep in mind: If we say that Christians should endorse same-sex relations, then we will need to recreate a rather un-Jewish Jesus and an un-Jewish New Testament. Most Christians today, however, are rightly trying to get back in touch with our Jewish roots, not away from them. But we can't have it both ways.

There is a chance that Christianity could depart from its Jewish context with regard to same-sex relations. But the New Testament would have to make this clear. We'll have to work through the next three chapters to see if it does.

CHAPTER FIVE

WHOM WOULD
JESUS LOVE?

Homosexuality and the Savior

Where does Jesus stand on the question of homosexuality?

This could be a very short chapter for one simple reason: Jesus never mentions same-sex relations. Not once. Jesus never directly addresses the question of whether two men or two women could fall in love, get married, and have sex.

Some people spin Jesus' silence into an affirmation. Since he never said anything, Jesus would have endorsed same-sex relations. Or, if he were dragged into the modern debate and asked: "Where do you stand, Jesus?" he would have shrugged his messianic shoulders with indifference and told his debaters to go feed the poor. Others say that since Jesus condemned fornication, he really did denounce same-sex relations. After all, the word *fornication* (*porneia*) is an umbrella term for all Old Testament sex-laws, which includes same-sex behavior.[1]

Like the poor child caught in the middle of a divorce, Jesus has been wooed by guardians on both sides of the homosexuality debate.

I actually do believe that Jesus' words and actions should profoundly shape how we approach our topic. But like the child who shakes free from the clutches of his divorced parents and tells them *both* to "stop it!" Jesus challenges the affirming and nonaffirming crowd alike. Here's how.

JESUS' CHALLENGE TO THE AFFIRMING CROWD

Jesus was a Jew. He wasn't some blond-haired, blue-eyed, pasty-white Norwegian man typical in most of our portraits. He was a short-haired, brown-skinned, Hebrew-speaking Jew.[2] He spoke a little Greek, though probably with a thick accent. And he didn't know a lick of English.

I fear that the affirming writers, who enlist Jesus to support their view, have ripped him out of his Jewish context. As we saw in the last chapter, the Judaism that existed for five hundred years on either side of Jesus unequivocally condemned same-sex behavior. And the condemnation is unqualified and universal, scattered across many diverse sects of Judaism. Never once do we see a Jewish leader, thinker, writer, or rabbi sanction any form of same-sex erotic behavior. They condemned pederasty, same-sex peer relations (both male and female), and even same-sex marriages, although the latter were rare in those days—rare but not nonexistent as some have argued.[3] One would have to create a rather un-Jewish, pasty-white Norwegian, Western Jesus before they recruit him to support same-sex relations.

ARGUMENT FROM SILENCE?

So why didn't Jesus address same-sex behavior? We have to be careful making definitive claims about why Jesus did or didn't talk about topics he never mentions. No one has access to Jesus' motivations. If we revisit Jesus' world, however, we could probably discover, with caution, some reasons why the topic never came up.

Remember, Jesus lived and ministered in Israel. Most of the people he talked to were Jews; only rarely did he talk to Gentiles.[4] Since same-sex relations weren't a matter of debate within Judaism, it's not surprising that the topic never came up. Or if it did, it was never recorded in the four Gospels.

Some say that this is an argument from silence and therefore invalid. Since Jesus never said anything about same-sex relations, then there is no way to know what he would have said had the question been raised.

This is a fair critique. It's true, it is an argument from silence to say that Jesus would have stood against same-sex relations if someone had asked him about them. However, there are good arguments from silence and bad arguments from silence. Not all arguments from silence are incorrect. Good arguments from silence look at other historical and culture details based on evidence to help explain why there is silence. Not all arguments from silence are the same.

And for what it's worth, I haven't said that Jesus did condemn same-sex relations. I've only said that if he did endorse them, he would have been the only Jewish person in more than a thousand years to do so. It's not impossible, just highly unlikely.

Plus, Jesus is silent on a whole host of other ethical questions, but I don't think his silence meant that he was indifferent. Jesus never mentions incest. Logically, therefore, it's an argument from silence to say that he had an opinion on the matter. Jesus never mentions rape. Perhaps he was for it, or maybe he was against it. We just don't know without making an argument from silence. Jesus never spoke out against bestiality. Only an argument from silence can say he would have frowned upon the act.

There are good arguments from silence—ones that are based on historical evidence—and bad arguments from silence that are created out of thin air. It would make much more historical and cultural sense to conclude that Jesus stood with the rest of Judaism on the question of homosexual relations.

But there are more points to consider.

JESUS' BIBLE AND HOMOSEXUAL RELATIONS

Jesus never read the New Testament; it wasn't around yet. Jesus' Bible was what we now call the "Old Testament." And Jesus' Bible clearly, from an ancient Jewish perspective, prohibited male same-sex intercourse. Modern people debate the meaning of Leviticus 18:22 and 20:13, but no ancient Jew ever did. At least, not that we're aware of. Whenever Jewish people discussed these passages, they took them as forbidding same-sex relations.

The fact that Jesus' authoritative Bible prohibited male same-sex intercourse suggests that Jesus would have believed the words of Leviticus had the question come up.

Now you may wonder, didn't Jesus do away with the Old Testament Law? Didn't he say that the Law, which includes Leviticus, is no longer binding on Christians?

I used to hold this view and some Christians still do. The fact that our New Testaments are worn ragged while the pages of our Old Testaments are crispy new shows that many Christians have little time for the Old Testament. And all those funky laws about menstruation and other bodily discharges avert us from discovering spiritual meat worthy of our morning devotions.

But look closely and you'll see that Jesus was a law-abiding Jew. He told his disciples: "Do not think that I have come to abolish the Law or the Prophets; I have not come to abolish them but to fulfill them" (Matt. 5:17). And again: "Anyone who sets aside one of the least of these commands and teaches others accordingly will be called least in the kingdom of heaven, but whoever practices and teaches these commands will be called great in the kingdom of heaven" (Matt. 5:19). When he heals a leper, he commands him to go see the local priest, just as Leviticus 13 says (Matt. 8:1–4). There are times, of course, when Jesus seems to correct the law. But if you look closely, you'll see that Jesus isn't usually correcting the law but a Pharisaic interpretation of the law.[5]

There are only a few places where Jesus may have improved upon an Old Testament law. In Matthew 19, he seems to correct what Deuteronomy 24 says about divorce. However, Jesus doesn't clearly go against what Deuteronomy says. Rather, he shows that Moses' words were a mere concession in light of Israel's hard hearts. Instead of correcting or overturning Old Testament law, Jesus actually draws out the true intention of the law when he says that a man should not divorce his wife.[6]

Jesus also reconfigured the law of retaliation ("eye for an eye and tooth for a tooth") and the dietary laws, but in both cases it's not as clear as you may think.[7] Jesus on the whole didn't do away with the Law. He certainly released us from the Law's condemnation, and he fulfilled the sacrificial system through his death and resurrection, and he corrected a pharisaic misinterpretation of the Law. But he didn't walk around scoffing at the Old Testament laws as some dusty relics of his bygone Jewish past. Jesus was a Jew through and through. He loved and cherished his Father's Law.[8]

Even if Jesus corrected (or improved upon) a few laws, he always makes this clear. That is, we have textual reasons, with chapters and verses, for saying that we should no longer poke out someone's eye if they poke out ours. But when it comes to same-sex relations, there is nothing explicit nor implicit suggesting that Jesus corrected, improved upon, or did away with the sexual commands in Leviticus 18:22 and 20:13. Nothing. There is no evidence.

JESUS' STRICT SEXUAL ETHIC

Even though Jesus never mentions homosexuality, when it came to sexual matters in general, he took a very strict stance compared to other rabbis of the day. You may have heard that there were two main schools of thought in Judaism around the time of Jesus: the school of Hillel and the school of Shammai, named after their respective founders. Both believed in the Mosaic Law, but they interpreted it differently. The school of Hillel was known for being more lenient, while the school of Shammai was more rigorous.

For instance, when it came to divorce, Shammai said that divorce was never permissible except in cases where the wife has committed fornication. As for Hillel, he said that a man could divorce his wife if she simply cooks a bad meal.[9]

Jesus, of course, takes the more strict view of Shammai: "Anyone who divorces his wife, except for sexual immorality, and marries another woman commits adultery" (Matt. 19:9). Some say he goes even further than Shammai by not allowing divorce at all (Mark

10:2–12). When it comes to adultery, Jesus takes a very strict interpretation by saying "that anyone who looks at a woman lustfully has already committed adultery with her in his heart" (Matt. 5:28).

So in sexual matters that were debated within Judaism, Jesus takes a stricter stance and not a more lenient one. While he never mentions homosexuality, I think it's fair to say, in light of what he says about other sexual laws, that it's much more likely that he would have upheld this sexual law rather than take a more lenient interpretation of it. Upholding it would fit the pattern of how he approached other sexual laws.

A good argument from silence or a bad one? You make the call.

I don't want to put words in Jesus' mouth. But I also don't want to recreate Jesus in our twenty-first-century, Western, postmodern, do-whatever-feels-right-for-you image. Jesus is not some ethical Gumby that we can bend around our personal desires. He wasn't a moral jellyfish, nor did his radical love toward sinners mean that he couldn't care less about their sin. Jesus' Sermon on the Mount (Matt. 5–7) still stands as one of the most stringent, demanding ethical speeches in all religious history. Jesus didn't shrink back from preaching repentance and yet he held to a very high ethical standard[10]—so high that he had to be crucified and walk out of a grave for us to attain it.

Jesus cares deeply about obedience. Not man-made, legalistic obedience cooked up by twentieth-century American fundamentalism, but that radical, counterintuitive, life-giving obedience to our gracious Creator.

But Jesus pulls repentance and obedience out of our souls, not by laying down the law, but by laying down love. And this is where Jesus challenges the nonaffirming crowd.

JESUS' CHALLENGE TO THE NONAFFIRMING CROWD

I've been shocked recently at Jesus' radical love toward the marginalized and outcast. Oh sure, I've always known that Jesus reached out to tax collectors, sinners, widows, and poor people. But until recently, I hadn't appreciated the scandal of *how* Jesus reached out to them. Jesus rarely started a relationship with the law, and he never offered his "stance" on political issues. He usually began the relationship with love and always showed acceptance, especially with those rejected by the religious elite.

Immediately after Jesus preaches the most rigorous ethical speech of all time (Matt. 5–7), he heads off to meet people in the surrounding villages (Matt. 8–9). His approach in relating to these people is astonishing.

In Matthew 8, Jesus meets a military leader of an oppressive empire—a centurion. The Romans had conquered Israel a hundred years earlier, and now the foreign invaders were ruling over the Jewish people. Many righteous Jews had tried to oust the pagans violently from their land and did so with much religious zeal. Many Old Testament leaders fought off and killed their heathen oppressors and were chalked up as heroes of the faith (Heb. 11). So when the Roman centurion steps up to the Jewish Messiah, everyone expected a righteous rumble.

But they are quickly let down. Although Jesus could have destroyed his enemy and would have been just in doing so, he chooses rather to conquer the centurion with love. When he asks Jesus to heal his servant, Jesus responds not with a sword but with grace: "Shall I come and heal him?" The centurion responds with great faith, and Jesus gladly welcomes him into the kingdom.

No doubt, the religious people were stunned. The Roman military was well known for its debauchery, paganism, and oppressive violence. Some say that centurions acted as virtual pagan priests, conducting religious ceremonies to Roman gods. Historically speaking, the centurion would have been a walking pile of sin, and yet Jesus never mentions any of it. Although Jesus takes a firm stance against violence in Matthew 5, he doesn't tell the centurion, "Well, okay, I'll go ahead and heal your servant, but I must first tell you where I stand on the issue of violence." Or "We can be friends and all, but if you want to be a Christian, you'll have to drop all your pagan practices and change your vocation before you can be my disciple."

Jesus doesn't lead with the law. He leads with love—love without footnotes.

Sure, Jesus was against paganism, violence, and many other habits in a centurion's life. But he doesn't feel the need to create a thick wall of moral conditions for the centurion to leap over in order to receive love. Jesus' love comes without a background check.

The same goes for Matthew the tax collector (Matt. 9:9–13). Jesus sees "a man named Matthew sitting at the tax collector's booth" and says to him: "Follow me." Immediately, "Matthew got up and followed him" (9:9).

It's tough for us to feel the shockwave of this passage, since we don't have a contemporary category for first-century tax collectors. They were not just shady IRS agents who struggled with greed; they weren't greasy used-car salespersons with too much teeth. Tax collectors were Jewish sellouts to the oppressive Roman Empire, who had taken over and unjustly occupied their country. Picture something like the Russian takeover in the old *Red Dawn* movie (or North Korea in the much lamer new *Red Dawn* movie). Tax collecting was legalized political and religious treason.

Moreover, tax collectors had a reputation for living excessively immoral lives. Religious Jews considered them to be worse than thieves and murderers, and on par with dung collectors. Yes—*dung collectors*. And they were thought to be past the point of repentance. If God's grace has a leash, it stopped short of reaching tax collectors, according to Jewish tradition.[11]

A modern-day parallel might be a pimp, who is also a drug dealer, who runs a porn studio on the side, and funnels his profits to support terrorism around the world. What would you say if you stumbled into someone like this?

Jesus says: "Follow me." Matthew gets up and follows Jesus.

Jesus doesn't say, "Well, you can attend our church service, but you first need to know where we stand on the issue of extortion." He doesn't say, "I can love you, Matthew, but I hate your sin." Jesus doesn't lead with the law—and there were a lot of laws he could have fronted with a thug like Matthew. Instead, he fronts love. "Come follow me." Jesus invites him to be his disciple without rubbing Matthew's face in his sin.

Is Jesus against extortion? Of course. Does Jesus desire that Matthew stop robbing people? I know, an argument from silence, but I think at some point, in the context of a relationship and love, Jesus probably said to Matthew, "So, about this whole tax-collecting gig ..."

There was a massive first-century culture war over tax gathering, but Jesus cuts through the clutter with radical love. Love without fine print. Jesus desires obedience, but to get that obedience he fronts love.

GAY IS THE NEW TAX COLLECTOR

In no way am I comparing gays and lesbians with tax collectors. I'm only trying to look at how Jesus approached people whom his religious society considered to be sinners. The fact is: religious people today treat LGBT people the same way that ancient religious people treated tax collectors. Therefore, Jesus' encounter with tax collectors should inform and challenge our approach to gay people.

Jesus meets another tax collector in Luke 19 named Zacchaeus. He's even more depraved than Matthew because Zacchaeus is a *"chief* tax collector and was *wealthy"* (Luke 19:2, emphasis added). He wasn't just an extortionist, but a very good one. Zacchaeus was hated by all—even by other tax collectors. When Jesus passes through Jericho, he looks beyond all the other people and tells the extortionist: "Zacchaeus, come down immediately. I am under divine compulsion to befriend you in your own home."[12] And, of course, all the religious people got upset.

Religious people always got upset whenever Jesus befriended people who they thought were terrible sinners. If you're a Christian who is trying hard to love LGBT people, and if this ticks off a lot of religious people, perhaps even those really close to you, then take comfort. You're in good company. Jesus knows exactly how you feel.

It's fascinating that Jesus only speaks twice in his encounter with Zacchaeus. First he says: "Zacchaeus, come down immediately. I must stay at your house today" (19:5). And then, after Zacchaeus repents, Jesus says: "Today salvation has come to this house, because this man, too, is a son of Abraham. For the Son of Man came to seek and to save the lost" (19:9–10). Take note: It wasn't Jesus' "stance on extortion" that led to Zacchaeus' repentance. It was Zacchaeus' encounter with the otherworldly love of Christ—love without footnotes—that pushed repentance out the other side. And Jesus never had to tell Zacchaeus where he stood on the issue of tax collecting.[13]

Some of the most beautiful, wise, loving, moral people I know are gay. So again, in no way am I drawing a parallel between the lifestyle of Zacchaeus with the behavior of all gay people. Tax collectors were simply considered to be really bad sinners by the religious leaders of the day. In the same way, many religious people today consider LGBT people or "the gay agenda" to be sinful and destructive; just like first-century religious people considered FCTG (first-century-tax-gathering) people and "the Roman agenda" to be sinful and destructive. Still, for some reason, "tax collectors and sinners were all gathering around to hear Jesus" (Luke 15:1).

Think about that. *They*—tax collectors and sinners—were drawing near to Jesus. They found something so compelling about Jesus that they drew near to hear him. And it wasn't because he was some postmodern poet who thinks that love means letting everyone do whatever feels right to them. That's the pasty-white, blond-haired, modern Jesus, not the Jewish rabbi of the New Testament. Jesus was able to preach hard-hitting, biblically saturated, ethically demanding sermons. And yet sinners and tax collectors were drawn to the presence of Christ.

It wasn't because their behavior was affirmed. It was because their humanity was affirmed.

UNCONDITIONAL WELCOME

We see the same pattern in almost every scandalous encounter Jesus has with "sinners." The father (= God) "felt compassion, and ran and embraced" his prodigal son before he knew that his son was repentant (Luke 15:20). Jesus declared to the woman caught in adultery, "Neither do I condemn you" before he said "go and sin no more" (John 8:11).[14] Jesus forgave the many sins of the prostitute that was washing his feet without ever mentioning her sins (Luke 7:36–50).

Did Jesus affirm everyone's sin? Of course not. Did he broadcast their sin when loving them? Biblically speaking: no.

Let me get real with you. I have become so discouraged over the years at how evangelicals have postured themselves against the LGBT community. And it's not just my isolated experience. According to the statistics, when young non-Christians were asked about the first thing that came to mind when they thought of evangelical Christianity, you know what they said? Ninety-one percent said that the first thing that comes to mind when they think of Christians is that Christians are "antihomosexual."[15]

Really? *Anti*homosexual? Is that what defines us? Would tax collectors ever be drawn to Jesus if their perception of him were that he was *anti*taxcollector?

The next two perceptions are that Christians are "judgmental" (87%) and "hypocritical" (85%). And most of the people surveyed had some personal contact with a Christian church. Their responses were largely from firsthand experiences.

Where did these perceptions come from? How can the most common perception of Christ-followers be that we are antihomosexual, judgmental, and hypocritical, when Jesus, who showed us how to live, railed most ferociously against hypocritical, judgmental religious people—and he never mentioned homosexuality?

Of course we all fall short of Jesus' standard. But to be known for the very things that Jesus stood against? That doesn't make any sense. I'm afraid that the way in which the evangelical church has taken a stand against homosexuality has watered down our good news. Our "stand" against homosexuality has been perceived as a stand not against sin but against humanity.

Jesus—the biblical Jesus—took a stand. But it was a stand on love.

If you are a nonaffirming Christian—who believes that practicing gay and lesbian people are living in sin and that homosexual relations are among the most sinful things a person could engage in—then, if you truly desire to follow Jesus, you should have more LGBT friends and not less.

You should be frequenting the gay district in town, inviting gays and lesbians over to your house, and asking to stay with gay and lesbian friends in their houses. If Jesus could dine with a person like Zacchaeus, then certainly you could bring yourself to enter into a humanity-affirming relationship with gay and lesbian people. A relationship without footnotes. A loving friendship that doesn't begin with "where you stand" on the issue of homosexuality, since Jesus didn't take this approach. Take a stand—yes. But take a stand on love. That radical, countercultural grace that drew sinners and tax collectors to Jesus. Jesus actually did talk about that.

WHEN TWO LESBIANS COME TO YOUR CHURCH

I read a story a while back about two lesbians who decided to go to church one Sunday just to make Christians mad.[16] "Let's just go for fun! We'll see how much we can push their buttons," Amy told her girlfriend. "I hear their motto is 'Come as you are'," Amy scoffed. "I just want to prove that they're 'come as you are ... unless you're gay.'"

Are our churches sending that signal? If you're greedy, slanderous, pugnacious, or addicted to drugs or alcohol, then "come as you are." But if you're gay, you're not welcome? Amy got that from somewhere. And according to the statistics, she's not alone. The evangelical church is considered to be *anti*homosexual and therefore *anti*Amy.

But Amy and her girlfriend went to church. They flirted in front of everyone, held hands, and made it very clear that they were lesbians. How did the church respond?

"Instead of the disgusted looks of contempt we expected, people met eyes with us and treated us like real people," Amy recalls. When I first read Amy's words, I was excited to see how this church fronted love. But there is a word that Amy uses that makes my heart break.

Expected.

"Instead of the disgusted looks of contempt we expected," they "treated us like real people." Amy and her girlfriend were shocked that these Christians thought they were human beings and not monsters.

Why was this shocking?

What else would they expect from a bunch of sinners saved by grace?

How else should divine image-bearers plugged into a lifeline of undeserved favor treat two human beings who are drawing near to the body of Christ?

Expected. They expected Christians to treat them like some subspecies of the human race. Instead, they were shocked that followers of Christ actually acted like Christ.

Most gay people I know have been involved in church at some point. Their testimonies are almost identical: I grew up in the church. I tried to follow Jesus. When I hit puberty, I experienced unwanted same-sex attraction that caused me unbearable pain and confusion. When I tried to talk about it, I was shunned, confronted, and made to feel like a monster. I became depressed, which led to isolation, which led to more depression, which led to fleeing the church in search of love.

For a staggering number of gay teens, growing up in church has led to the grave.

Teens who experience same-sex attraction are two to seven times more likely to attempt suicide than teens who don't. And unfortunately, the teens who seek help from religious leaders are *more* likely to kill themselves than those who seek help from nonreligious counselors.[17] Quibble over statistics all you want, but this is still frightening. I seriously doubt that the tax collectors and sinners who were "drawing near to Jesus" (Luke 15:1) walked away wanting to kill themselves.

LGBT people who grew up in the church, who didn't commit suicide, often end up leaving the church in search of a community that would value them as humans. But it's not just gay people who have left the church. A growing number of younger straight people are leaving Christianity based on how the church has treated gay people. And it's usually not because of the church's nonaffirming view of same-sex behavior, but their nonaffirming posture toward gay and lesbian people. It's not too much truth but too little love that's driving gay and straight people away from the bride of Christ.[18]

And I am not talking about a thin type of love that doesn't care about holiness. I am not talking about the superficial, secular love trumpeted by our twenty-first-century Western culture. I am talking about first-century Jesus-love. The love that seeks one's holiness but isn't contingent upon one's holiness. The *agape* love that Jesus showed. The love that told an extortionist, "Follow me" and stood up for a woman fresh off her steamy affair and said, "I don't condemn you." The love that demands, "If you love me, keep my commandments," but not "If you keep my commandments, then I will love you."[19]

Jesus-love is neither permissive nor conditional. It expects and enables obedience but doesn't require obedience as its prerequisite.

The fact is, most LGBT people I know didn't leave the church because their behavior wasn't affirmed—"I want to sleep with people of the same sex, and if you don't affirm this I'm gone." It was because their humanity wasn't affirmed.

"AN ABOMINATION TO THE GOD I ADORED"

My friend Lesli, for instance, is biologically a woman, but from the time she was four, she felt like a boy. She didn't "choose" this; it was a preconscious desire. She felt like a boy, had emotions like a boy, and played like a boy. Lesli figured that she had been stuffed in the wrong body at birth.

Lesli also had accepted Jesus at a young age and loved him with all her heart. It wasn't until her teenage years when she realized that she didn't fit the mold of who people wanted her to be. She realized that she was transgender—biologically female but everything else male.

Lesli loved Jesus and was passionately involved at her church. But toward the end of her freshman year in high school, her pastor began preaching on homosexuality, and this is when her world fell apart. She recounts:

> My pastor began a sermon series that included the evils of homosexuality. He condemned all homosexuals to hell. God had no forgiveness for such deviants. Even worse was the mentally ill trans community. He spoke in detail about men becoming women and women becoming men. These people were an abomination in God's eyes. They were unsavable. We must protect our children from their evil ploys. My friends shouted "Amen" and showed appropriate levels of disgust . . . I was ashamed that I was such an abomination to the God that I adored.

Ashamed. That she was such an *abomination.* To the God she adored.

We cannot let our hearts become so callused over by fear-driven sermons about the evils of the "gay agenda" that we forget that homosexuality is about people, not an issue.

Lesli was convinced that neither the church nor that church's

God accepted her, so she did what hundreds of thousands of LGBT people have done: she left the church and found a form of love in the LGBT community where her humanity was affirmed and cherished.

Thanks to the grace of God mediated through another pastor many years later, Lesli came back to Christ and now ministers to teens wrestling with their gender identity. But many LGBT people don't come back. They remain jaded by the church. They keep hearing about some "good news" papered over with a thin veneer of grace, but it's a gospel that lacks the scent of Calvary. It only bears the stench of Christianese rhetoric that dehumanizes beautiful people created in God's image.

TRUTH ~~VERSUS~~ AND LOVE

Love doesn't mean affirming one's behavior. Jesus would not have high-fived Matthew as he was on his way to beat someone's face in and take their tax money. Love means accepting one's humanity without affirming everything they do. Love confronts as much as it forgives. The same Jesus who loved Matthew also preached the Sermon on the Mount, and I don't think Jesus was schizophrenic. Loving people in spite of their behavior doesn't mean affirming their behavior.

But this is the fear for many nonaffirming Christians. You think that if you show radical Zacchaeus-shaped love to LGBT people, that they will think you affirm everything they do. Actually, they won't. If they know you're a Christian, there's a good chance that gay and lesbian people already assume you don't agree with their sexual identity. In fact, they probably assume that you hate them and think they are disgusting people. Showing them radical love and not racing to inform them about your "stance" on homosexuality will only convince them that you believe they are human.

Remember, repentance doesn't lead to God's kindness. It's God's kindness that leads to repentance (Rom. 2:4). In the same way, nonaffirming Christians should flood LGBT people with kindness, and such kindness will lead to repentance. But if it doesn't, the kindness doesn't stop. Because "our Father who is in heaven ... makes his sun rise on the evil and on the good, and sends rain on the just and on the unjust" (Matt. 5:45). And he doesn't shut up the skies when the unjust don't repent. He keeps refreshing them with scandalous rain.

The evangelical church needs to get this. I am not calling on the church to give up its convictions. I am calling on the church to change its posture, to be convicted about Christ's stubborn one-way love that he called us to mediate to others.

So where does Jesus stand?

He stands on love. He stands on compassion. And he therefore stands on truth.

He stands in solidarity with the woman caught in adultery, taking on her shame and sin, and declaring: "Neither do I condemn you."

CHAPTER SIX

FALL SHORT OF GOD'S GLORY

Homosexual and Heterosexual Sins in Romans 1

Romans 1 is probably the most important passage in the debate about same-sex relations, since Paul describes them in some detail. This is also the only place in the Bible where female homoeroticism is mentioned. Before we jump in, let's sum up the most salient points we have observed thus far, so that we don't get lost in a forest of information.

The Bible only mentions heterosexual marriages, which isn't sufficient in itself to draw any conclusions. However, in several passages (Gen. 2:18; Matt. 19:4–5; and especially Ephesians 5:21–32), it seems like sexual difference is necessary for marriage.

The account of Sodom (Gen. 19:1–9) is largely irrelevant for understanding what the Bible says about same-sex relations, since it talks about attempted gang rape not mutual love.

Leviticus 18:22 and 20:13 prohibit male same-sex intercourse and don't appear to describe a particular form of same-sex relations (such as rape or prostitution). These verses use general language that would include all forms of male homosexual sex. And it seems that these commands are still relevant today.

Judaism unanimously and unambiguously condemned same-sex relations even though such relations were widely accepted (with certain conditions) in their Greco-Roman environment.

Jesus never explicitly mentions homosexuality, but his Jewish background and his posture toward the marginalized challenge people on both sides of the debate.

I don't believe that any one of these points alone carries enough weight to form a conclusion. And even though the weight of evidence thus far appears to support the nonaffirming view, we need to look at the rest of the Bible and consider different counterarguments before we form our conclusion. Homosexuality is too important of a topic—because people are too important—to form a view prematurely. If we race to form a conclusion too quickly, this only shows that we already had our minds made up before we study the authoritative Word. In which case, the Scriptures are not all that authoritative. Just a handy supplement.

GAY AND STRAIGHT— DAMNED WITHOUT CHRIST

Romans 1 actually condemns both gay and straight people—a point that is sometimes missed when homophobic Christians unsheathe the chapter and wield it against the LGBT community. Beginning in verse 24, Paul writes:

> Therefore God gave them over in the sinful desires of their hearts to sexual impurity for the degrading of their bodies with one another. They exchanged the truth about God for a lie, and worshiped and served created things rather than the Creator—who is forever praised. Amen. (Rom. 1:24–25)

The reference to "sexual impurity" here is not limited to same-sex relations. It's a general statement that includes sex outside of marriage, adultery, rape, and all sorts of other sexual sins committed by both gay and straight people. So if you're straight, let's make sure you don't read the next couple verses with a massive log sticking out of your eye. There's a good chance you've already violated Romans 1 even before you get to verse 26:

Because of this, God gave them over to shameful desires. Even their females exchanged natural sexual relations for unnatural ones. In the same way the males also abandoned natural relations with females and were inflamed with passion for one another. Males committed shameful acts with other males, and received in themselves the due penalty for their error. (Rom. 1:26–27 my translation)

The entire context of Romans 1–3 is important for understanding these verses. Paul launches into an argument that sweeps from Romans 1:18 all the way to 3:26, which basically says we're all damned without Jesus. Literally. The first part (1:18–32) sums up the sins of the Gentiles, while the second part (2:1–29) accuses the Jews of being just as wicked.[1] The third part (3:1–20) concludes that we're all up the creek, Jew and Gentile, since we are *all* under sin (3:9). What is worse, we can't work our way out of our mess by pulling ourselves up by our moral bootstraps in order to obey the Law (3:19–20). All people are under God's wrath—something we have chosen for ourselves (Rom. 1:19–23).

But Paul is not all doom and gloom. In Romans 3:21–26, he paints a life-giving portrait of the atoning work of Christ, which erases all previous wrongs and ushers believers into a covenant relationship with God. All the junk we did—whether Jew or Gentile, gay or straight, murderer or moralist, porn addict or pride addict—has been stuffed in a coffin and thrown into the sea.

There is absolutely no room for moral pride here. It's an offense both to Paul and to the cross of Christ to look down your spiritual nose at the homosexual acts in Romans 1 and ignore your own greed, slander, envy, covetousness, and judgmentalism, which are also mentioned in Romans 1. As Christians, we're all a bunch of beggars trying to show other beggars where to find bread.[2] A beggar who is proud that he found the loaf first is nothing more than a damned beggar. If you're thrilled to read this chapter in order to find biblical artillery to blast your affirming friend, then please stop reading.

Stop. Pray. Confess. Repent. Then return with tears: tears of gratitude to the One who delighted in you; tears of sorrow for those who have not found the Bread of life; tears of pain as you weep with those who wrestle with their faith and sexuality.

HAVE WE MISUNDERSTOOD ROMANS 1?

At first glance, Romans 1:26–27 seems like a rather straightforward critique of same-sex relations. I remember first hearing about people who didn't think this passage prohibited such relations: I scrunched my eyebrows and thought they were nuts. I couldn't see how this passage could be read any other way than condemning same-sex relations.

But then I started to pay attention to the actual affirming arguments and saw where they were coming from. In fact, as I have combed through scholarly defenses of an affirming view of Romans 1, there were at least a few points that threw me back in my chair and forced me to question the traditional view. As I've said throughout this book, it's not about being affirming or nonaffirming; it's about being biblical. It's about submitting to God's Word even if it critiques and offends what you've always believed.

I have studied through this passage extensively and considered every interpretation as fairly as I could. I have even written a rather lengthy scholarly article that wrestles with what I believe to be the strongest affirming interpretation.[3] Still, after many hours in books and conversations, I believe that the nonaffirming interpretation of this passage best represents what Paul is saying.

In this chapter, I will explore the meaning of Romans 1:26–27 and interact with what I think is the best affirming argument against the nonaffirming view. In order to be thorough and fair, I have added an appendix at the end of the book that critiques other significant affirming interpretations of this passage.

SAME-SEX RELATIONS IN ROMANS 1:26–27

As we look at Romans 1, there are three significant observations that are relevant for our discussion. The first one is brief; the last two are long.

THE LANGUAGE OF MUTUALITY

First, Paul considers both people involved in the sex act to be doing something wrong in Romans 1:26–27. The last part of verse 27 says: "Men committed shameful acts with other men, and received in themselves the due penalty for their error." Paul's previous statement about women in verse 26 is not as explicit, but given the parallel between verse 26 and 27, it is likely that both females are equally guilty as well. Plus, historically speaking, female homosexual relations were for the most part consensual in the ancient world. They weren't pederastic or driven by power differences like many male same-sex relations were.[4] When Paul condemns female homoerotic behavior in verse 26, and parallels it with male homoeroticism in verse 27, it would seem that Paul's words apply to consensual same-sex acts in both verses. Paul doesn't use language that suggests exploitative same-sex relations or a power differential. He doesn't refer to rape or to pederasty. He doesn't limit his words to men having sex with male prostitutes. The language is all-inclusive and suggests mutuality. He doesn't single out the active partner nor does his language reflect the typical dominator/dominated paradigm. Surely Paul's words include all of these, but his language is too general to be limited to a particular form of same-sex relation.[5]

The next two observations are very important. I'll discuss them in more detail.

GOD'S DESIGN IN CREATION

Second, Paul salts his argument with many allusions to the Creation account in Genesis 1 and 2.[6] For instance, Paul refers to

God as "the Creator" in Romans 1:25, which points the reader back to Genesis. Earlier Paul said that God has been revealing himself "ever since the creation of the world" (1:20). Again, this alerts the reader to Genesis 1 and 2. Paul also uses gender specific terms to describe men and women, that is "males" (*arsen*) and "females" (*theleiai*) in Romans 1:26–27. These two terms were first paired in the Greek translation of Genesis 1:27, a passage that highlights the different genders of humanity: "God created man, according to the image of God he created him, *male* [*arsen*] and *female* [*thelu*] he created them" (Gen. 1:27).[7] Paul is not just talking about people having illicit sex with people, but females having illicit sex with females, and males with males.

What's the point? It seems that Paul draws attention to God's creation of humans into different biological sexes. Therefore, Paul considers same-sex relations to be a departure from God's intention in creation—which would be nothing novel for a Jew like Paul to say. The same-sex acts in 1:26–27 violate gender boundaries, which goes against the way they were created as *males* and *females*. Every first-century Jew would have yawned at Paul's point. Remember—this wasn't a matter of debate within Judaism.

We'll return to that gender point below. But there is one more allusion to Genesis that is worth noting. In Romans 1:23, Paul says:

> [They] exchanged the glory of the immortal God for images [*eikonos*] *in* the likeness of [*homoomati*] mortal mankind [*anthropou*] and birds [*peteinon*] and animals and reptiles [*herpeton*].

This verse uses five of the same Greek words used in Genesis 1:26 LXX:

> Then God said, "Let us make mankind [*anthropon*] in our image [*eikona*], in our likeness [*homoiosin*], so that they may rule over the fish in the sea and the birds [*peteinon*] in the sky, over the livestock and all the wild animals, and over all the *reptiles* [*herpeton*] that move along the ground."

This can't be anything other than intentional. Paul pens Romans 1:23 with an eye on Genesis 1:26. His logic is not too far from Genesis 1, where God commissions mankind (male and female) to rule over the earth. In Romans 1, Paul says that instead of worshiping God by ruling over the earth, they have idolized the things of the earth and turned their back on their Creator. Mankind has departed from God's original intention; the way God designed them to be as gendered humans. Notice the pattern of exchange in Romans 1. Humankind "exchanges" the Creator for creation; females exchange sexual relations with males for females; males exchange sexual relations with females for males. And all of this seems to stem from a departure of the way God designed us, as seen in Genesis 1–2.[8]

Let me make a simple observation so we don't get lost in a sea of technicalities. If Paul situates the same-sex relations (Rom. 1:26–27) in the context of departing from the Creator's intention, then this suggests that Paul's words are not limited to some cultural way of behaving. That is, Paul doesn't say that certain types of same-sex relations were taboo in his Greco-Roman environment and therefore they are wrong. He says, or seems to assume, that what is wrong with same-sex relations transcends culture. Violating God-given gender boundaries is universal and absolute. They go against the way God created males and females and intended them to relate to each other sexually.

AGAINST NATURE

This brings us, thirdly, to perhaps the most important phrase in this passage: Paul considers same-sex intercourse to be "against nature" or "unnatural," as some translations have it (1:26). The Greek phrase is *para physin* and it has been butchered by people on both sides of the debate.

Some nonaffirming people look no further than the English translation "unnatural" and think this settles the debate. Gay sex is unnatural; therefore it is wrong. And maybe it is. But what does "unnatural" mean? Assuming a particular meaning of "unnatural" and reading it back into the text is not a responsible interpretation. Paul says later that God grafted Gentiles in to the covenant promises of God, which was "contrary to nature" (*para physin*; Romans 11:24). Does this mean that God too is "unnatural" and therefore sinful?[9]

Nonaffirming Christians can't just quote Romans 1 and think that this settles the debate. Everyone knows what Romans 1 says; the debate is over what it means. We have to do the hard work of interpretation and not sluggishly rely on quotation.

Affirming writers usually say one of two things about *para physin*. Some think Paul believes that same-sex intercourse is wrong because it can't procreate.[10] Paul believes, so the argument goes, that the only valid form of sex is that which seeks to bear children. *Para physin*, therefore, refers to any form of nonprocreative sex—heterosexual or homosexual.

If this is what *para physin* means, then of course this would condemn not only same-sex relations, but also a huge swath of evangelicals who use condoms, take the pill, or get snipped in order to have sex without the burden of child-bearing.

But does Paul say that homosexual sex is "unnatural" because it can't procreate?

No. He never says it. In fact, Paul discusses marriage and sex quite frequently, and yet he never mentions procreation (1 Cor. 7:1–40; Eph. 5:22–33; Col. 3:18–4:1). He even talks about having sex for the purpose of pacifying sexual urges in 1 Corinthians 7. Still, no mention of procreation. This would be rather odd if Paul believed that sex is only valid if it seeks to bear children. To assume that Paul thought homosexual sex was "unnatural" because it can't procreate is just that—an assumption. It's not in Romans 1, and it's not in any of Paul's letters. So this probably is not what the phrase *para physin* means.

Other affirming writers say that *para physin* means "against culture," or against the way Paul's culture expects people to act. James Brownson says that the phrase *para physin* means to go against "what we would call 'social' realities." According to Brownson, "Male-male sex in particular was 'unnatural' because it degraded the passive partner into acting like a woman."[11] Brownson believes that Paul's "moral logic," which underscores his use of *para physin*, is loaded with misogynist assumptions about women. When a man has sex with another man, he makes that man act like a mere woman. And *that* is unnatural.

The implication, of course, is that Paul's assumptions about the inferiority of women should not be observed today. And if Paul had such a low view of women, then I agree. (Although this makes me wonder about other caveman-like assumptions Paul may have had.) My main question is: Did Paul really think women were inferior? Yes, his fellow Greco-Roman and even Jewish writers believed some pretty awful things about women.[12] And yes, some ancient writers revealed these terrible assumptions about women when they critiqued same-sex relations.[13] But did Paul agree with them? Is there anything in Romans 1 that hints at this? Or is there anything in his letters that slams on women the way other people in his culture did?

Maybe you think Paul was a chauvinistic pig, I don't know. I've always been struck by Paul's high view of women, especially when measured against his environment.

Contrary to his fellow Greco-Roman and Jewish writers, Paul seems to have a rather high view of women. He calls several women "co-workers" (Rom. 16:3–4; Phil. 4:3), "workers in the Lord" (Rom. 16:6, 12), deacons (Rom. 16:1–2; 1 Tim. 3:11), prophets (1 Cor. 11:5; cf. Acts 21:9), and he calls Phoebe a "patron" (Rom. 16:2) who apparently funded much of the early Christian mission. He possibly calls Junia an "apostle" (Rom. 16:7), though translations differ. In Christ there is neither "male nor female" (Gal. 3:28) and women have just as much authority over their husbands' bodies as their husbands have over theirs (1 Cor. 7:3–5)—a revolutionary statement in its own right. Find me another statement among Paul's contemporaries who said something as radical as: "The husband does not have authority over his own body but yields it to his wife" (1 Cor. 7:4).

Even if Paul advocates for different roles in marriage (Eph. 5:22–33, for example), he commands men to self-sacrificially serve their wives, and he never suggests that females should submit to their husbands because they are inferior to men. Instead, Paul says that submission reflects the beauty and equality of the Triune God. And I don't think Paul had a low view of Christ and the Spirit.

It's unlikely that Paul considered same-sex intercourse to be "unnatural" because it can't procreate or because it makes the passive partner act like an inferior woman. Both of these views assume things that are neither in Romans 1 nor in his other letters.[14]

So what does *para physin* mean?

The phrase *para physin* has a long history, going as far back as Plato who first used it in reference to same-sex intercourse.[15] The phrase became popular among Greco-Roman moral philosophers and Greek-speaking Jews, who believed that same-sex intercourse was contrary to the will of God (or the design of nature).[16]

To be sure, many of these writers also believed that all forms of nonprocreative sex were wrong. Some condemned masturbation. Others prohibited sex during menstruation or even sex with an infertile wife. Some considered any sex that sought pleasure instead of parenthood to be sin. Or, as we'll see below, some moral philosophers argued that out-of-control passions leading to sex were immoral—even within a heterosexual marriage.[17]

Musonius Rufus was a Roman philosopher who lived around the same time as Paul. Rufus was more conservative than a KJV-only preacher living in the Bible Belt. He says that sex is justified "only when it occurs in marriage and is indulged in for the purpose of begetting children, since that is lawful, but unjust and unlawful when it is mere pleasure-seeking, even in marriage."[18] I would have hated to be Rufus's teenage son listening to his talk on the birds and the bees. What is important is that Rufus goes on to say: "But of all sexual relations those involving adultery are most unlawful, and no more tolerable are those of men with men, because it is a monstrous thing and contrary to nature [*para physin*]."[19]

Notice that Rufus considers all forms of nonprocreative sex to be immoral, but only sex between men is considered *para physin*. That's the pattern we see throughout ancient uses of *para physin*.

As far as I can tell, the phrase *para physin* is never used to speak of immoral forms of heterosexual sex.[20]

Philo, for instance, distinguishes between sexual lusts between men and women, which are "passions recognized by the laws of nature," and passions that are "felt by men for one another."[21] According to Philo, all nonprocreative sex is wrong. But only homosexual sex is "against nature."[22]

This is the pattern we see time and time again.[23] Various ancient writers critiqued all sorts of immoral sexual behavior. And yes, many of them believed that only procreative sex was valid. But when discussing sexual immorality, the phrase *para physin* was reserved for same-sex erotic behavior. Paul is simply reflecting the typical meaning of a widely known phrase. Richard Hays, a professor at Duke University, says it well:

> In Paul's time the categorization of homosexual practices as *para physin* was a commonplace feature of polemical attacks against such behavior, particularly in the world of Hellenistic Judaism. When this idea turns up in Romans 1 (in a form relatively restrained by comparison to some of the above examples), Paul is hardly making an original contribution to theological thought on the subject; he speaks out of a Hellenistic-Jewish cultural context in which homosexuality is regarded as an abomination, and he assumes that his readers will share his negative judgment of it.[24]

I actually don't like the way Hays worded his last sentence: "homosexuality is regarded as an abomination." As I said earlier, the term *homosexuality* is a modern one and way too broad. The word *abomination* is only used to describe the male-male sex act, not gay or lesbian people (Lev. 18:22; 20:13). But Hays wrote this more than twenty-five years ago. I am almost positive he would reword this today.

The rest of what Hays says rightly sums up everything I've seen. *Para physin* was simply stock language used by other Roman and Jewish writers to condemn same-sex relations. Extramarital or marital,[25] consensual or nonconsensual,[26] pederastic or peer[27]: *para physin* was used to critique same-sex relations as against the design of nature or, in Paul's view, against the design and intention of the Creator. The fact that Paul uses *para physin* in a context saturated with allusions to Genesis 1–2 suggests that this meaning is most likely what Paul has in mind.

WAS PAUL CRITIQUING EXCESSIVE LUST?

Some writers argue that Paul does not critique all same-sex relations. He only condemns those that result from excessive lust and uncontrollable passions. Therefore, Romans 1 does not apply to loving, consensual, nonlustful same-sex marriages—which is what affirming Christians are arguing for today.

I believe that this is by far the most persuasive affirming interpretation of Romans 1 that's out there. If you're familiar with their work, you'll notice that this is the view of Matthew Vines and James Brownson, along with other scholars such as Dale Martin and David Fredrickson. While I respond to other affirming interpretations in the Appendix, I need to deal with this one here since it is the most convincing.

This view correctly points out that many Greco-Roman writers believed that same-sex eroticism was the byproduct of excessive lust. That is, some men got bored with having sex with women, and from an out-of-control passion for the exotic and erotic, they started to penetrate other men. There's no denying this: same-sex male relations were often critiqued on the grounds that they were the byproduct of excessive lust.[28]

But I don't think that Paul believes that homosexual sex is wrong simply because it's the byproduct of excessive lust. Here are four reasons why.

First, while many ancient writers believed that same-sex relations were the result of excessive lust, other writers did not. Excessive lust was one of many reasons why some Greco-Roman writers thought that same-sex relations were wrong. In fact, Plutarch's *Dialogue on Love* records a speech by a guy who argues that heterosexual, not homosexual, sex is the byproduct of excessive lust.

According to ancient writers, excessive lust is one of several things that pushed people to engage in same-sex intercourse. As we saw in chapter four, some people even thought that same-sex desires were fixed at birth. And the entire project of pederasty was not (in its more noble forms) driven by lust but a desire to educate the youth. The point is: just because some ancient writers believed that same-sex intercourse resulted from excessive lust does not mean that they thought it was wrong simply because it resulted from excessive lust.

Second, the excessive-lust view doesn't work for Paul's critique of female same-sex relations in Romans 1:26.[29] Even if Greco-Roman writers critiqued male-male same-sex acts on the basis of excessive lust, the same argument wasn't used for female same-sex acts. Female same-sex relations were rarely (if ever) considered to be the byproduct of excessive lust.[30] And yet, Paul still says that they are "against nature."

I cannot emphasize enough how important 1:26 (female homoeroticism) is for interpreting this passage. Female homosexual relations were mutual, nonpederastic, and not the result of an out-of-control sex drive. Still, Paul says they are against nature.

Third, the phrase "against nature" does not help the excessive-lust interpretation. Everything we've seen with *para physin* above would have to be refuted in order for the excessive-lust view to stand. In other words, Paul never said that same-sex eroticism was wrong because it results from excessive lust. But he does say it was "against nature," and "against nature" does not mean "excessive lust." Given the context of creation in Romans 1, together with the emphasis on gender (male and female), it seems more likely that Paul uses *para physin* according to its typical meaning: same-sex relations go against the way God created men and women to relate sexually.

It would be tough to argue that consensual, same-sex relations, that did not result from excessive lust—and we have ancient examples[31]—would have been considered perfectly fine by Paul.

Lastly, while Paul uses the terms "passions" (1:24, 26) and "desire" (1:27) in Romans 1, he never talks about "excessive passion" in the same way that his Greco-Roman contemporaries do. James Brownson disagrees with this. He says that "it is not desire itself that Paul opposes, but excessive desire, which directs itself toward what is not rightly ours, overcoming self-control and obedience to God."[32] Brownson, however, spices up what Paul actually says in Romans 1 when he argues that Paul's primary critique is against "self-seeking desire," "excessive desire," "desire" expressed "in increasingly extreme and destructive ways," "desire that is out of control," "human desire in its extremity," and "self-seeking lust that demeans the other and advances one's own agenda."[33]

Self-seeking lust? Demeans the other? Advances one's own agenda? Where is this in the text? All of these qualifying phrases bend Paul's actual words in the direction that Brownson wants them to go.

It is not excess desire that Paul condemns. He condemns the actions that result from sexual desire.[34] "Desire" (*epithumia*) and "passion" (*pathos*) are considered wrong in Romans 1 not because such desires are excessive—Paul never says they are excessive—but because they grow into sinful sexual actions.[35] Both *epithumia* and *pathos* are considered wrong in Romans 1 since they are satisfied in an object contrary to God's will.[36] It is the action, not the desire, that Paul considers *para physin*.[37]

The excessive-lust view raises some good points and has forced me to go back to the text to see if I have understood the passage correctly. After looking at all the evidence, however, I think the excessive-lust view creates more problems than it solves.

Having said that, if we could climb inside of Paul's imagination, I seriously doubt that he was picturing a gay couple getting married after many months of nonsexual courtship when he penned Romans 1. I can see why Christian gays and lesbians read this passage and say, "That doesn't describe me!" While the stuff going on seems to be consensual (as we saw above), Paul is describing same-sex acts that fit the historical context of Corinth (where he is writing from) and Rome (where his audience lives). The same-sex acts in Romans 1 also fit the rhetorical context of people turning their back on God and pursuing all sorts of sinful activities. Remember: Paul is emphasizing sins of a pagan environment that has rejected God.

However, the reason Paul condemns the same-sex erotic behavior—that it is against nature and violates the Creator's intention for male-female relations—shows that Paul's language applies to all forms of same-sex intercourse. In a similar way, when Paul describes other pagan vices, such as murder, envy, deceit, covetousness, and slander in Romans 1:29–31, this does not mean that these acts are fine if they are committed by loving Christians. It's the act that Paul condemns. The specific colors Paul uses to paint the portrait, such as "burning with passion for one another" (1:27), don't limit Paul's critique to a specific form of same-sex sex.

The honest interpreter should recognize how general Paul's language is. He doesn't describe homosexual prostitution, men having sex with boys, or reckless orgies. Nor does he bemoan the "passive partner" in male-male sexual encounters as many of his Greco-Roman contemporaries did. Paul doesn't draw attention to violating the social pecking order of the Roman class system as other authors did. And contrary to the opinion of modern scholars, Paul does not showcase a low view of women here.

Rather, Paul uses basic terms and language of mutuality—male and female, natural and unnatural, one another—to describe consensual same-sex acts.

SUMMARY

As Bible-believing Christians, we have a responsibility to accurately interpret, believe, and respond to God's Word. I only hope and pray that I have done that in this chapter, and I genuinely invite feedback and critique if I have not done so. I hope that I have done nothing more than accurately convey Paul's words. And if I've read anything into this passage, then please dismiss it. In fact, you have a spiritual duty to dismiss anything I've said that does not convey Paul's original intention.

If I have rightly interpreted Paul, then this would logically mean that it would be more destructive, not less, to encourage people to fulfill their desire for sexual intimacy with a person of the same sex. It may seem to satisfy a person's felt needs and desires. It may appear to be the most loving thing to do. It may feel like you're looking out for the person's best interest and wanting them to flourish as human beings. But what if the opposite is true? If God is love, and if God wants humans to flourish, and if Romans 1 accurately reflects the will of God, then it is not loving nor would it cause a person to flourish as a human to encourage them to pursue same-sex sexual intimacy.

But let's remember the context of Romans 1. Paul doesn't write this chapter to condemn gay people. He writes it to condemn all people. Reading Romans 1 without reading Romans 2–3 (or the rest of the letter) is like walking out of a theater five minutes after the movie started. Any discussion, debate, sermon, or lecture on homosexuality that doesn't showcase the scandalous grace that beams from the rest of Romans is itself a scandalous disregard of the gospel. Until we find our own self-worth in Jesus, cling to his righteousness and not our own, pry every log from our eyes right down to the last splinter, assault every species of judgmentalism and hypocrisy lurking in the corners of our pharisaic hearts, trumpet the majesty of the cross and the triumph of the vacant tomb above all our good deeds—which are by-products of God's grace, though salted with our own sin—and pummel the insidious notion that we straight people are closer to God than "those" gay people over there—until we do these things, we will never view homosexuality the way God does.

CHAPTER SEVEN

LOST IN TRANSLATION

Homosexuality in 1 Corinthians 6:9 and 1 Timothy 1:10

First Corinthians 6 and 1 Timothy 1 mention some form of same-sex behavior, but there is a massive debate over what Paul is talking about. It all comes down to how we interpret two Greek words, *malakoi* and *arsenokoites*, which have been translated with more than twenty different English words. In fact, I don't know of any other pair of Greek words in the New Testament that has been subject to such a wide range of translations than *malakoi* and *arsenokoites*. And this is not just some ivory-tower discussion. Translations have real life implications and sometimes very expensive ones.

AN EXPENSIVE TRANSLATION

In 2008, Michigan attorney Bradley Fowler sued Zondervan Publishing House for 60 million dollars, since they published the NIV that translated *arsenokoites* as "homosexual offenders" (1984 version).[1] Fowler said that this translation caused him years of "anxiety, loss of sleep, appetite, self-esteem and the ability to re-establish any family bonds."[2] Fowler didn't win the suit, but he did give a healthy reminder that translations matter, especially if you want to avoid a hefty lawsuit.

I actually think Fowler has a point. "Homosexual offender" is not a good translation, as we will see. Many people are considered "homosexual" (that is, same-sex attracted) but this doesn't mean they are having sex. And what does "offender" mean? Whom have they offended? The law? Their neighbor? Straight people? God? And if a "homosexual" is celibate, then what is the offense? Is it their existence that is an offense before God? As you can see, the translation "homosexual offender" is dangerously ambiguous and potentially destructive.

But most translations have been updated with more precise language. Here's how these words are translated according to the NIV's updated version:

> Or do you not know that wrongdoers will not inherit the kingdom of God? Do not be deceived: Neither the sexually immoral nor idolaters nor adulterers nor *men who have sex with men* [*malakoi* and *arsenokoitai*] nor thieves nor the greedy nor drunkards nor slanderers nor swindlers will inherit the kingdom of God. (1 Cor. 6:9–10)
>
> We also know that the law is made not for the righteous but for lawbreakers and rebels, the ungodly and sinful, the unholy and irreligious, for those who kill their fathers or mothers, for murderers, for the sexually immoral, for *those practicing homosexuality* [*arsenokoitai*], for slave traders and liars and perjurers—and for whatever else is contrary to the sound doctrine that conforms to the gospel concerning the glory of the blessed God, which he entrusted to me. (1 Tim. 1:9–11)

We will look at other translations at the end of this chapter, but first, let's try to understand what the Greek words mean.[3]

Now, I know we just completed a very heady discussion of Romans 1, but let me warn you upfront that this chapter is going to be equally deep. If you don't want to engage in lengthy discussions about the meaning of Greek words, then this chapter will be a bear. If, however, you're not willing to perch up in your chair, roll up your sleeves, and turn your phone off for a couple hours to study these two words, then I'd say you should not form a strong opinion about homosexuality. When asked what you think, at least be honest and say, "I'm not too sure, since I don't want to take the time to understand what the New Testament actually means."

For those of us who do care, we need to understand what the Greek words *malakoi* and *arsenokoites* say about same-sex relations. Let's begin with 1 Corinthians 6:9 where both words are used.

MALAKOI AND ARSENOKOITES IN 1 CORINTHIANS 6

The relevant phrase in 1 Corinthians 6:9 (NIV) is "men who have sex with men," which is an interpretation of the Greek words *malakoi* and *arsenokoitai*. But this is only one of many ways that scholars interpret these words.

Affirming scholars generally argue that these words are too ambiguous; their meanings are simply unknown. For instance, Daniel Helminiak says, "Nobody knows for certain what these words mean, so to use them to condemn homosexuals is really dishonest and unfair."[4] Likewise, Dale Martin, a brilliant New Testament scholar at Yale University, wrote a detailed article on these two words and concludes (regarding *arsenokoites*): "I am not claiming to know what *arsenokoites* meant. I am claiming that no one knows what it meant."[5]

When affirming scholars take a stab at interpreting these words, they usually say that *malakos* and *arsenokoites* refer to exploitative sex, such as male prostitution or pederasty. After Dale Martin acknowledged that no one really knows what *arsenokoites* means, he says that the best option is that it refers to "some particular kind of economic exploitation."[6] If this is true, then these two passages are largely irrelevant for the modern question about consensual, loving, monogamous same-sex relations.

Nonaffirming scholars usually say that the first word, *malakoi*, refers to the passive partner in male homosexual intercourse, while *arsenokoites* refers to the active partner. According to this interpretation, these two words describe men who are actively engaging in male same-sex intercourse.

So what do these words mean? Let's start with *malakoi.*

MALAKOI

Malakoi is the plural form of *malakos,* which simply means "soft" or "delicate." For instance, it is used in the New Testament to describe "soft" clothing (Matt. 11:8). But in 1 Corinthians 6:9, the word describes a certain kind of person, and in context there is some sort of sinful action tied to these *malakoi.* Look at the rest of the words in Paul's list: sexually immoral, idolaters, adulterers, thieves, and so on. The *malakoi* are likewise defined by something that is sinful. They are not just wearing a fluffy sweater.

Unfortunately, Paul never uses *malakos* in his other letters, so we can't crosscheck his other uses. To understand what Paul is talking about, we need to look at how this Greek word (and its Latin equivalent, *mollus*[7]) is used in its Greco-Roman environment. After all, Paul is writing to people living in Corinth—an incubator of Greco-Roman thought—and he is trying to communicate to them in terms that would have been familiar to them.

While *malakos* means "soft," it was most often used to describe men who looked and acted like women, that is, effeminate men. By *effeminate,* though, I am not talking about guys who can't throw a football. I am talking about men who fundamentally confused gender distinctions.[8] They acted like women or talked like women, perhaps smelled like women, or they had sex like women; that is, they received sex from other men.

Philo, for instance, uses the word *malakoi* to describe certain "men-women," as he labels them, who "desired wholly to change their condition for that of women." Such change includes wearing heavy makeup and thick perfume, getting their hair curled, dressing in women's clothes, getting castrated, and playing the passive role in sexual intercourse with other men—something Philo considers to be "contrary to nature."[9]

A Roman writer named Lucan described boys who were castrated as "unhappy youth, softened [Latin, *mollita*] by the blade, their manhood cut out."[10] Another author named Phaedrus wrote a popular fable about one of the gods who got drunk while creating men and women. Inebriated, the god accidentally attached female genitalia to men and male genitalia to women. The latter were called "soft men" (*mollus*; Greek, *malakoi*)—though they looked like men on the outside, everything else about them was feminine.[11]

To be clear, the word *malakoi* does not in itself mean "the passive partner in male homosexual intercourse." The word is much broader than that.[12] For instance, men who shaved their chest hair were considered *malakos*, since thick burly chest hair was a sure sign of manliness. However, if a man was willing to shave the manliness growing from his chest, this often raised questions about what other unmanly acts such a *malakos* was willing to engage in. Roman satirist Martial, for instance, points to a man's depletion of his body hair as sure evidence that he played the passive role in sexual intercourse with other men.[13]

While *malakos* often described effeminate men in general, the accusation usually included the assumption that he also played the passive role in sexual intercourse. Put differently, not every person accused of being a *malakos* necessarily engaged in sex with other men, but every man who played the passive role in homosexual sex could be called *malakos*.[14] Therefore, *malakos* doesn't have to refer to same-sex intercourse, but it often did.

The word *malakoi*, however, occurs in 1 Corinthians 6:9 without further explanation. All we can say about the word, as it stands alone, is that it probably refers to effeminacy in the Roman sense; that is, a man who is trying to be a woman. Whether or not this sense includes some sort of sexual sin depends partly on the meaning of our next term: *arsenokoites*.

ARSENOKOITES

And here's where the real debate begins. Scholars differ widely on what this word means since this is the first time it occurs in all of the ancient Greek literature we have. To make matters worse, the word *arsenokoites* occurs in a list of vices in 1 Corinthians 6:9–10, which makes it hard to interpret. It would have been much easier if Paul had said, "And the *arsenokoites* walked into a room, locked the door, grabbed his male partner, and kissed him." Such context would remove all ambiguity in figuring out what Paul meant by *arsenokoites*. But here, Paul simply lists the word among other words, and all that we know is that a person who is an *arsenokoites* is identified by something sinful (1 Cor. 6:10–11).

So how do we move forward to interpret this word? Here are four questions we must answer:

What do the different parts of the compound word *arsenokoites* mean by themselves?

Does the Old Testament contain any similar words or phrases that may inform Paul's use of the word *arsenokoites*?

Does the word occur anywhere in later Jewish literature?

What does the word mean in later Christian literature?

1. THE MEANING OF *ARSEN* AND *KOITE*

Arsenokoites is actually a compound word made up of two Greek words: *arsen* and *koite*.[15] *Arsen* simply means "male" and not "man" (that is, adult male) as many translations have it. It refers to the male gender irrespective of age.

The other half of the compound word is *koite*. This word simply means "bed" or it can have the verbal force of "to sleep with" in a sexual sense. Other compound words that have *koite* in them often carry an explicit sexual meaning. So *doulokoites* is formed by *doulos* ("slave") and *koite* ("bed"), and it means "one who sleeps with slaves." Or *metrokoites* comes from *meter* ("mother") and *koite* ("bed") and means "one who sleeps with his mother."[16] Therefore, if we just add up the meaning of the two parts of the compound word, *arsenokoites* refers to someone who sleeps with other males.

However, we've got to be very careful determining the meaning of a compound word based on its individual parts. As Dale Martin rightly points out, words may have a completely different meaning than the sum of its parts: to use his own example, the word "understand" has nothing to do with "to stand under."[17]

But this doesn't mean that *arsenokoites* can't mean "one who sleeps with other males." After all, *playwright* refers to a person who writes plays, *fishermen* means men who fish, *birdwatcher* means, well, you get the point. Martin's caution, though, rightly shows that we can't determine the meaning of *arsenokoites* just by looking at its parts. We need to look at other pieces of evidence.

2. SIMILAR USES IN THE OLD TESTAMENT

The Old Testament was written in Hebrew, but it was also translated into Greek about a hundred years before Christ. Most New Testament writers actually read from this Greek translation (now called the "Septuagint") rather than the Hebrew. The exact word *arsenokoites* does not occur in the Septuagint. However, a similar phrase does. In fact, we see both *arsen* and *koite* in close proximity in at least two verses in the Old Testament. Not just any two verses, but the only two verses that mention same-sex relations. That is, Leviticus 18:22 and 20:13. Here is my translation of how the Greek of these passages reads. I'll mark in bold the relevant Greek words:

Leviticus 18:22:

*kai meta **arsenos** ou koimethese **koiten** gunaikeian*
"and you shall not lie with a male with the lying of a woman"

Leviticus 20:13:

*kai hos an koimethe meta **arsenos koiten** gynaikos ...*
"and whoever lies with a male with the lying of a woman ..."

You don't need to know Greek to see the resemblance, especially in Leviticus 20:13. The two words *arsenos* and *koiten*, which form Paul's compound word *arsenokoites*, occur right next to each other. Now, Paul doesn't wave a huge banner saying, "Look, look, my word *arsenokoites* comes from Leviticus!" But the parallel is striking. So striking that it appears to be intentional. Could it be that Paul uses a word (perhaps even creates a word) based on how the two parts of the compound word are used in Leviticus 20:13?

Put differently, is it possible that Paul uses a compound word *arsenokoites*, the parts of which can conceivably mean "one who sleeps with males," and does not have Leviticus 18:22 and 20:13 in view—the only two verses in the entire Old Testament that talk about men sleeping with males?

I guess it is possible that Paul does not have Leviticus in view. I find it very unlikely. However, you make the call.

I am honestly shocked that some affirming writers give such little attention to the connection between *arsenokoites* and *arsenos koiten* in Leviticus 18 and 20. John Boswell devoted several pages to the word *arsenokoites* in his groundbreaking book on homosexuality, but he doesn't even mention the connection.[18] Affirming scholar James Brownson, who recently wrote what is arguably the best defense of the affirming view, mentions the connection but says it is "speculative and lacks external confirming evidence."[19]

But what is "speculative" about connecting *arsenokoites* to one of the only places *arsen* and *koite* occur together in the Bible?[20] This doesn't seem too speculative to me. I appreciate the more balanced view of affirming writer Matthew Vines, who says that "it's possible that Paul coined the term *arsenokoitai* based on his familiarity with the Greek translation of Leviticus 20."[21] Likewise, affirming scholar Robin Scroggs argues thoroughly and convincingly that Paul almost certainly has Leviticus in mind when he pens *arsenokoites*.[22] He doesn't dance around the apparent connection because it might hurt his argument. Both Vines and Scroggs, however, believe that despite the Leviticus connection, *arsenokoites* probably refers to pederasty—men having sex with boys. We will see later why this interpretation is unlikely.

For now, let's cautiously conclude that Paul pens *arsenokoites* with an eye on Leviticus.

3. *ARSENOKOITES* IN LATER JEWISH LITERATURE

Since there is no use of the specific term before Paul, we should look to writings after Paul to see if they use the term. The next time we see *arsenokoites* used is by a Greek-speaking Jew who uses it as a verb: "Do not *arsenokoiten*, do not betray information, do not murder. Give one who has labored his wage. Do not oppress a poor man."[23]

Here we have a shotgun of moral commands that tell us little about the specific meaning of *arsenokoites*. All we know is that a Jew living around one hundred years after Paul uses the same word. And since he is a Jew, he probably didn't discover the word by reading 1 Corinthians! Maybe he too derived the word from Leviticus 18 and 20, but we don't know for sure. In any case, it's tough to know how this particular writer understood *arsenokoiten*, since there is little from the context that colors in its meaning. All we know from this text is that the word was used by a Jew apart from just getting it from Paul.[24]

We also know that many other Jewish writers used a Hebrew phrase *mishkab zakur* ("lying with a male"), which is equivalent to the Greek phrase *arsen koite*. This Hebrew phrase reflects the original wording of Leviticus 18:22 and 20:13 and was widely used in Judaism to describe same-sex relations.[25]

Why is this significant? It's significant because the Hebrew equivalent of *arsenokoites* seems to have been in play around the time of Paul or not long after. It's quite possible that Paul's seemingly rare use of *arsenokoites* is simply a Greek version of a Hebrew phrase that was already in use; namely, *mishkab zakur*. Think about it. Both the Hebrew phrase and the Greek phrase are almost identical to the wording of Leviticus 20:13. Paul is bilingual; he knows Hebrew and Greek. But he's writing to an audience in 1 Corinthians that only knows Greek. So he uses—perhaps invents—a Greek phrase, based on Leviticus 20:13, that parallels a Hebrew phrase that may have been used within Judaism to describe men "who sleep with [*mishkab*] other males [*zakur*]."

Are you still with me? I know this discussion is complicated, so I hope you're reading slowly. If you need to refill your coffee, now's the time. Again, figuring out the meaning of *arsenokoites* is crucial for understanding what the New Testament says about homosexuality. So we need to comb through the actual evidence to make sure we know why English translations differ so widely on its meaning.

Let's sum up our third point before we move on. The Hebrew phrase *mishkab zakur* was a catch phrase that describes male same-sex relations. The Greek equivalent is *arsen koite*, which appears to be the basis for Paul's word *arsenokoites*.

So far, there's good reason to translate *arsenokoites* as "men who have sex with males." Still, we want to be cautious until we examine all the evidence, so let's continue to hold our conclusion with an open hand.

4. ARSENOKOITES IN LATER CHRISTIAN LITERATURE

Arsenokoites is used sporadically in Christian literature after Paul.[26] Now, to state the obvious, these references weren't known by Paul, so they can't be used as possible sources for Paul's understanding of the word. What they can tell us is how other Christian writers understood the term.

There are many uses of *arsenokoites* that we can label "undefined," since they occur in contexts where the writer is simply quoting 1 Corinthians 6:9. Or a writer may list *arsenokoites* with a bunch of other sins without giving us any clues from the context that explains what the word means.[27] Therefore, we will look at passages where Christian writers offer some sort of explanation of *arsenokoites*.

One of the earliest references comes in the work of early church theologian Hippolytus (AD 170–235):

> The serpent (*Naas* from Hebrew *naas*, "snake") approached Eve

and after deceiving her committed adultery with her, which is contrary to the law; and he also approached Adam and possessed him like a boy, which is also itself contrary to the law. From that time on, adultery and *arsenokoitia* have come into being.[28]

What? Your Sunday school teacher didn't tell you about Satan having sex with Adam? Yeah, neither did mine.

This tale, of course, has no basis in the Bible, but it still explains how a writer understands the term *arsenokoitia* (a form of *arsenokoites*). Given the fact that the term parallels Satan "possessing" Adam (sexually) like a boy, *arsenokoitia* could refer to pederasty. Adam, however, was a man, so I don't think we can limit *arsenokoitia* to pederasty even though it certainly includes having sex with boys. Plus, if the author wanted to limit the sexual sin to pederasty, why not use one of the main terms for pederasty such as *paidophthoros* ("corruptor of boys")? *Arsenokoitia* here probably refers to men who have sex with other males regardless of age.

Bardaisan (AD 154–222) lived around the same time as Hippolytus and also uses the term *arsenokoites*.

> From the Euphrates River all the way to the ocean in the East, a man who is derided as a murderer or thief will not be the least bit angry; but if he is derided as an *arsenokoites*, he will defend himself to the point of murder. [Among the Greeks, wise men who have male lovers are not condemned.]

Bardaisan's words here are recorded by a later church historian named Eusebius (AD 265—340).[29] This is important because it is probably Eusebius, not Bardaisan, who added the words in the brackets: "Among the Greeks, wise men who have male lovers are not condemned." Eusebius, therefore, added these words to explain the meaning of *arsenokoites*: A man who has a "male lover." Most of the time, such male lovers were teenagers, but in some cases they were partners of equal age, as we saw in chapter 4. In any case, *arsenokoites* almost certainly means "men who sleep with other males" in this passage.

Origen (AD 184–253) was a famous theologian and biblical scholar who used the word *arsenokoites* on several occasions. In some cases, it's hard to figure out what he means, since the word occurs in a list of vices or a quote from 1 Corinthians 6:9.[30] However, there is at least one place that may help us see how Origen understood *arsenokoites*:

> On the other hand some were roaming widely—adulterers, temple prostitutes and thieves will receive judgment; some wander outside—the ones who pursue lusts contrary to nature, who *arsenokoitein* and any other parade of forbidden things they can receive; see that there is no accusation against an holy man. Anyone who can't keep still but roams, shares in the accusation of the shameless woman.[31]

Origen's use of the verb *arsenokoitein* further defines his previous phrase "pursue lusts contrary to nature." This latter phrase almost certainly comes from Romans 1:26–27, where Paul describes same-sex intercourse as "contrary to nature." And as we saw, the phrase "contrary to nature" includes all forms of homosexual sex.

It's tough to know if Origen has a specific type of same-sex relation in view. Was he thinking about male prostitutes? Pederasty? Or same-sex relations in general? It's impossible to say for sure. But since there's nothing in the context that clearly limits its meaning, all we know is that Origen uses *arsenokoites* to refer to men having sex with other males—especially if he was thinking of Romans 1 when he wrote this.

Along with uses of *arsenokoites* in early Christian writers, we can also look at how ancient translations of the New Testament rendered the word *arsenokoites*. The first few centuries after Christ witnessed many different translations of the Bible, as the gospel went forth into foreign lands. Looking at these translations might help us understand how some Christians interpreted the term *arsenokoites*.

Some of the most important early translations of the New Testament are the Latin, Coptic, and Syriac versions. Now, I know a little bit of Latin, but I've never studied Syriac or Coptic, so I've relied on other scholars who have. Early Latin translations most often translate *arsenokoites* with the phrase *masculorum concubitores*, which means "men who have sex with males." There's no ambiguity here. Latin translators understood *arsenokoites* to refer to the active partner of male same-sex intercourse.

As far as the Coptic and Syriac versions go, I emailed my former PhD supervisor Dr. Simon Gathercole to find out how they translate 1 Corinthians 6:9. Simon is a professor at Cambridge University and has been reading ancient languages since he was nine years old. While most British lads were out playing cricket, Simon was poring over ancient texts. (He is actually darn good at cricket as well.) I'll never forget when he taught himself Coptic and Syriac while I was studying under him for my doctorate. Simon is one of those guys who catch languages faster than I can catch a cold.

Needless to say, I felt confident emailing him about the Coptic and Syriac versions of 1 Corinthians 6:9. This is what Simon said:

> Coptic has for *malakos* just "malakos" transliterated, and for *arsenokoites* "sleeper with male." Syriac has for *malakos* a word that I think means "corrupt" and for *arsenokoites*, like Coptic, "those who sleep with males."[32]

In other words, both versions translate the Greek word *arsenokoites* exactly like the Latin version: "men who sleep with males."

SUMMARY

Let's circle back around and sum up what we've seen so far. First, the two words that form the compound word *arsenokoites* mean "men who sleep with males." Second, it seems to have been derived from Leviticus 18:22 and especially 20:13, where *arsen* and *koite* also occur and are used to prohibit male same-sex intercourse. Third, the Hebrew equivalent *mishkab zakur* ("lying with a male") was also coined as a technical term for same-sex intercourse based on

Leviticus 18:22 and 20:13. Fourth, later Christian uses of the term *arsenokoites* (and its equivalents) also understand the term, with minimal variation, to refer to men who have sex with other males.

As has been the spirit in this book so far, I don't think that any one of these points can stand alone in determining the meaning of this Greek word. But taken together, it seems like there is good evidence for understanding *arsenokoites* to refer to men who have sex with other males. Also, Paul lists *malakoi* right before *arsenokoites*, which probably means that *malakoi* refers to men who significantly cross gender boundaries by receiving sex from other men. *Arsenokoites*, then, would refer to the active partner in same-sex intercourse.

Some affirming scholars agree with this, but say that the *malakoi* are "call boys" who sell themselves to other men, and that *arsenokoites* are the men who hire out the *malakoi*.[33] Other scholars say that 1 Corinthians 6:9 refers to pederasty. Certainly Paul's words include such people, but I don't think these words can be limited to pederasty. After all, there were other Greek words that were widely used by Christians, Jews, pagans, and anyone else who knew Greek, to refer to pederasty. For instance, the Greek word *paiderastes* was widely used to refer to "the love of boys," as was *paidophthoros* ("corruptor of boys") or *paidophtoreo* ("seducer of boys").[34] Jewish authors especially used the latter two terms to condemn the practice. Another pair of Greek words, *erastes* and *eromenos,* were often used to describe the older man (*erastes*) and his boy-lover (*eromenos*).

If Paul had pederasty in view, why didn't he use one of the many terms available that refer specifically to pederasty?[35] That would be like me saying, "I love sports" even though what I really mean is "I love baseball." If all I meant was a specific type of sport—baseball—then I would have used a word that clearly conveys that specific sport. Likewise, Paul uses a general term that means "men who sleep with males." If he had a more specific type of men or males in view, there's a good chance he would have said so. But he doesn't. Instead, Paul uses the term *malakoi*, which highlighted the gender confusion inherent in the sex act (men acting like women) and a generic term, *arsenokoites*, to refer to the active partner in the male-male sex act.

1 TIMOTHY 1:10

Paul uses *arsenokoites* one other time in 1 Timothy:

> We also know that the law is made not for the righteous but for lawbreakers and rebels, the ungodly and sinful, the unholy and irreligious, for those who kill their fathers or mothers, for murderers,[10] for the sexually immoral, for *those practicing homosexuality* [*arsenokoitai*], for kidnappers and liars and perjurers—and for whatever else is contrary to the sound doctrine [11] that conforms to the gospel concerning the glory of the blessed God, which he entrusted to me.

Like 1 Corinthians 6, *arsenokoites* occurs in a list of vices, though without the term *malakoi*. What is interesting about the list in 1 Timothy is that Paul prefaces it with a reference to "the law," which refers to the Mosaic Law; that is, the laws contained in the first five books of the Old Testament. When Paul gets into his list of vices, he seems to follow the order of the Ten Commandments.[36] For instance:

> Killers of parents refer to the fifth commandment: "Honor your father and mother."
> Murderers refer to the sixth commandment: "You shall not murder."
> The sexually immoral and the *arsenokoites* both refer to the seventh commandment: "You shall not commit adultery."
> Kidnappers violate the eighth commandment: "You shall not steal."
> Liars and perjurers refer to the ninth commandment: "You shall not bear false witness."

Now, you may say that *arsenokoites* is quite different than adultery, and technically you would be right. Adultery refers to having sex with someone else's spouse. The Ten Commandments, however, were believed to be the fountainhead for all other laws that come after it. That is, all the laws in Exodus, Leviticus, Numbers, and Deuteronomy are in some way connected to one of the Ten Commandments. In this sense, the seventh commandment against adultery was understood to encompass all forms of sexual immorality. And in Jewish tradition, homosexual intercourse was described as a form of adultery.[37]

It appears that Paul is grouping these vices under the Ten Commandments as was common in Jewish and Christian tradition.

Since the Ten Commandments were believed to sum up the entire Old Testament law, it's possible that Paul tethers Leviticus 18:22 and 20:13 to the seventh commandment by means of the word *arsenokoites*. It's impossible to jump inside Paul's head and say for sure. But no first-century Jew would have batted an eye at this suggestion. Linking same-sex prohibitions to the seventh commandment was common.

Paul's use of *arsenokoites* in 1 Timothy doesn't seem too different from his use of the same word in 1 Corinthians 6. It refers to men who play the active role in same-sex intercourse.

TRANSLATING *MALAKOI* AND *ARSENOKOITAI*

The word *malakos* refers to men who significantly blur gender distinctions. Given the sexual context of 1 Corinthians 6 and its close association with *arsenokoites*, the word probably includes the sexual meaning of "males who have sex (passively) with other men." *Arsenokoites* refers to men who have sex with other males and does not appear to have a narrow meaning of a male prostitute or a man who has sex with boys, although it certainly includes these acts.

When it comes to English translations, several versions really butcher the meaning of these two words. The New American Standard Bible (NASB) translates *malakoi* as "effeminate," which isn't a bad translation as long as we don't understand effeminacy through the lens of a high-school locker room. According to ancient Roman culture, effeminacy meant a radical distortion of one's gender. The NASB goes on to translate *arsenokoites* as "homosexuals," which is a terrible translation. Today, many people are considered "homosexual" (that is, gay) regardless of whether they are having sex with other men. And while the word "homosexual" includes both men and women, *arsenokoites* only refers to men. Many same-sex attracted teens have killed themselves because their feminine traits solicited names like "fag" and "homosexual" from bullies, regardless of whether they are having intercourse with other males. I know several self-identified gay men who are attracted to men but would never have sex with other men because they believe the Bible condemns such an act. None of them are *arsenokoites*.

Translating *malakos* or *arsenokoites* as "homosexual" is not only linguistically wrong and historically naive; it is pastorally destructive.

Other translations also miss the mark. The King James Version translates *arsenokoites* with "abusers of themselves with mankind," which is way too broad. So is Eugene Peterson's rather sweeping "Those who use and abuse each other, use and abuse sex, use and abuse the earth and everything in it" (*The Message*), which presumably includes those who don't recycle. The English Standard Version has "men who practice homosexuality" for *arsenokoites*; the added word "practice" is a good qualification. The New International Version's "men who have sex with men" translates both *malakoi* and *arsenokoites* together. This is a good translation as well except for one major flaw: it is limited to male same-sex adult relations. But remember, *arsenokoites* does not mean "men who have sex with (adult) men" but "men who have sex with *males*." This, of course, includes adult relations but isn't limited to them.

Malakoi refers to men who thoroughly cross gender boundaries by receiving sex from other men. *Arsenokoites* refers to men who have sex with other males.

So, are all gay people going to hell?

No.

I'll explain why in chapter 10.

INTERLUDE

A Summary

So what does the Bible really say?

It says that it's a sin. It's damnable, evil, and could exclude a person from God's kingdom (1 Cor. 6:9–10). It's so bad that God destroyed an entire city that was engaged in it (Gen. 19), and Jesus says that those who practice it are liable to face judgment rather than salvation when he returns (Matt. 25). And those who think they can continue to practice it and still think they are genuine followers of Christ are deceiving both themselves and others.

Still, our culture has accepted it as a virtue instead of a vice. Even our Christian culture is letting it slip into our churches unnoticed. We sometimes applaud it and place people in leadership who are too weak to preach against it. Many churches, if they are not actively endorsing it, try to remain neutral. But neutrality is nothing more than endorsement covered in sheep's clothing.

I'm not talking about homosexuality.

I'm talking about the misuse of wealth—the sin that's condemned in more than two thousand passages in God's inspired Word. When overfed and overpaid straight Christians condemn gay people while they neglect the poor, stockpile wealth, and indulge in luxurious living, they stand on the wrong side of Jesus' debates with the Pharisees. As we move forward and summarize our discussion, let's make sure we are on the hunt to slaughter all types of sins, especially those in our own lives. Then, and only then, should we address the sins of others.

With that in mind, let's review what we have learned about the Bible and same-sex relations. We will begin by summing up the arguments that support a nonaffirming position.

121

ARGUMENTS FOR THE
NONAFFIRMING POSITION

First, the Bible talks a lot about marriage yet only affirms hetero-sexual marriages. This isn't decisive in itself, but in Genesis 2 Eve's femaleness seems to be a necessary prerequisite for her marriage to Adam—a marriage that becomes the prototype for all God-sanctioned marriages (Gen. 2:24–25).

Second, Jesus highlights sexual difference in marriage, even when he didn't need to (Mark 10). Paul does talk about homosexual relations and when he discusses marriage he sometimes highlights sexual difference as necessary if marriage is to reflect the character of God (Eph. 5; cf. 1 Cor. 11).

Third, Leviticus 18:22 and 20:13 state in absolute terms that men should not have sex with other men. A close look at the larger context, and the repetition of similar statements in the New Testament, suggests that these verses are still binding on believers.

Fourth, the Greeks and Romans (ca. 500 BC–AD 400) engaged in various types of same-sex relations. Most of these relations exhibited some sort of power difference—the dominant and the dominated—but we do see some evidence of consensual relations especially between women. Still, every Jewish writer who spoke about same-sex relations during this time condemned them.

Fifth, the New Testament and early Christianity grew out of Judaism and shared much of Judaism's sexual ethics. If Christians were going to depart from Judaism's clear stance against same-sex relations, we would expect it to be rather clearly stated in the New Testament.

Sixth, while Jesus never mentioned same-sex relations, he displayed a rather strict sexual ethic in other matters. It would make more sense that Jesus, being a Jew, stood with his Jewish contemporaries on their view of same-sex relations. He didn't mention such views because no one in his Jewish audience contested them.

Seventh, Romans 1 echoes the well-known ethic among Jewish

and Greco-Roman writers, who believed that same-sex relations were "against nature." Paul's main reason for prohibiting same-sex eroticism is that it goes against the Creator's intention for male-female sexual relations. Romans 1 can't be limited to a particular type of same-sex relation since he uses general language ("males with males," "with one another," etc.). Moreover, Paul's reference to female same-sex relations almost certainly includes consensual relations, since female homoeroticism wasn't pederastic nor did it clearly exhibit power differences.

Eighth, Paul's term *malakos* ("effeminate") in 1 Corinthians 6:9 is capable of different meanings. However, it commonly referred to men who significantly altered their gender, which often included playing the passive role in intercourse with other men. *Arsenokoites* ("men who sleep with males," 1 Cor. 6:9; 1 Tim. 1:10) is probably derived from Leviticus 18:22 and 20:13, where same-sex relations are forbidden. Given the Hebrew parallel *mishkab zakur*, which is derived from these passages, it is likely that *arsenokoites* means "men who sleep with males." This meaning is confirmed by its later Christian uses, which seems to mean "men who sleep with males" in contexts where other terms clarify its meaning.

We could also add a ninth argument that we haven't mentioned since it is not a biblical argument but a historical one. For two thousand years, orthodox Christianity has believed that marriage is between a man and woman and that such sexual difference is necessary.[1] This is an argument from tradition, of course. As I said earlier, I am not opposed to overturning tradition if the Bible demands it. But given the previous eight arguments, it would take a rather earth-shattering series of arguments to overturn such well-established tradition.

So have there been any earth-shattering arguments? Some nonaffirming Christians I know don't even want to entertain, let alone acknowledge, the strengths of affirming arguments. But I find this approach to be intellectually naive and biblically anemic; it only shows that our presuppositions are more authoritative than

Scripture. In order to be biblical, we should always test our fallible interpretations against other interpretations that might render them inaccurate.

Here are the best affirming arguments I have wrestled with.

ARGUMENTS FOR THE AFFIRMING POSITION

First, none of the Bible's positive statements about heterosexual marriage were originally addressing homosexual relations. It's not as if the Pharisees asked about Joey and Frank's forthcoming wedding and Jesus responds by saying, "God designed marriage to be between a man and a woman." Jesus and Paul do highlight sexual difference in marriage but not in the context of addressing homosexuality. Still, as I said in chapter 2, I don't think that the marriage passages are irrelevant. I just think they should be used with caution.

Second, the excessive-lust interpretation of Romans 1 raises some good points and I don't think Paul envisions homosexual marriages when he writes Romans 1. As we have seen, though, his language is so broad that it ultimately applies to all same-sex relations. While I think that the excessive-lust interpretation reads too much into the passage, the strength of this view should prevent Christians from simply quoting Romans 1 and thinking that this solves the debate.

Third, while there is some evidence for same-sex marriages around the time of Christ, most homosexual erotic behavior was extramarital, exploitative, pederastic, or exhibited unhealthy power differences that are deemed immoral by all Christians today. Affirming writers have been pointing this out for years, and I don't think many nonaffirming Christians have considered (or been able to refute) the implications of this argument. Many affirming writers agree that the Bible condemns the forms of same-sex relations that were popular in its day. But the forms available to the biblical writers are not the forms that affirming Christians are arguing for today: consensual, monogamous, same-sex unions.

This argument has some strengths, although ultimately I believe it is overplayed. As we have seen, Leviticus 18, 20, and Romans 1 use language that is all-inclusive. Neither Leviticus nor Romans mentions pederasty or power differences, rape or prostitution; both Leviticus and Romans use language of mutuality in their same-sex prohibition. Moreover, Paul's reference to (consensual) female same-sex relations solidifies this point: Romans 1 does not clearly reflect the dominant versus dominated sexual paradigm. Plus, Paul grounds his prohibition in the creation account, which highlights God's opposite-sex design for sexual relations.

I have tried to treat the Bible as fairly and cautiously as I can. Still, in light of the nine arguments above, I do not see the Bible affirming same-sex sexual relations.

CHALLENGES FOR NONAFFIRMING CHRISTIANS

But the Bible also challenges several nonaffirming assumptions.

First, a bad argument used to support the right view is still a bad argument. "Adam and Eve not Adam and Steve" type of arguments are unhelpful, unchristian, and a poor use of our God-given intellect. They are not funny and they are not intelligent. Please stop using this stupid argument.

Second, "gay pride is" not "why Sodom fried." I don't think it is wise to use the Sodom story to prohibit consensual, loving, same-sex unions today. That's like comparing apples with orangutans. When Christians race to quote Genesis 19 to condemn same-sex unions, it feels like they are not interested in what the Bible actually says, but only want to load their gun with proof texts that have little to do with the current discussion.

Third, Jesus' encounter with people who were considered sinners by the religious elite provides a good model for how nonaffirming Christians should relate to non-Christian LGBT people. Jesus didn't open up a relationship by giving his stance on a person's sin. Rather, he opened it up with love. If we desire for people to live holy lives, then we need to begin with love.

Fourth, homosexual sins are never mentioned in isolation. They are always brought up in contexts where many other sins are mentioned—greed, slander, gossip, and others. To consider your own sins as not as bad as those of LGBT people is to join hands with Pharisees whom Jesus condemned to hell. And that's not a safe crowd to run with.

NOW WHAT?

For the remainder of this book, I will approach various questions that often come up in the discussion. Are people born gay? Can they change? *Should* they change? Can gay people become Christians and still be gay? Is same-sex attraction sinful or just same-sex behavior? Is it unloving to demand celibacy from same-sex oriented believers? And a whole host of other questions that I've been asked over the years. Since I believe that the Bible does not sanction same-sex relations, I will assume this position throughout the rest of this book.

Let me be honest. I'm a biblical scholar and a pastor. I'm not a psychologist, a sociologist, or an anthropologist. Heck, I'm sometimes a terrible counselor, though I'm trying to be a better one! Therefore, I'm not going to assume I'm an expert in all the different fields of study that help inform our knowledge of homosexuality. I've tried to read as broadly as I can and as much as I can, and I've enlisted the help of people who are experts in these other fields. But I'm not going to cook up some airtight answer to every single question, especially when tough questions resist simple answers. But I will do my best to apply the Bible and Christian logic to the many questions that people are wrestling with.

Like you, I am on a journey. Maybe in five, ten, or fifteen years, I will have a better answer, or maybe I will have changed my mind on the answers I give in this book. For now, here is how I am thinking through the questions you've probably asked.

Let's start with nature versus nurture. Are people born gay?

CHAPTER EIGHT

"BORN THIS WAY"

Does God Make People Gay?

The title of this chapter is a loaded question, but it's often raised in conversations about homosexuality. The logic often goes: If someone is born gay, then God must have made them that way, and if God made them that way, then being gay must be okay.

Some nonaffirming Christians respond by asserting the opposite: People are not born gay, but choose to be gay. And since they choose it, God is not responsible for their same-sex orientation.

This debate is often framed in terms as "nature versus nurture." Some say that *nature* determines whether someone will be gay. That is, some people are born with a same-sex orientation that is fixed at birth. Others say that we are all born heterosexual, but nurture (life circumstances, family upbringing) sometimes cultivates gay desires: sexual abuse, an absent father, a domineering mother, or too many sisters that treated little Bobby like a doll growing up.

So are people born gay? Or do they choose to be gay? Or did something happen in their upbringing that made them gay?

NATURE AND NURTURE

To answer these questions we need to ditch the word *gay* first. We will bring it in later, but for now it is best to leave it out. The actual question we're asking is: Are people born with a same-sex orientation even though they may not realize it until later?

Again, some people come down very strongly on either the nature or the nurture side, presumably because this will help justify their position. If people are born with same-sex attraction, then such attraction is God-given. If they are not born with same-sex attraction, they must have chosen it at some point in their life.

I actually think that both views are overstated. I have read a lot of research by people on both sides of the debate and the most credible conclusion—now widely agreed upon—is that both nature and nurture play a role in cultivating same-sex desires. While multiple studies have investigated a genetic link for same-sex attraction, all of the results remain inconclusive—there is no clear evidence for a clear genetic cause. What we do know is that the question of what causes same-sex attraction is more complex than we realize. The American Psychological Association (APA), for instance, concludes that both nature and nurture have a part in creating same-sex attraction:

> There is no consensus among scientists about the exact reasons that an individual develops a heterosexual, bisexual, gay, or lesbian orientation. Although much research has examined the possible genetic, hormonal, developmental, social, and cultural influences on sexual orientation, no findings have emerged that permit scientists to conclude that sexual orientation is determined by any particular factor or factors. Many think that nature and nurture both play complex roles; most people experience little or no sense of choice about their sexual orientation.[1]

The most important line here is "nature and nurture both play complex roles." The APA's statement is shared by several studies that come to the same conclusion.[2] Nature *and* nurture play a role in forming one's same-sex desires, and it's unlikely that one's desires are produced solely by any one biological or societal factor.

Likewise, it's true that some people who have a same-sex orientation had been sexually abused. Therefore, many people like to say that this is always the root cause of same-sex desires. But again, same-sex desires are rarely the by-product of any single cause. After all, what about all the people who have been sexually abused yet end up straight? Or what about the LGBT people who actually had a very good upbringing? (I've met quite a few.) If sexual abuse automatically caused same-sex attraction, then you would expect it to happen all the time, or at least most of the time. But the facts don't support this.

A good friend of mine is totally straight; he doesn't experience any same-sex desires. He's married to a beautiful wife, has two kids, teaches Bible at a Christian university. Still, when he was a young teenager, he had an abusive sexual relationship with an older boy for several years. The experience messed him up, and he's still working through the implications. But his experience didn't automatically create same-sex desires in him. Same-sex behavior, even abuse, doesn't always lead to same-sex attraction.

Nature and nurture both play a complex role in forming same-sex desires. It seems wrongheaded to try to locate the cause of same-sex attraction entirely in either nature or nurture.

Plus, there are many feelings and desires that you think are inborn but have actually been shaped more by the environment you grow up in. Why is it, for instance, that most American boys are attracted to girls with big boobs and skinny waists? You may think it's because they are simply boys—good old, heterosexual boys. But in other cultures, men are more attracted to heavy-set women than skinny women, and the size of boobs is largely irrelevant except for the hungry infant.

I'll never forget hearing about my cousin's experience as a missionary in Papua New Guinea. She said that she could've walked around without a shirt, and the native men wouldn't have batted an eye. But if she wore jeans in public, there's a good chance she would arouse the men, even if she wore a large coat that covered her chest. In that culture, a woman's pelvic area, though covered in denim, is much more provocative than a woman's breasts, even if her breasts were as bare as Eve's.

The fact is, one's culture subconsciously influences our desires.

Anthropologist Pat Caplan says, "What people want, and what they do, in any society, is to a large extent what they are made to want, and allowed to do. Sexuality . . . cannot escape its cultural connection."[3] Our desires and choices are never independent from our cultural influences—influences that are usually unnoticed. The lines between our choice, our biology, and influences from our culture are often blurred and tough to separate completely.

In some cases, biology doesn't shape choices; choices shape biology. A few years ago, I talked with a physician-scientist friend of mine who has researched this topic extensively. I learned from him that neuroscientists have discovered that certain actions and habits can actually physically alter the shape of your brain. This is based on the brain's plasticity, which:

> Refers to alterations in neural pathways and synapses which are due to changes in behavior, environment and neural processes, as well as changes resulting from bodily injury. The brain actually *changes*, neurons shift and grow, chemical levels rise or fall, depending upon experiences, actions and patterns acquired throughout the course of our lives.[4]

Certain behaviors, if practiced over time, can change the size and shape of our brain. Porn addicts, for instance, alter their brain through excessive use of porn. If all we did was look at the biology and saw different types of brains in porn addicts, we could conclude that such addiction is the by-product of their anatomy. But actually, their anatomy is the by-product of their behavior.[5]

I'm not saying that same-sex behavior will reconfigure your brain. That's not my point. But I am saying that the interplay between biology and choice, nature and nurture, desire and action, is incredibly complex and it is unhelpful (and unscientific) to try to pin down same-sex attraction as just the by-product of the way people are born.

The one lesson I've learned is that the claim "I was born gay, and therefore it's okay" is not only theologically wrong; it is scientifically naive.

DOES IT MATTER?

It's important to understand that solving the nature-versus-nurture question doesn't solve the ethical question. Just because someone is born with a particular desire—even a seemingly fixed desire—doesn't mean it is automatically moral to act on that desire.

I love how affirming writer Justin Lee puts it:

> Just because an attraction or drive is biological doesn't mean it's okay to act on . . . We all have inborn tendencies to sin in any number of ways. If gay people's same-sex attractions were inborn, that wouldn't necessarily mean it's okay to act on them, and if we all agreed that gay sex is sinful, that wouldn't necessarily mean that same-sex attractions aren't inborn. "Is it a sin?" and "Does it have biological roots?" are two completely separate questions.[6]

I think Justin is spot on here. And Justin is the leader of the Gay Christian network; coming down hard on the nature side might help his cause. Still, Justin has chosen good reason over bad arguments to support his view.

The same goes for John Corvino, another affirming writer, who says:

> The fact is that there are plenty of genetically influenced traits that are nevertheless undesirable. Alcoholism may have a genetic basis, but it doesn't follow that alcoholics ought to drink excessively. Some people may have a genetic predisposition to violence, but they have no more right to attack their neighbors than anyone else. Persons with such tendencies cannot say "God made me this way" as an excuse for acting on their dispositions.[7]

So even if all the medical research showed that same-sex desires were biological (which it doesn't), this still wouldn't mean that it's okay to act on those desires. Biblical Christianity has always taught that people are born with a sin nature, which affects our whole being: our intellect, bodies, emotions, and desires. Paul describes humanity as those who live "in the passions of our flesh, carrying out the desires of the flesh and the mind" (Eph. 2:3). We have passions and desires that are etched into the fabric of our "flesh," a term that most often denotes "our sin nature." Likewise, Jeremiah says, "The heart"—the core of our desires and affections—"is deceitful above all things, and beyond cure. Who can understand it?" (Jeremiah 17:9). Earlier the prophet said that our sin is "engraved on the tablet of our heart" (17:1) and etched into our being like spots on a leopard's coat (Jer. 13:13). Ezekiel says that the human heart is made of stone and is dead (Ezek. 1 36:26–27). This doesn't mean that all of our desires and passions are wrong. But it does mean that some of them very well could be, and we need God's revelation to sort out which ones are right and which ones are sin.

Again, the logic that if same-sex desires are biological they are therefore okay to act on is not a Christian logic. Remember the words of Lee: "'Is it a sin?' and 'Does it have biological roots?' are two completely separate questions."

Now someone could agree with this but argue that Christians have redeemed hearts and renewed passions. Therefore, if a Christian still has same-sex attraction after getting saved, then these desires are the product of, not antithetical to, God's redeeming work.

For this logic to work, though, we must in principle affirm every postconversion desire that springs from the hearts of Christians, since their hearts have been redeemed.

That would be scary.

The fact is, Christians still struggle with sinful desires, even though we have been redeemed from sin. Paul commands the Christians at Rome: "Let not sin therefore reign in your mortal body, to make you obey its passions" (Rom. 6:12). This command would be ridiculous—a waste of parchment—unless the Roman Christians were obeying the sinful passions of their sin nature. Paul tells the Galatians that the "desires of the Spirit are against the flesh," and the Spirit works "to keep you from doing the things you want to do" (Gal. 5:17). That is, sometimes what we "want to do" is at odds with what God's Spirit says we should do. This side of heaven, our desires cannot be fully trusted.

Christian theology has always taught that our desires are tainted by sin and are terrible instructors of morality. The fact that people, even Christians, have same-sex desires does not change the ethical question: Is it God's will to act on those desires?

WHAT DOES GAY MEAN?

Let's come back to the term *gay*. I said that I don't think it's helpful to use this term in the nature-versus-nurture debate. We need first to understand how *gay* relates to other concepts such as same-sex attraction, same-sex orientation, and same-sex behavior.[8]

Same-sex attraction refers to "an enduring pattern of emotional, romantic, and/or sexual attractions to" someone of the same sex and includes other nonsexual relational bonds such as "affection between partners, shared goals and values, mutual support, and ongoing commitment" (APA).[9] Such attractions are not chosen or created by the person. They are simply felt. If you are straight, then ask yourself: When did you choose your opposite-sex desires? The fact is, you didn't. At some point in the sixth grade, you saw that girl with the soft blond hair or that boy with a cute smile and you felt something. The feelings came upon you. The same is true of same-sex attraction.

Whether or not this attraction was shaped by nurture or produced by nature doesn't change the fact that when the person first experiences such attractions, they do not consciously choose them. It's not as if they woke up one day as a thirteen-year-old and made a conscious decision: "I think I'll be attracted to ... let's see. How about ... boys." Why would any junior high kid choose that? Most schools are not very sympathetic to boys who like boys or girls who like girls. Even if it is cool to be viewed as gay in some schools, one's sexual impulses will eventually trump coolness and reveal that they really are straight.

Same-sex orientation is sometimes used as a synonym for same-sex attraction, and I'll use it synonymously in my following discussion. Technically, however, same-sex orientation usually conveys a stronger, more fixed attraction. It basically refers to "the amount and persistence of their own attraction."[10] In other words, someone could experience some level of same-sex attraction while not being same-sex oriented, but everyone who is same-sex oriented experiences same-sex attraction. It is always important to recognize that same-sex attraction is not limited to sexual attractions and cannot be equated with a desire for sex.

Same-sex behavior refers to acting on one's same-sex attraction. This includes lustful thoughts, which are sinful regardless of your orientation, and pursuing sex (or sexual conduct) with someone of the same sex—something not every same-sex attracted person does. For what it's worth, the Bible only directly addresses, and prohibits, homosexual sex and *not* same-sex attraction. But we'll explore this a bit more in the next chapter. Same-sex behavior, unlike same-sex attraction or orientation, is a choice.

So how does the term *gay* (or *lesbian*) relate to same-sex attraction, same-sex orientation, and same-sex behavior? It all depends on the person using the term. Some people use the term *gay* in a strong sense of capturing their core identity, while others use the term in a *soft* sense to describe their experiences as a same-sex attracted person. For the latter, *gay* is a virtual synonym for "same-sex attraction" or "orientation." The term *gay* does not in itself mean that someone is engaging in same-sex behavior or thinks that it would be right to do so—even in the context of marriage.

When talking about homosexuality, it is absolutely crucial to distinguish between same-sex orientation (or attraction) and same-sex behavior.

For instance, a friend of mine who is attracted to the same sex has never engaged in sexual behavior. He is a Christian who is committed to lifelong celibacy because he believes that same-sex behavior is a sin. He told me about a painful experience he had when he came out to his elders. When he told them that he was attracted to the same sex, some of them responded: "We can't approve of your lifestyle."

Lifestyle? What lifestyle? His lifestyle was marked by sexual purity—he had never even kissed another person. The elders confused same-sex attraction with same-sex behavior. Or they assumed that if someone is attracted to the same sex, then they must be "really gay" and therefore having lots of gay sex and marching in gay parades. This is why the words we use are so important. And this is why actually listening to what a person is saying is even more important. Same-sex attraction and same-sex behavior are two different things. While someone may experience same-sex attraction, this does not mean they are engaging in same-sex behavior.

It is so important to get to know what people mean when they say, "I am gay" or "I am lesbian." Labels are easy; relationships are hard work. Quick categorizations are anemic; listening to one's narrative is rich and exhilarating. And it is much more Christian.

Just the other day, a pastor friend of mine got a text from a woman checking out his church, which said:

Hello, I'm looking for a church that will accept my daughter as a lesbian ... If you are that church please let me know, we would love to come to a church where she is not shamed.

How would you respond to this text? Some people would simply say, "Thank you for your text. While we would love for you to visit, you must know that we do not accept lesbians in our church." But would Jesus respond this way? "Thank you for your text, Zacchaeus. While I would love for you to visit, you must know that we do not accept tax collectors in our church."

What would a Christian response look like? There are a couple things we need to know before we reply to this text.

First, what does she mean by "lesbian"? Is she attracted to the same sex or engaging in same-sex behavior? If so, is she married?

And how long has she been out as a lesbian? And does *she* call herself a lesbian, or is it just her mother's label? All of these are important questions to answer before you fire off a text about your stance on homosexuality. Chances are, there is a story here that is worth getting to know before you answer the question.

Second, what does she mean by "accept"? Does she mean accepting all forms of sexual behavior? (In which case, many straight people aren't "accepted" at his church.) Or does "accept" mean accepting her humanity? Notice that she correlates nonacceptance with being shamed. Why does her mother fear that a Christian church might shame her? Have churches shamed her in the past? Chances are, they have.

My good friend Lesli (the one who grew up transgender) gave me some good advice that I think would help us respond to this text. Lesli constantly befriends people who are LGBT, and they often ask her, "Do you think homosexuality is a sin?" Knowing firsthand all the baggage that underlies the question, Lesli learned how to respond with relational savvy: "That's a good question, and I want to answer it. Can I buy you coffee every week for the next four weeks so that we can get to know each other first? I want to know your story, and I want you to know mine. And then we can talk about our question."[11]

Lesli is not avoiding the question. She simply knows that there is so much pain, anger, and misunderstanding that drives the question. If she simply answered yes to the question "Is homosexuality a sin?" it would for some people immediately translate into "gay people are abominations, disgusting, and the worst of all sinners." The simple yes to the question, when filtered through a life story that probably contains dehumanizing words from Christians, will mean something very different than what Lesli intends.

And the same might be true for the mother who sent my pastor friend that text. *Will you accept my daughter, or will you shame her as a perverted, subhuman "other"?* You can't actually answer that question without getting to know her and understanding what she means. Here is one way he could respond that I think would be both loving and faithful:

> Thanks for your text! I'm very excited that you and your daughter are interested in coming to our church. Since God accepts all people, even straight people, yes of course, we would accept your daughter. But I would love to sit down with you and your daughter to hear her story and let her know more about our church and the God we worship. Can I buy you both a coffee?

Maybe the mother would think he's blowing off her question and would move on to another church. But chances are, she would take him up on the offer and end up encountering the scandalous grace of God from the heart of a pastor who cared enough to listen to their story.

TIP OF THE ICEBERG

You see, the text message was a mere tip of the iceberg, as it usually is when people come out. A pastoral approach that only looks at the tip, yet fails to explore the larger story, will fail to love people the way Jesus does. This is so important for parents, friends, family, or anyone else who has a loved one who comes out as gay. Most people get shipwrecked in how they approach the declaration because they don't listen to the story lying beneath the waters.[12]

Imagine with me for a moment. Picture yourself in the seventh grade, and while all your friends are hankering after the opposite sex, for some reason you feel nothing. You don't fit the stereotype of how a boy or girl should act. Soon, your "friends" realize that you are different, and they let you know it. Your name becomes "fag" or "dyke" or "homo," and even your family begins to act weird around you. They too know something is wrong, but it's too awkward for you and them to talk about it. Silence and strange looks replace what once was love.

So you try to meet new friends at church. But your church friends don't act much differently. You see people whispering to each other with grins as they stare at you from across the room. You try to talk to people, but you are met with superficial conversations and it's clear that people want nothing more than to escape your presence. After all, if they linger around you too long, they too may be considered "different."

You pray, you cry, you beg God to change your desires, but nothing happens. You feel alone, depressed, and unvalued. You hear kids use the term *gay* to describe music they don't like or clothes they would never wear. And last Sunday at church, the pastor made several off-handed remarks about those "abominations" who are corrupting our society and are after our children. So you wonder, "Am I going to turn into a pedophile? Is that where these desires will lead? Could God love someone as disgusting as me?"

Then you meet a friend. A real friend. Someone who looks you in the eye and listens to your story. You don't talk about your pain, not yet at least. But there's this weird sense that your new friend already knows your story. Finally, after weeks of hanging out, your friend takes your hand and leans into you with a stare that pierces your soul and says, "I know you have a lot of pain built up and that people have hurt you and made you feel terrible. I just want you to know that I'm here for you. If you need anything, let me know. I think you're a wonderful and beautiful person, and you have so much to offer. I enjoy being around you, and I'll be here for you—no matter what."

Soon, your friend introduces you to several other friends who also care for you. They welcome you with open arms into their community and reaffirm their love and commitment to you. Several of these friends are gay; others are not. But all of them accept you for who you are and make you feel like you are actually human—and valuable. And none of them seem like the abominations that Christians say they are. Around them, you can be yourself. You can talk about your pain. You can talk about your fears. And you can be open about your same-sex attraction without being observed as a creep. After all, several of these new friends feel the same way.

But you want to give this Christian thing one last shot. Deep down you want to love the Christian God, but you can't love a God who could never love you back. So you go to church and knock on the pastor's door and say, "Pastor ... um ... I'm gay, and I want to know if I can still come to church?"

This is the tip of the iceberg.

Now imagine that you are that pastor. What do you say? Do you confront? Do you give your stance on homosexuality? Do you quote Leviticus?

No. Instead, you listen. You ask questions. You look beneath the waters. You learn about the deep, painful, joyful, confusing story that has driven this marvelous soul *from* church and now *back* to church. You look them in the eye. You take them by the hand. You smile, you cry, you hug, and you show the love of Christ that drew tax collectors and sinners to him. "Thanks for being so honest with me. I'm honored that you would be willing to share this with me. I'm sorry that I haven't gotten to know you better. Can I take you out to coffee? I've got another appointment right now, but let me cancel it. There's nothing I'd rather do right now than just get to know you better."

Yes, you confront. You confront with the otherworldly love of Christ, which is far superior and way more humanizing than any other love they will find in the world. Or so we say.

The point is, people don't just wake up one day and say, "I think I'm going to be gay." The journey from experiencing same-sex attraction to engaging in same-sex behavior or embracing a gay identity is not a quick and simple one. The declaration "I am gay," especially in the strong sense of one's core identity, often stands upon a massive block of ice submerged beneath the sea—especially with kids who grow up in the church. Until you understand that deeper narrative, you won't understand why they have come out as gay. If you only address the declaration—"You can come to church, but you'll have to stop being gay"—there's a good chance you'll only confirm that true love and value is found outside the church.

This scenario, of course, is only one of many possible reasons why someone ends up leaving the church and embracing a gay identity in place of a Christian identity. In my experience, though, it's frighteningly common. Having listened to countless stories of LGBT people, I now understand better why people with same-sex attraction have left the church in search of love. Because people will gravitate to where they are loved the most. And if the world out-loves the church, then we have implicitly nudged our children away from the loving arms of Christ.

CHAPTER NINE

GAY AND CHRISTIAN

Can Someone Be Both?

Maybe you've heard the label "gay Christian" and thought that it's a contradiction. If a person is gay, they can't be Christian. And if they're Christian, they should not call themselves gay—even if they experience same-sex attraction.

In this chapter, we will explore several questions that surround the phrase "gay Christians." Let's begin with the most basic question: Should nonaffirming same-sex-attracted Christians call themselves gay?

SHOULD SAME-SEX ATTRACTED CHRISTIANS CALL THEMSELVES GAY?

As you recall, in the last chapter I made a distinction between a *strong* and *soft* sense of using the term *gay*. A *strong* sense refers to one who uses the term *gay* to describe their core identity, central to who they are, a primary aspect of their existence as a human. I have a hard time seeing how this can be reconciled with the gospel, which shatters and shackles all other identities and submits them to Christ. We are slaves of King Jesus and find our ultimate identity in his death and resurrection (Eph. 2:4–7; cf. Gal. 3:28).

Some people, however, use the term *gay* in a *soft* sense of simply describing an aspect of how they experience the world. For instance,

I am a straight man. And both my straightness and maleness affect the way I see the world. In the same way, some of my friends are also men, but attracted to the same sex, which adds a very different lens through which they see and experience the world.

So is it okay for them to call themselves "gay Christians"?

This has been a major point of contention among nonaffirming Christians. And to be honest, I've gone back and forth on my view. Let me open up a window into my brain to show you how I've thought through this question.

On the one hand, I don't call myself a "straight Christian." Why then should same-sex attracted Christians call themselves "gay Christians"? We are all just Christians. All other identities have the potential of muffling our primary identity in Christ. The first thing that should follow the phrase "I am" should be "Christian."

On the other hand, God values diversity and we have all sorts of identities that are good and true and reflect God's colorful image. Yes, my ultimate identity is in Christ. But I am also a man, an American, and a Dodgers fan—for better or worse. I am a writer, a professor, a husband, and a father. I am a pastor, a scholar, and I like to run, so sometimes I call myself a runner. When I use these labels, I always intend them to be secondary, not primary. They are all part of who I am, not the central core of my existence. These secondary labels simply describe how I experience the world, even though they are all subordinate under my primary identity: "I am in Christ."

So here's where I am on this question. If someone uses the term "gay" simply to mean that they are same-sex attracted, then I think it's fine in itself. It's simply a true statement about how they experience the world. I don't think it is necessarily wrong to describe yourself as "gay," if you are using the term not to speak of your core identity but your unique experience as a same-sex attracted person.

However, I also think it can be confusing and potentially misleading if your audience doesn't know what you mean by the term and ends up reading into it a connotation you don't intend. When we use language, we need to consider not just what *we* mean by our words, but how those words will be understood in the ears of others. That's just good communication. For instance, if I referred to myself as a "warrior Christian," this could mean different things to different people. Am I violent? Am I aggressive? Am I going to punch you in your face in the name of Christ? "No, no, I only mean that I did three tours in Iraq for the Marine Corps." Okay, so maybe I'm not violent or aggressive, just a sacrificial patriot. In any case, the phrase "warrior Christian" will most likely *mis*communicate what I am trying to say about myself.

Or more relevantly, when I tell people that I'm "nonaffirming," this could be terribly misleading too, unless I explain exactly what I mean. It doesn't mean that I don't affirm people; it simply means that I don't affirm the sanctity of same-sex sexual relations. Left unexplained, the word *nonaffirming* could come off as dehumanizing. Explained, the word means that I love and value all people the same, while maintaining a traditional Christian sexual ethic.

When I lived in Israel, the Jewish believers told me not to call myself a "Christian," but rather use the term "believer." I was initially appalled at their hypocrisy—*I'm a Christian and everyone in Jerusalem is going to know it!* But then they told me why they don't use the term "Christian." "When local Jews hear 'Christian,' they think back to many years of history when so-called 'Christians' killed Jews who didn't convert to Christianity." This is why they use the term "believer" instead of "Christian." It conveys the same thing, only without all the baggage.

In the same way, the term *gay* may simply mean that a person experiences same-sex attraction, and therefore the label is not inherently wrong. But it also carries the potential of communicating something that the person doesn't intend. We need to be careful about using labels that could be misleading given their wider cultural meaning.

All in all, I think we need to be sensitive to our audience when we use certain terms—especially terms that mean different things to different people. When my nonaffirming gay Christian friends use the term, I know what they mean, so I don't bat an eye. But many people don't know what they mean, and they are likely going to read all sorts of things into the term *gay.*

Whether or not you use the term *gay* (to describe yourself or other people), the most important thing is to look past the label to the person who is using it. If you are gay, then make someone get to know you first before they try to stuff you in a box and strap it with a label. People are way too prone to minimizing the diverse and colorful experiences of others.

Since we've taken the time to unpack the meaning of *gay* and examine its nuances, I'm going to use the term *gay* interchangeably with *same-sex attraction* for the rest of this book.

IS SAME-SEX ORIENTATION SINFUL?

Another question that often comes up is: is same-sex orientation itself sinful, or just same-sex sexual behavior? And by *sinful,* I mean a morally culpable sin and not just a product of the fall, like being born blind. A morally culpable sin is a concrete act of disobedience that people need to repent from. Some people say yes, same-sex orientation is a morally culpable sin. For instance, my friend Denny Burk says that same-sex orientation is itself sinful, since the Bible condemns desires that are directed at sinful objects. In his own words:

> Homosexual orientation describes one who experiences an enduring sexual attraction to persons of the same-sex [sic]. Because the Bible teaches that it is sinful to have a desire for illicit sex, homosexual orientation is by definition sinful.[1]

Burk points to several texts to support his view (Matt. 5:27–28; Mark 7:21), but the one that is most pertinent is Romans 1:26–27, which we've seen before:

> Because of this, God gave them over to passions of dishonor, for even their women exchanged natural sexual relations for

unnatural ones. In the same way the men also abandoned natural relations with women and were inflamed with lust for one another. Men committed shameful acts with other men, and received in themselves the due penalty for their error.

According to Burk, this passage shows that "Sexual desire that fixates on the same sex is sinful, and that is why God's judgment rightly falls on both desires and actions."[2] Therefore, same-sex behavior and same-sex orientation are both sinful.

Denny Burk is a good scholar and has thought through the question of homosexuality quite thoroughly.[3] However, I think he is wrong on this question for several reasons.

ROMANS 1:27 DOES NOT REFER TO ORIENTATION

First, we can quickly dismiss Romans 1:27 since it's not talking about same-sex orientation but same-sex lust. Paul uses a unique phrase in 1:27 ("burned with passion") that refers to passions that accompany and drive sexual arousal.[4] But this phrase is a far cry from what people mean by same-sex orientation today.

THE MEANING OF SAME-SEX ORIENTATION

Second, I don't think it is accurate to equate what people mean by same-sex orientation to what the Bible says about sexual desire. Same-sex orientation is a general disposition, regardless of whether someone is acting on it or even thinking about.

For instance, when I say that I have an opposite-sex orientation, that means that I am attracted to women. It describes my sexual orientation. Whether I am sleeping or awake, studying or at the beach, I never cease to be heterosexual. I am attracted to females; that is my orientation. This doesn't mean that I am slobbering around 24/7 wanting to hump every female I see. That would be lust, not attraction.

Put differently, my experienced (conscious) desire to have sex with someone is a narrow part of my opposite-sex orientation, but it doesn't constitute it. Being heterosexual also doesn't mean that I am only opposite-sex attracted to my wife. That is not what opposite-sex orientation means. My opposite-sex orientation certainly includes my wife but isn't limited to my wife. I am opposite-sex attracted to females, although I am in love with and (should only) sexually desire my wife.

Therefore, living in the constant state of opposite-sex orientation is not sinful, even though it is only okay for me to act on that orientation with only one member of the female species. Likewise, living in the constant state of same-sex orientation doesn't mean that someone is living in a 24/7 state of morally culpable sin. Again, one doesn't cease to be same-sex oriented when they are sleeping. If it were a morally culpable sin, then they would need to be repenting all throughout the night. So I don't think that our modern concept of same-sex orientation can be neatly mapped onto the sinful "desires" that the Bible talks about.

SAME-SEX ORIENTATION IS NOT JUST ABOUT SEX

Third, it would be wrong to reduce same-sex orientation to a desire to have sex. As we saw in the last chapter, same-sex orientation refers to a persistent emotional, romantic, and/or sexual attraction to someone of the same sex and includes other non-sexual relational bonds such as "affection between partners," shared goals and values, mutual support, and ongoing commitment."[5] Same-sex orientation is not just about wanting to have sex.

This is a serious confusion of categories that can be quickly solved by actually listening to LGBT people. Being gay doesn't mean you walk around wanting to have lots of gay sex any more than being straight means that you walk around wanting to have lots of straight sex. Having a same-sex orientation includes a wealth of other virtuous emotions and desires toward members of the same sex; it cannot be narrowly reduced to a volcanic hunger for sex. Same-sex orientation includes a desire for conversational intimacy, same-sex physical touch, emotional bonds, companionship, doing life together, and expressing mutual affection toward members of the same sex. And if all of this sounds "gay" to you, then David and Jonathan really were gay, since I am alluding to 1–2 Samuel.[6]

David and Jonathan weren't gay. But they did experience deep-seated, same-sex affection, and nonsexual intimacy toward each other. Same-sex oriented Christians experience similar desires only to a greater degree.

My lesbian friend Julie Rodgers, for instance, describes her same-sex attraction as

> an overall draw toward someone of the same sex, which is usually a desire for a deeper level intimacy with those of the same sex. Just like a heterosexual orientation can't be reduced to a desire for straight sex, a gay orientation can't be reduced to a desire for gay sex. This longing for intimacy is usually experienced as a desire for nearness, for partnership, for close friendship, rich conversation, and an overall appreciation of beauty.[7]

Julie goes on to say:

> Over the course of the 10,080 minutes that go by in a given week, very few of those minutes (if any at all) are likely comprised of sexual thoughts about other women, and moments when one dwells on those thoughts (lust) are even more rare. In those instances—those rare instances—when one dwells on lustful thoughts, we can all agree that it's sinful.[8]

Most gay Christians I know say the same thing. Same-sex attraction is much broader than just a drooling desire for gay sex. Such attraction includes a virtuous desire to be intimate—in the David and Jonathan or Jesus and John sense of the phrase—with people of the same sex.[9] I wonder if it's an athletic, militaristic, MMA, independent, self-made, muscular version of (American) Christianity that has stiff-armed the very idea of two men having an intimate and affectionate relationship with each other without being labeled gay. Maybe, just maybe, straight men can learn a good deal from gay Christian men about what it means to be *Christian* men, who can say to each other, as David said, "Your love to me was extraordinary, surpassing the love of women" (2 Sam. 1:26).

I've interacted with several people who disagree with me on this issue, and I think our disagreement comes down to a confusion of categories. When I hear people talk about same-sex orientation or attraction being sinful, and I ask them to describe what they mean by such terms, they almost always describe them as an active desire for sex. But that is not what same-sex orientation means. An active desire for sex may spring from one's orientation, but it is not the same as their orientation. Again, someone can be same-sex oriented and yet not think about sex during most hours of the day. And if being same-sex oriented is sinful, then what would repentance look like? Every second of every day confessing the sin of your very existence and waiting for God to make you straight? That's not realistic, biblical, or pastoral.

Repent from illicit sexual desires—yes! But same-sex orientation is not the same as illicit sexual desire.

ROMANS 1 PROHIBITS THE ACTION

Fourth, Romans 1 appears to conflate *desire* and *action*. That is, Paul doesn't seem to view a naked desire apart from a sinful action. (But same-sex attraction can exist without being acted upon.) Notice that when Paul mentions the "passions of dishonor" in 1:26 he immediately explains these desires by describing an action: "for (*gar*) even their women exchanged natural sexual relations for unnatural ones." Paul is talking about women having sex with women. He doesn't consider the "passions of dishonor" separate from the act. It is the entire event—the act and the desire that fueled the act—that is considered to be sin.[10]

Paul is not talking about some sort of orientation that is not acted upon. He's not talking about Julie's orientation that still exists when she's asleep at night or while she's living the 10,000 minutes during the week where she's not thinking about sex yet continues to be oriented to the same sex. That is, Paul doesn't have in mind a general orientation toward members of the same sex: the preconscious, unchosen, unacted-upon orientation of Christ followers. He is describing a sinful act and includes the desire that led to that act. But he doesn't view the general orientation that's not acted upon as sin. That's not what Paul is talking about.

I think this is where James 1:13–14 is helpful: "Each person is tempted when they are dragged away by their own desire and enticed. Then, after desire has conceived, it gives birth to sin; and sin, when it is full-grown, gives birth to death." Notice that James distinguishes between a desire and desire that "gives birth to sin."[11] A woman may give birth to a child, but the woman herself is not the child. Likewise, in James' own words, desire may give birth to sin, but this means that desire itself is not sin.[12]

Same-sex orientation can be a product of the fall—like blindness—and yet not be a morally culpable sin. Like blindness, one's orientation might be part of a disordered creation but still contain the positive potential for uniquely seeing the world. And the same is true for gay Christians. For instance, such people often recognize more clearly the deep human need for intimate, same-sex relations. This is something all people need but few people realize. Gay Christians also experience a stronger realization that one's primary familial identity is in the church and not in one's nuclear family. The gay Christians I know cling to and celebrate *God's* focus on the family, which was reconfigured when Jesus said, "Whoever does the will of my Father in heaven is my brother and sister and mother." Believers aren't just *like* a family. They *are* a family. Gay Christians get this and often long for such familial intimacy more than straight Christians.

God could hijack a person's same-sex attraction and bend it to cultivate a better way of seeing and experiencing the world. Yes— God might just be that sovereign.

HOW SHOULD NONAFFIRMING CHRISTIANS VIEW AFFIRMING CHRISTIANS?

This is by far one of the hardest questions I've had to think through as I wrestled with this topic. It's one thing to weep with those who experience same-sex attraction but think it's wrong to act on it. But what about those Christians who have studied the Bible and disagree with my interpretation?[13] They love Jesus, believe in God's Word, and yet interpret the passages we've looked at differently. They believe that consensual, monogamous, faithful, loving, Christ-centered marriages between same-sex couples can be God-honoring.

This is, perhaps, one of the most pressing ethical questions facing the church today. A couple of decades ago, affirming Christians were a small minority. Today, a growing number of evangelical believers affirm the sanctity of monogamous same-sex unions. My guess is that it won't be long before nonaffirming Christians will be in the minority. Whether we realize it or not, the evangelical church is on the verge of a catastrophic split. People on both sides of the debate need to think deeply about how they view those on the other side.

Are affirming Christians heretics? Wolves in sheep's clothing? False prophets? Or is this a secondary issue that believers can disagree on—like keeping the Sabbath and baptism—and still join hands in worship? Does it come down to a simple disagreement on how to interpret a few passages? Or is it a gospel-issue that is a threat to orthodoxy?[14]

I don't think I can chisel my answer in stone just yet. I am still working through all the implications of my (ongoing) study, and I am sure I will be thinking through this question for many years to come. To be clear, the more I study the Scriptures, the more I am convinced that the Bible doesn't sanction same-sex unions. But that doesn't in itself answer the question about how to relate to those who disagree. So instead of codifying my thoughts on Sinaitic tablets for all to obey, let me offer some conversational reflections that may help you think through this all-important question: How should nonaffirming Christians view their affirming brothers and sisters? And are they brothers and sisters?

It's important to note that not all affirming Christians are the same. This point seems so obvious that I hesitate even saying it. But I still hear people talk about affirming Christians as if they are all from the same womb. Affirming Christians are not all the same. They may all affirm consensual, monogamous, same-sex relations, but they may have arrived at this view for many different reasons.

I've met some people who don't really care what the Bible says. Experience and science (or a distorted and naive view of science) is their authority. Their Bible is: "Gay people are born gay; therefore, it's right for them to act on it," or "It would be unloving to tell a gay person that they can't act on their desires," or "If I marry a person of the same sex, God will forgive me, so I'm going to go ahead and do it."

None of this is Christian logic, and it makes God out to be more of a sexy cheerleader on the sidelines than the King of creation who commands our morality. Before you make a judgment call about affirming Christians, you should find out why they are affirming, since not all affirming Christians ignore the Bible and crown human desire as the lord of right and wrong.

I'll never forget reading Justin Lee's account of how he arrived at an affirming position. It blew my socks off. Justin was raised in a healthy, loving, conservative Christian family and has been sold out for Christ since he was young. But when he hit puberty and was overwhelmed by same-sex attraction, he was devastated. He spent night after night, weeping and praying that God would take these desires away. Still, he remained attracted to men. Finally, Justin set out to truly study what the Bible said. He recalls:

> If God was calling me to celibacy, I would be celibate, but I needed to be sure. To settle this issue once and for all in my own mind, I had to ignore the half-baked ideas on both sides

and go straight to the source—not just a quick perusal of what the Bible had to say, but an honest, prayerful, in-depth study.[15]

As I read Justin's testimony, I couldn't help but wonder how many nonaffirming Christians have had such a humble and open posture toward God's Word? How many traditionalists have come before God with a clean slate and said: "God, whatever your Word says, I will believe it. I'm going to thoroughly study your Word and see what it actually says about homosexuality. And whatever it says, I will believe—at all cost."

I know of only a few.

But Justin did this, and he ended up leaning toward an affirming view. I obviously disagree with Justin's conclusion, but any true Bible-believing Christian should be impressed with his heart and humility.

I don't actually know Justin, though I hope to meet him someday. The only "Justin" I know is through the words of his book. But from what I can see, it seems like he has a high view of Scripture, submits to its authority, embraces the gospel, and loves Jesus.

Maybe he doesn't. Maybe he's an impostor. Maybe *you* are an impostor. Only God knows. I just don't think it's healthy to sweep every single affirming Christian under the same rug of heretics that don't believe the Bible. As I have said before, the debate is not about what the Bible says but what the Bible means.

I know some of my nonaffirming Christian brothers and sisters will disagree. But I still think there is room for dialogue and fellowship with those who hold different views on this topic. Maybe I will change my mind on this. But for now, I want to hold to my biblical convictions and not demonize or condemn everyone who disagrees with me about homosexuality.

WHAT ABOUT 1 CORINTHIANS 5?

Now we come to the million-dollar question: Should we "1-Corinthians-5" gay people from church?

I get really nervous when I see Christians transform whole chapters into verbs. We "Matthew-18-ed" this person and "1-Corinthians-5-ed" that person like some sort of gunslinger from the wild, wild West. We need to make sure we're paying close attention to the specific situation explained in these chapters so that we don't rip them out of context, shove them in our guns, and fire them at modern situations that may not reflect what Paul was thinking of.

In 1 Corinthians 5, Paul rebukes the Corinthian church for celebrating an incestuous affair between a son and his stepmother. Paul points out that this is a clear act of sexual immorality, and it is assumed throughout the passage that the person has not repented from it. In fact, the Corinthian church never addressed the sin; instead of confronting the fornicator, they boasted in the act. Paul therefore commands the church, "Expel the wicked person from among you" (1 Cor. 5:12).

Does the same command apply to gay people in the church?

Ah, did you catch it? Hopefully you didn't answer yes or no to the question. Instead, you should have asked, "What do you mean by 'gay people'?" After all, the phrase "gay people" includes people who experience same-sex attraction but are not acting on it, or who have engaged in same-sex behavior but are trying to repent from it.

Let's reword the question: Does 1 Corinthians 5 apply to people who are actively engaging in sexual relations with people of the same sex and have no desire to repent from it?

Now, let's make sure we understand what is going on in 1 Corinthians 5 before we apply it to people actively engaging in same-sex intercourse. First, this is a local church matter. The church at Corinth had probably twenty to fifty members—real members, not just folks who filled a pew on Sunday morning. The guy who was sleeping with his stepmother is "among" (5:1, 12) the Corinthians in the sense that he was an active part of the local community.

A good friend of mine from church has a daughter who is a lesbian, and my friend was wrestling with the implications of 1 Corinthians 5. Her daughter lives on the other side of the country and is not involved in a church. She has only a vague faith commitment but not a firm desire to follow Christ. "Should we '1-Corinthians-5' her?" my friend asked with tears pooling up in her eyes. What would you say?

As we began talking, I acknowledged that this was a tough question. (And anyone who thinks there's an easy answer probably hasn't thought through it very thoroughly.) I then pointed out that *if* her daughter were actively engaging in a sexual relationship with another female, and *if* she were a member of our church, and *if* she publicly claimed to follow Christ, and *if* she had no desire to repent from her actions, then yes, 1 Corinthians might apply. But since she is not a member of our church—let alone any church—and since it's not clear that she is even following Christ, I have a hard time applying 1 Corinthians 5 to her situation.

Second, if 1 Corinthians 5 does apply to professing believers who are actively engaging in same-sex relations, then to be consistent, we also need to apply it to everyone "guilty of sexual immorality or greed" and to the "idolater, reviler, drunkard, or swindler" (1 Cor. 5:11). If we are inconsistent in the values we choose to enforce, we are no better than the Pharisees, who "preach, but do not practice," who "strain out a gnat but swallow a camel" and are "full of hypocrisy" (Matt. 23:3, 24, 28).

So if we "1-Corinthians-5" everyone who is engaging in same-sex relations, then we also need to "1-Corinthians-5" all the greedy, who hoard their wealth and have no concern for the poor; and the revilers, who drop unchristian bombs in blog comments and Facebook posts, and who stab others with dehumanizing words that tear down instead of building up; and the swindlers, who cheat on their taxes and illegally download copyrighted content off the internet.

I am not saying that we leave all the other immoral people alone. Not at all. I am only saying that we need to be consistent and not single out certain sins that we think are worse than others. Jesus condemns few things more harshly than hypocrisy and selective religiosity. So if we are being pharisaical about how we decide which sins to enforce, then maybe somebody should "1-Corinthians-5" *us* out of the church.

I am still wrestling with the implications of 1 Corinthians 5, and I probably will be for some time. But let me be clear: *If* God's Word is inspired and authoritative, and *if* greed, reviling, drunkenness, and sexual immorality (including same-sex relations) are sin, and *if* someone is engaging in these behaviors and doesn't have desire to repent, and *if* your church agrees with all of these things (it's not just one person's opinion but is shared by the leaders of the church), then yes, in the context of love and tears and truth: the perpetually unrepentant greedy, revilers, drunks, and sexually immoral who claim to be a Jesus-follower should be "put out of your fellowship" (1 Cor. 5:2).

Even as I say those words, it feels unloving and sends chills up my spine. But even more unloving would be to cherry-pick verses from the Bible that feel right to us and ignore the rest that don't feel loving to us. To think you are loving your neighbor without first loving God and obeying his Word is to mock the Creator's will and scoff at true love. If *we* are the ultimate judges of what is right and wrong, and if *we* think we have a better, more updated understanding of what love is, then we are doing nothing more than replicating the sin of Eden and becoming our own moral authority—determining what is right and wrong. And God help us all.

CHAPTER TEN

ON THE SIDE OF THE ANGELS

What Does Christian Faithfulness Look Like?

Throughout my study, I've become friends with many Christians who experience same-sex attraction and also embrace a nonaffirming view. Their stories and friendship have forever affected my life. Much of what I wrestle with in this chapter is not just theory. It is the daily experience of many people dear to my heart. I don't approach the following questions from a distance, but with real stories etched into my bones. The stories of Nick, Matt, Nate, Amy, Brian, Lesli, Sam, Lindsay, Wes, Sarah, and others—all of whom are attracted to the same sex but believe that it is wrong to act on their attractions. Imagine that your dreams of getting married and having kids were crushed by the thought that you could never be with the man or woman you desire. Like waking up from a nightmare but realizing it wasn't a dream, gay Christians battle daily with temptations and struggles that most Christians will never experience. It is time for straight Christians to lay aside the culture war and election ballots and become life-giving agents to brothers and sisters who are hungry for love yet often come up short when they search for it in the church.

So what are the options for nonaffirming same-sex attracted Christians? For the most part, there are three.[1]

REPARATIVE THERAPY

If I wrote this book twenty years ago, or even five, I might have been more enthusiastic about this first option. As you may know, Exodus International was a Christian ministry that used to help same-sex attracted Christians reverse their orientation and cultivate desires for the opposite sex. The so-called "ex-gay" ministry was founded in 1976 by Gary Cooper and Michael Bussee, who had a heart to help Christians overcome their same-sex attraction, something both of them struggled with. At its height, Exodus had grown to become an umbrella agency to hundreds of similar organizations in the U.S. and in other countries. But in 2013, Exodus closed its doors.

Alan Chambers, the president of Exodus when it shut down, apologized for the many lives that have been harmed while trying to help people change their orientation. While Exodus trumpeted the slogan "Change is Possible," the reality is that many people didn't experience the change they were expecting and sometimes promised.[2] Exodus' failure to deliver what it assured was, perhaps, foreshadowed most graphically in 1979, when co-founders Bussee and Cooper fell in love and became partners.

As you can imagine, trying to change someone's sexual orientation has received a bad rap over the years. Most people now have a negative view of "reparative therapy"—the therapeutic method of trying to change one's same-sex orientation. Many people consider reparative therapy to be unethical and destructive. LGBT people mock fundamentalist Christians who think they can "pray the gay away." Older reparative treatments, such as electric shock to the genitals, are now viewed as silly, if not barbaric.[3] Many parents have been devastated by persistent efforts by counselors who convince gay teens that their upbringing is the cause of their homosexuality. I recently read two different stories about gay teens who were brainwashed into thinking that they had been sexually abused by their fathers, even though they actually never had been.[4]

Some people say that more harm than good will result from

those who try to change their orientation. Still, there are some people who say they have been blessed by reparative therapy, even though their voices are often muzzled and mocked by the tidal wave of opposition both inside and outside the church.

I have a friend who is part of this snuffed out minority. He is a licensed psychologist with a PhD and works for a secular practice that helps gay men change their orientation. Please note: this is not Exodus International; it's not even a Christian practice. At least half of the men who come to him are not religious. This is quite different from most ex-gay ministries, who hire nonprofessional counselors to help Christians crucify their same-sex attraction.

I asked him about the success rate of his practice. And he said that approximately 50 percent of the gay men that come to him experience full, ongoing change in their sexual orientation, and another 25 percent experience a significant degree of change, while 25 percent experience little to no change.

I literally laughed out loud in Starbucks when he told me this. "What? There's *no way* that's possible!" I had been reading a lot of books that mocked reparative therapy and celebrated the death of Exodus, waving the banner that change is impossible and devastation is likely. My friend said, "Look, I know what all the websites say. But I can only tell you what I've seen in the hundreds of clients that have come to me. I didn't get this from books; I got it by dealing with real people."

Again, my friend's practice is secular; many of his clients aren't Christian. He has no theological investment for needing these men to change, and he doesn't go around trumpeting the claim that "change really *is* possible." He's just telling me what he has observed through his medical practice. And he's not shocking anyone's genitals or "praying the gay way."

I asked him what he thought about Exodus International, and he said that he wasn't too surprised that most people didn't actually experience lasting change. "Helping people change their sexual orientation is an in-depth and somewhat complicated psychological process. Exodus International was filled with well-meaning but non-professional counselors who didn't have the necessary credentials."

Now, some of you want to throw this book across the room at the mere suggestion that 50 percent of his clients have changed their orientation. Others may be tempted to Tweet: "@PrestonSprinkle says change really is possible!" But please don't. Don't throw the book. Put your phone down. I never said I agree with my friend. Maybe he was lying. Maybe he was telling the truth. Maybe his clients will return to their homosexual desires after twenty years, I don't know.

I only mention my friend's experience to show that there are other professional voices out there that should counterbalance the anti-change, "good riddance, Exodus!" opinion that has all but monopolized the conversation.

From what I've seen, I think that Mark Yarhouse takes the most fair-minded approach to sexual orientation change efforts. Mark is a leading Christian psychologist who has done a ton of research in sexuality—specifically, homosexuality. In fact, Mark and his former colleague Stanton Jones performed one of the most in-depth studies on the effectiveness of Exodus International.[5] While some people say that change is destructive and others say that change is quite probable if done the right way, Yarhouse says that change *is* possible, although radical change is rare. But we have to first define what we mean by *change*.

If by *change* we mean total conversion from gay to straight, then it is extremely rare that people will experience this sort of change. And yes, potential harm is always a possibility. But there are other types of change that people have experienced with a good measure of success. People have experienced change in identity, where they develop an improved sense of who they are. Or a change in behavior, where they cultivate a stronger ability to resist acting on their desires. Or they experience some measure of change in same-sex attraction. Not a complete enter-the-phone-booth-and-walk-out-Super-(Straight)-Man type of change, but some degree of reduction in same-sex attraction, and possibly even the beginnings of opposite-sex attraction.[6]

That said, there are two very important things to understand before anyone seeks to change their sexual orientation. First, be realistic with your expectations. This is one of the reasons why Alan Chambers said that Exodus failed. They often (not always) gave people unrealistic expectations about the degree of change the person could expect. The slogan "Change is Possible" was interpreted as "If I go to Exodus, I'll come out straight!" And when the large majority did not experience this, it induced a lot of pain, especially for those who ended up getting married to someone of the opposite sex only to find out later that they were still very much gay.

Be realistic with your expectations. Some change is possible; very little change is likely, as is no change at all.

Second, the person who experiences same-sex attraction must desire the change. No one should force another person to change their orientation. Parents, listen up! Everything I've read and everyone I've talked to from all the different perspectives on the topic say the same thing: *If* someone should seek reparative therapy, *they* need to be the one who desires it. Not their friends, not their pastor, and especially not their parents. Forcing your kid who just came out to go to reparative therapy will probably lead to more pain and frustration, and it will almost inevitably damage your relationship with your child.

All in all, it is important to make sure that we don't preach a gospel of heterosexuality, as if the good news of Jesus is that he can make you straight. Wholeness and salvation should not be equated with becoming straight, but becoming more like Jesus, which is possible if a person remains totally attracted to the same sex from cradle to grave.

MIXED-ORIENTATION MARRIAGE

The second option for a same-sex attracted Christian is to pursue a mixed-orientation (MO) marriage. That is, to marry someone of the opposite sex.

This option may be just as hotly debated as reparative therapy. The fact is, many people would say that the odds of a gay person becoming happily married to someone of the opposite sex are about the same as a straight person being married to someone of the same sex. So if you're a straight dude, first imagine yourself being married to another dude before you tell your gay friend, "Come on, just find a sexy woman and it'll all work out."

I've seen a few marriages end in destruction because of one partner finally coming out. I've also heard of other marriages where one partner said they "used to be gay," but after going through reparative therapy, they tied the knot, only to find out a few years later that the ex-gayness wore off or never really took root. Both spouses ended up with an insurmountable mountain of pain and confusion as they signed the divorce papers. Some therefore say: Since same-sex orientation is fixed at birth, the possibility of a mixed-orientation marriage is impossible and harmful—another by-product of a backwoods theology destined to do more harm than good.

It's tough to know for sure why some MO marriages fail. After all, many Christian heterosexual marriages fail, and some of the ones that stick it out are plagued with loneliness, depression, and porn addiction—till death do them part. Does this mean that heterosexuals shouldn't attempt to get married? You can see the hypocritical logic here. The frequent failure of marriage doesn't mean that it is inherently destructive. Perhaps we're going about it all wrong.

It is definitely true: many MO marriages have failed. Much of this probably has to do with problems related to the issue of orientation. But this doesn't mean that it isn't still an option that could end in a beautiful, joyful, yet difficult relationship. But that's true of all marriages, right? Beautiful. Joyful. *Difficult*.

I have two gay friends who are in MO marriages. Nathan is a

same-sex attracted Christian married to Sara, and Brian is a same-sex attracted Christian married to Monica. Both Nathan and Brian will tell you that it hasn't been easy, and there are many unique challenges that accompany their marriages. Yet both of them describe their marriages as relationally and sexually fulfilling—even though they both still have a strong same-sex orientation. In fact, Nathan says that while he only had the beginnings of romantic interest in Sara when they were dating, this interest grew into a more intense emotional and physical attraction as their relationship progressed. Nathan says, "By the time we were married, I hadn't become 'straight' because I still experienced same-sex attractions. At the same time, a 'one-woman' orientation had been developing within me during my relationship with Sara, so marrying her felt like the most natural thing to do and what my heart had in fact grown to long for."[7]

Brian and Monica's story is similar. Their relationship was grounded in a deep friendship that grew into an intimate marital bond—one that was rooted in honesty, friendship, and unconditional love. Both Brian and Nathan tell me that they hesitate talking about their marriages for fear that gay Christians will think that getting married will make them straight or that all MO marriages will look like theirs. In fact, Nathan and Brian often say that if both partners are not completely honest with each other from the beginning, the relationship will likely end in disaster. The same-sex attracted partner needs to be totally transparent about their attractions, and the opposite-sex attracted partner must be real about their struggles and fears. MO marriages can only succeed if they are grounded in a rich, radically authentic, relational bond. And it's very important that a same-sex attracted person doesn't feel outside pressure to pursue such a marriage. It must be their own choice; it shouldn't be forced upon them. But hey, all this sounds like a healthy foundation for all marriages. Maybe MO partners could teach us all a good deal about godly matrimony.

But if you can't change your orientation and don't fall in love with someone of the opposite sex, what is your other option?

CELIBACY

The third option is, perhaps, the most difficult. I have met so many beautiful and faithful celibate gay Christians over the past few years, and our friendship has forever changed my life. As I've been writing this book, there's not a page that goes by where I don't have their names and faces and stories swirling around in my head. I have become a much better person as I've shared many meals and drinks with my celibate gay friends. Needless to say, what I'm about to write is deeply personal.

The celibacy option has fallen under attack by affirming people both gay and straight. Some see it as dehumanizing; many see it as cruel. "Forced celibacy," as they call it, is nothing more than brutal blowback from conservative religious thought. The only reason why gay Christians would choose celibacy is because they have been brainwashed by religious conservatives into thinking that they must choose celibacy. And this is demeaning, destructive, and unchristian.

Matthew Vines, for instance, comes down pretty hard against celibacy in his book, *God and the Gay Christian*. He says that "Celibacy is a gift, and those who do not have the gift should marry."[8] Telling people who don't have the gift of celibacy to remain celibate "requires gay Christians to build walls around their emotional lives so high that many find it increasingly difficult to form meaningful human connection of all kinds."[9] "To deny to a small minority of people, not just a wedding day, but a lifetime of love and commitment and family is to inflict on them a devastating level of hurt and anguish."[10] Vines believes that "mandatory celibacy" hinders gay Christians from fully expressing the image of God through marriage: "When we reject the desires of gay Christians to express their sexuality within a lifelong covenant, we separate them from our covenantal God, and we tarnish their ability to bear his image."[11] In the end, "embracing a nonaffirming position makes [gay Christians] less like God."[12]

When I read Vines' words, pain wells up in my soul as I wonder: Is my nonaffirming position hindering people from fully expressing

God's image? Am I denying humans the relational fulfillment they need? As a man who is happily married, I hesitate even talking about celibacy. After all, what do I know?

This is why I think it's important to listen to people who are actually pursuing celibacy. I honestly think that Vines misrepresents (or doesn't try to represent) those who have chosen this path. He paints celibacy with a gloomy brush and doesn't consider the testimony of people who are actually celibate. This would be like if I wrote a book on homosexuality and never listened to people who are actually gay.

Dan Mattson, for instance, is a celibate gay Christian, and he says:

> My life isn't a "life of misery," and I'm not "doomed to celibacy," or a life of heart-breaking loneliness. I reject the representation of a life striving for celibacy as miserable, and part of my mission in life is to debunk all of the dreary, droopy tropes out there of what celibacy is all about."[13]

Ron Belgau is another very thoughtful celibate gay Christian. I love his honesty about the struggles of celibacy:

> Is celibacy difficult? Yes (so is marriage; so is grad school; life *is* pain, princess). Is it frustrating at times? Yes (but watch someone raising toddlers sometime and it may change your perspective on the challenges of celibacy). Have there been times when I wanted to give up? Yes. But is it worth it? Yes. And do I regret it? No.[14]

Ron doesn't candy-coat celibacy and make it sound super peachy. It's not. But pain often accompanies holiness, and holiness unearths uncanny joy. Holiness is a difficult path for every Christian—gay or straight, married or single—and each path toward holiness comes with its own unique struggles. I would never say that married people have the same struggles that singles do. Yes, they are different. But marriage is not the solution to all of our relational longings. And marriage certainly isn't the only way or even the best way to bear

God's image, as Vines believes. We bear God's image because we are human, not because we've tied the knot.

If you think that marriage is the solution to loneliness and depression, then I would highly recommend you don't get married—gay or straight. I know many married people who are incredibly lonely and depressed. Just look at the number of people who get divorced, have an affair (emotional or physical), or become addicted to porn after they get married. Some of the loneliest people I know are married. That is because marriage was not designed to solve a person's loneliness.[15]

As Ron says elsewhere:

Although Christian discipleship is costly, it need not be lonely. Our culture has become very fixated on sex, but sex and romance are not the same as love. Nor is Christian love the same as the kind of casual friendship that is common in our culture.[16]

My friend Andrew Thomas is a celibate gay Christian and he says that "gay Christians may be called to live without sex, but no one can survive without healthy friendships and emotional intimacy."[17] Tim Otto says the same thing: "Being gay, I had felt that 'social solidarity' and 'family' were impossible for me." Tim could have run off and gotten married to another man to solve his loneliness. Instead, he realized that he was already married to a relationally intimate Bride.

Yet with my brothers and sisters in the Church of the Sojourners, I felt like I was suddenly coming to the surface and encountering light after years of living in an underground cave. I was living in a New Testament family, in which I was loved, and in which others needed my love.[18]

Dan, Ron, Andrew, Tim, and many others whom I don't have space to mention, all disagree with the way that affirming Christians equate celibacy with loneliness and lack of relational intimacy. Again, no one is saying that celibacy is easy and will always experience life-giving intimate relationships. But from their own testimonies, the celibate gay Christians I know do not say that their singleness inevitably leads to loneliness and an inability to love and be loved. The claim that the nonaffirming view inherently denies gay Christians "a lifetime of love and commitment and family," thus inflicting "on them a devastating level of hurt and anguish" and cultivating "pain in other people's lives," is not based on a biblical view of love and turns a deaf ear to the ones who are actually pursuing such a faithful life that's rooted in and reflects the life of our single Savior.

LOVE AND SEX

Because love—true, biblical, life-giving *agape* love—is not the same as sex. One could have sex and not have love, and one can experience love that lifts you to the heavens and never have sex or romantic intimacy. Jesus told us to love our neighbors, but this doesn't mean we need to have sex with them.[19] Or as my friend Nick Roen says: "We all have a deep, deep need for love. And that love is just as legitimately available within celibacy as it is in sexual expression. In our hyper-sexualized culture, that message will turn some heads." And Nick speaks out of real life. He is yet another celibate gay Christian who enjoys love and intimacy, even in the absence of sex.

When affirming Christians talk about celibacy in the worst possible light, they not only misrepresent what celibacy is, but they reinforce a secular and rather thin view of love where intimacy is impossible without genital contact. But actually, some of the Bible's richest expressions of love have no reference to sex. David had all the sex he wanted, sometimes with whomever he wanted. But when David writes about rich, satisfying, intimate love, he talks about his best friend Jonathan: "Your love to me was *better* than the love of women" (2 Sam. 1:26). Jesus, John, and Paul all talked about life-giving love that fills your lungs with the breath of heaven without ever mentioning sex.

My friend Matt Jones is another celibate gay Christian who has a remarkable perspective on celibacy, but he didn't always have a positive outlook. In fact, he used to view celibacy as many affirming Christians do.

> For most of my college career I was haunted by a singular image that I thought would define the entirety of my existence: When I closed my eyes I saw, I *felt*, myself closing the door to a cold and dark apartment, entirely empty, devoid of anyone who would witness my life and show me that I was known and loved. The frozen silence of it all was terrifying.[20]

A "cold and dark apartment" is not the abundant life Jesus promises. We need people. We need relationships. We need to love and be loved. And all of this can be found apart from marriage.

Matt's perspective changed, however, when he began to see the beautiful freedom that singleness may bring. Marriage certainly comes with its own freedom—freedom of monogamous intimacy, sexual union, raising kids, and many other unique blessings. But singleness also opens up a different sort of freedom and joy that married people miss out on. Freedom to minister much more pervasively; freedom from the anxiety that accompanies the marriage and child-rearing; freedom to love the community of God's people with much more intensity that can't be matched by any responsible family man. Instead of a cold, dark apartment, Matt's future began to look like a sun-bathed playground with all sorts of unforeseen possibilities. Far from becoming a barrier to the good life, Matt's singleness enabled him to plunge his face into the well of the abundant life Jesus promises.

Matt changed his perspective by opening up his mind and heart to the richness of the gospel—the good news about a single Savior who provides abundant life for all who die with him. Matt stopped viewing his celibacy as a big fat no—no to joy, no to sex, no to intimacy—and a life-giving yes. Yes to relationships. Yes to friends. Yes to serving others and enjoying life to the fullest. "I had just somehow been blinded to how abundantly good and profound life could be as a single person."

Both marriage and singleness come with their own set of unique yeses and nos. I would never belittle the difficulty that comes with the distinctive nos of singleness. There are many blessings I've experienced that flow from my marriage. But if you think that marriage is the only way to say yes to life, yes to love, and yes to happiness, then you'll not only be disappointed if you get married, but you will also forgo the cruciform joy that is possible in your singleness. The gospel never promises happiness to married folk. It does promise joy for those who pick up their crosses and die with Jesus.

THE CHURCH AND SINGLENESS

But here lies the problem: The church doesn't know what to do with singles. Until the church can develop a better theology of singleness, it won't know what to do with celibate gay people in their midst. And this is a real crisis.

Most Christians view singleness as an interim stage, a period of life that you have to get through like standing in line for a ride at Disneyland. No one wants to be there, but we must grin and bear it so we can jump on a rocket and swirl around the Matterhorn. Singleness is rarely viewed in a positive light in American Christianity.

Much of this anti-singleness message is preached by our churches, sometimes with words, other times with actions. Sometimes the message is conscious; usually it is subtle and unintended. But single people hear it loudly and clearly: "You're incomplete until you get married and have at least two to four kids." (If you have more than four, then people think you are weird again.) Single people have a hard time feeling like a genuine, valuable part of our church communities. Shuffling them off to singles' ministry (so that they can find a spouse), cut off from all the other married people, often perpetuates the problem.

But don't take my word for it. Just ask any post-college single person at your church how they feel. Ask them if they feel like they are valued, honored, respected, loved, and invited into the lives and homes of other families of the church. Ask them if they are ever made to feel incomplete by off-handed comments ("How come you're not married *yet*?"), sermon illustrations that always draw from parenting, or stay-at-home moms huddled in the corner swapping toddler stories. Ask them how they feel on Mother's Day or Father's Day, when the calendar doesn't contain a Singles' Day. Ask them how they feel when their friends who used to stay up with them until two in the morning watching movies and pounding popcorn go off and get married and never have time for them anymore. "Sorry I haven't called you in six months. See, I'm now in charge of the young-marrieds group, and I've been *so busy*." The church oftentimes has no real space for single people other than to volunteer for the nursery, since they obviously have extra time on their hands. Being single and all.

The church needs to learn how to value single people. I know this. Because I've been guilty of it. I've ignored many single people at church and haven't taken the time to identify with their unique struggles and joys. I'll never forget hosting a community group a while back and we had fifteen people the first night. Ten minutes into the meeting, one guy got a phone call and left. I thought it was odd, but I kept on "doing community" with the fourteen of us. Then it dawned on me. The fourteen who remained were all married—there were seven couples. The one guy who left was single. And I seriously doubt that he actually had a phone call.

Did we do anything? No. But that's sort of the point, right? We didn't do *anything*. We didn't think of how awkward it must have been to be a single guy in the midst of a bunch of babies and breast pumps. We didn't make him feel included and valued. We were too busy swapping our parenting prayer requests that we didn't notice that the room must have felt like a cold and dark apartment for our single friend.

But this is typical in churches today. Statistically, single people are much less likely to attend church, get involved in a small group, or volunteer at church events compared to married people.[21] What's shocking is that the number of married people is rapidly declining in society while the number of single people is rising. There should be more single people involved in church, not less. Still, single people don't feel connected and valued, even though they are likely to volunteer at other nonprofits or social organizations that help people. But church? Church is for married people or those who are looking for a ring.

Until the church develops a more holistic vision for singleness, it will fail to be the family that celibate gay Christians need. Or as my friend Matt Jones says: "Unless a community is seriously modeling a commitment to hospitality and grace for all stages of life, its sexual ethic, no matter how 'orthodox' it may sound, will never seem viable or good in any meaningful way."

Singleness should never be seen as a stage to get through, but a unique gift intended to be used for God's glory.

FEELING CALLED TO CELIBACY?

Some of you may think, "But what if a person does not *feel* called to singleness?" Is it inhuman and unchristian to mandate celibacy for gay people who don't *feel* called to it? It's an interesting question, but it has many false assumptions about what it means to be called.

Christian thinking is often cluttered with buzzwords and spiritual phrases. We "invite Jesus into our hearts," live "missionally," "do community," and, of course, "feel called" to authenticate the decisions we make in life. We feel called to go to a certain college, but when we meet a girl at a different college, we feel called to transfer. We feel called to minister and called to marry. We feel called to work at Burger King instead of McDonalds, but when we land a higher paying job at Starbucks, we feel called to serve coffee.

The Bible actually does talk about being called, but the word *called* is almost always used in reference to salvation.[22] In other words, all Christians have been called by God, and we all have a call to live a faithful Christian life—even if you don't feel like it. There are only a few times when the word *call* is used of a specific vocation. Paul, for instance, talks about being called to be an apostle.[23] But the only "feeling" he had on the Damascus road was terror, not a warm sensation. Paul wasn't too jazzed about his new vocation, and neither was Ezekiel, Isaiah, or Jeremiah—all of whom were called to be prophets. Paul and the prophets were simply summoned into obedience by their Creator, and such obedience—which included a pile of suffering—came with unpredictable joy.

First Corinthians 7:17–24 does talk about being "called" in the context of marriage and singleness. However, a close look shows that the term *call* here refers to salvation and not a particular vocation. Paul is telling the Corinthians to remain in the position they were in at the time of their calling; that is, at the time when they were saved. "Was anyone at the time of his call already circumcised? Let him not seek to remove the marks of circumcision" (7:18).

The word *call* never refers to one's desire to be celibate, and it is never associated with a feeling.

Paul might implicitly refer to a "gift of celibacy" in 1 Corinthians 7:7 when he says: "I wish that all were as I myself am. But each has his own gift from God, one of one kind and one of another." Since Paul was unmarried—probably widowed—he might be referring to some sort of gift when talking about his singleness. The term *gift* here (*charisma*) is the same Greek word often translated as "spiritual gift" elsewhere, and Paul defines such gifts as "manifestations of the Spirit for the common good."[24] That is, all spiritual gifts—*charismas*—are given by God for the good of those around you. *Charismas* aren't primarily for *you*, and using those gifts doesn't depend on whether you feel like it—yes, even the gift of singleness. As Paul says later in the chapter, single people have been empowered by God to further his kingdom without the distractions and stresses of married life (1 Cor. 7:32–35).[25]

And since Paul was probably married at one point, this gift of celibacy does not refer to some crazy desire not to have sex, but to God's grace in Paul's life while he was (now) single. Barry Danylak, who did a PhD at Cambridge University on this topic and who is also single, says that Paul

> does not imply that those with the gift of singleness are asexual individuals with no interest in marriage or family life. But it is suggesting that they experience a genuine freedom that allows them to serve God with a whole heart, irrespective of whether they ever experience the fulfillment of marital intimacy and family life.[26]

One of the problems is that we think that people are either called to singleness for life, or they are called to be married. According to this way of thinking, if you are called to be married but are *not yet* married, then you are by definition not living out your calling; you are incomplete. But the Bible never says this. The Bible talks about living out your call *as a Christian* whether you are single or whether you are married (1 Cor. 7). As my friend Lance Hancock says, "The gift is not a desire or capacity to be single; the gift is singleness itself."[27]

How do you know if you are called to singleness? If you are single.

How do you know if you are called to marriage? If you are married.

That is, your call as a Christian while you are single is to be a faithful steward of your singleness. And your call as a Christian while you are married is to be a faithful steward of your marriage.

So I reject the notion that gay Christians must feel some sort of call if they are to remain single and celibate forever. They are called to be like Christ, to love Christ, to uphold Christ as supreme in their lives. Celibate Christians are called to love, to serve, to rejoice in their suffering as Christ rejoiced in his. They are called to pick up their cross and follow a Savior who has suffered more than any of us ever will, who calls us—married or single—to rejoice in our sufferings inasmuch as they broadcast his sufferings to the world.

Suffering and joy are not antithetical in God's kingdom. When God calls us to salvation, he calls us to partake in his Son's suffering, so that we can also partake in the Son's joy.

LOVE CRUCIFIED

The Christian faith is built on the notion that the fleeting pain in this life does not compare to the infinite joy awaiting us in the next. I do not belittle the real pain that accompanies the life of celibate gay Christians who desire a husband or wife of the same sex, who might never experience the exhilarating pleasure of having sex with another person. But I do want to put their struggles—your struggles—in the context of other broken people who are seeking to follow a mighty Savior who also was broken, and who called us to embrace our brokenness since we have the guarantee of wholeness through the resurrection.

Christianity is funny that way. We don't shy away from pain and suffering because Jesus embraced such sufferings and called us to walk the same road. Suffering is not antithetical to divine joy. I've seen a man named Nick Vujicic born with no arms and no legs rejoice in his suffering and further God's kingdom through his calling. I've wept with Carlos and Devin, whose sudden death of their seven-month-old child compelled them to go on and foster several children. I've held hands with beautiful lepers in Kathmandu, Nepal, who smile while they are rotting away because they've found a Savior worthy of life and worthy of death. And I've seen celibate gay Christians who never felt called to singleness find otherworldly pleasures in a life they never thought they could bear.

I don't buy the unchristian notion that denying gay people a same-sex spouse is tantamount to denying them a fulfilled life. I reject the myth that true love and intimacy are only found in a partner you can have sex with. And I despise the modern American evangelical lie that a marital spouse is the quintessential form of happiness, without which no one—unless she "feels called"—can experience true fulfillment as a human being. None of this is based on a Christian worldview, which finds its meaning in a single Savior who was spat upon, mocked, tortured, and killed, yet "for the joy set before him" endured the misery of the cross in order to taste the delights of resurrection life.

Jesus never promised us all the earthly blessings we desire if we follow him. But he did promise that every spark of loneliness, every tinge of pain, every dull ache of depression, every chill of isolation, will be redeemed when Jesus returns to restore his creation and reward the righteous with eternal life.

And only then will we be on the side of the angels, "who neither marry or are given to marriage," a resurrected state foretasted in this life by my celibate brothers and sisters.[28]

AFTERWORD

The Challenge

This book represents part of my journey in thinking through homosexuality; it's not the end of my journey. Calling the final chapter a "conclusion" would therefore be a misnomer. There are many more questions that I haven't addressed, and other issues that I have all but ignored—like what the Bible says about transgender, transsexual, or intersex people. Still, as I reflect on my interaction with the Bible and homosexuality, I see several challenges for nonaffirming Christians as we seek to be truthfully loving, and lovingly truthful, toward gay people inside and outside our church communities.

As I pointed out in the last chapter, the church needs to develop a much better theology of singleness. We cannot make single people feel less valuable, less gifted, or incomplete until they get married. Until we view single people as just as complete as married people, we will not know how to embrace celibate gay people.

In chapter 5 and elsewhere throughout this book, I have urged the Christian church to cultivate a richer and more authentic relationship with the unchurched LGBT community. When LGBT people are in need, or just need someone to talk to, their immediate response should be to go to the nearest Christian church. It is our job to broadcast the love of Christ in such a way that there is no doubt in their minds that Christianity is where love and salvation can be found. Love—biblical love—does not mean affirming everyone's behavior. Yet people will never have the power to change unless they first experienced genuine acceptance.[1]

I see several other challenges for nonaffirming churches.

1. CULTIVATE AN ENVIRONMENT WHERE PEOPLE WHO EXPERIENCE SAME-SEX ATTRACTION CAN TALK ABOUT IT

No doubt, there are people within your church walls who experience same-sex attraction. They are twelve, thirteen, sixteen years old. They are forty-five and married to an opposite-sex spouse and have three kids. There are many same-sex attracted Christians who remain closeted due to an unhealthy church environment that wouldn't know what to do with them if they talked about their struggle. Manly men, feminine women, guys who don't talk with a lisp and who could throw a football farther than you. Women who could get any guy they wanted but want nothing more than to feel the warm embrace of another woman.

The Christian church needs to get past the "us" (straight people) versus "them" (gay people) mindset and start cherishing the lives of the beautiful people that experience same-sex attraction. We need to create and cultivate a safe and honest environment where people who experience same-sex attraction don't feel gross or ashamed; where they can talk openly about their struggles in their small group and the room is not filled with cold silence and terrified stares. We allow people to admit their struggle with pride and a weak prayer life. But these are much more hideous—arrogance and lack of communion with God—than someone's attraction to the same sex. The latter should be easy. But we live in, and have created, a culture where it is terrifying to struggle with same-sex attraction.

I long for the day when preachers and teachers, deacons and elders, single college students and stay-at-home moms, can all talk about their same-sex attraction and not be viewed as animals. Unless you are a Pharisee who thinks you really are much better than the rest of those sinners over there, then you should be eager to love and walk with people who are attracted to the same sex.

One of the ways to cultivate such an environment is to avoid off-handed comments about "the gay agenda," "the homosexual community," or "the sin of homosexuality." All of these phrases—and many others—often get misconstrued and misinterpreted, especially by the thirteen-year-old who is scrambling to find a gun because he thinks he is an abomination before God. If you are a preacher, use your words carefully. Explain what you mean and what you don't mean. Don't sling out phrases that could mean many different things to many different people.

Personally, I don't normally mention homosexuality from the pulpit unless I carefully explain exactly what I mean. I don't use homosexuality as a quick example of sin, and I don't talk about culture wars from the pulpit. If I ever mention homosexuality from the stage, I always ask myself: "How would I hear this if I were a teen struggling with same-sex attraction, or a visitor who is a lesbian, or a parent of a gay son who just committed suicide?" Your audience is diverse. Their stories are unique. Your people have specific struggles and many of them are hidden. Preachers, make sure you consider all of these before you make off-handed comments about homosexuality.

2. LISTEN TO THE STORIES OF LGBT PEOPLE

In his song "Every Breaking Wave" on U2's 2014 album *Songs of Innocence*, Bono sings:

> And every shipwrecked soul, knows what it is
> To live without intimacy
> I thought I heard the captain's voice
> It's hard to listen while you preach

It is hard to love someone while you are talking; love is most authentically shown when you are listening. To listen is to love, and you can't love without listening.

A few years ago when I was writing my book on nonviolence, I read a lot of books on the topic. I studied all the relevant passages in the Bible, and I read lots of different books on the ethics of war.

I was trying to figure out whether Christians should ever fight in war or use violence as a last resort. But most importantly: I talked to dozens of people who served in wars. What was it like? How did it feel when you lost your friend in an attack? How did war make you think about violence and nonviolence? If all I did was read about the topic, my perspective would have been jaded, keeping at arm's length the people who are most affected by the very thing I am writing on. And the same is true of homosexuality.

I believe that every single Christian needs to think deeply about this issue. And since it is not an issue, but *people*, every Christian needs to listen to the stories of LGBT people.

I think the fear is that if you listen to someone's story, it means you agree with all of their decisions and actions in that story. But we don't treat other people like this, do we? Counselors listen to those who come to them for help. Doctors listen to patients. Lawyers listen to clients. Friends listen to their friends, if they are true friends. None of these listeners agree with everything they hear. Listening simply means that we care enough about the person to experience their life through reliving their story. And you can only do this if you listen.

A couple years ago, I taught a class on homosexuality, and one of the assignments I gave was for my students to interview someone who is LGBT. The rules for the assignment were that they were required to ask questions and just listen. Too often we are quick to jump in and correct, disagree with, or confront. So for this assignment, they were required to just ask questions and listen to their stories. What was the result? Not a single student changed their theological perspective on same-sex relations. But almost every student grew in compassion, love, and understanding for people who experience same-sex attraction.

To listen is to love, and you can't deeply love until you listen.

3. PUT HOMOPHOBIA TO DEATH

Homophobia refers to the dislike of or prejudice against LGBT people. When an LGBT person grows up in the church, they usually encounter homophobia—feeling that they are disgusting in the eyes of the Christian God because they have been treated this way by his people.

We need to put homophobia to death. Stab it. Kill it. And bury it in a grave. If it tries to resurrect, step on its head. Affirming Christians can't be the only ones concerned about homophobia in the church. Nonaffirming Christians should be just as relentless—if not more—in confronting the unchristian posture toward gay people that runs rampant in the church.

Evangelical leaders need to stand for truth. And putting homophobia to death is part of standing for truth. Jesus is truth, and Jesus is not adultererphobic, taxcollectorphobic, centurionphobic, and he is certainly not homophobic. Jesus does not have a prejudice against any human being. But if he did, it would be against judgmental, homophobic religious people.

We need to destroy homophobia. If someone tells a gay joke, kill it. Blurt out that line that will make everyone feel awkward, "That's actually not very funny. Do you worship Jesus with that mouth?" If people want to talk about some issue about "those people over there"—stop it. Don't let them. Stand up and be bold. Destroy homophobia. Don't squirm in your silent agreement. Take a stand for truth. Take a stand for people. Kill homophobia.

Some people will think you are "pro-gay" if you stand up for gay people, and that's fine. If people mistake your unconditional love for gay people as an affirmation of homosexual behavior, then don't worry about it. You're in good company. Religious people often thought that Jesus was a sinner because he had many friends who were sinners, yet he kept on befriending sinners. Don't let religious pressure from your friends or family force you to cowardly embrace the pharisaic ethic of homophobia. Don't buy the lie that if you love people too much, you must not care about sin. The gospel teaches us otherwise. Jesus cared so much about sin that he surrounded himself with sinners. Let us go and do likewise.

4. EDUCATE OTHERS ABOUT THE COMPLEXITIES OF HOMOSEXUALITY

One of the best ways to kill homophobia is to educate people about the complexities and humanness of homosexuality. Whether it is in personal conversations, Bible studies, sermons, or any other venue where the subject of homosexuality is discussed, Christians need to resist quick and easy answers that perpetuate a simplistic view of a very complex issue.

Whenever I give a talk on homosexuality to evangelical Christians, I immediately sense that many people become uneasy, even angry, if I don't begin by telling everyone where I "stand on the issue." But I resist the pressure. I go into detail about what it is we're even talking about. I try to humanize homosexuality so that we don't just banter around about concepts, verses, and political debates about gay marriage. I make sure that we all understand the intricacies of homosexuality and the diversity of people's experiences.

A posture based on truth delights in thinking deeply and critically about homosexuality. Such a posture believes that topics—or people—should be understood before they are evaluated. But a posture based on fear only wants assumptions to be reaffirmed. A fear posture doesn't want to think or be challenged, but only wants to be reinforced and validated. This fear posture has hindered our gospel witness on homosexuality and has led to a very thin understanding of what it is we are even talking about. A truth posture, however, seeks to listen, to understand, to learn the other side, and to be corrected by God's Word.

Nonaffirming Christians need to be eager to think and rethink what they assume they know about homosexuality. We need to come humbly before God's authoritative Word and invite the Spirit to show us where we need to be more like Jesus—because with homosexuality, we haven't been.

5. PROMOTE BIBLICAL (NOT CULTURAL) MASCULINITY AND FEMININITY

I met a guy a couple years ago who used to be a worship leader at a large church in California. We'll call him Tom. At the height of a thriving ministry, he came out as gay and ended up leaving the church, finding a partner, and hasn't been to church since. I recently had breakfast with Tom to hear his story and to see if there was anything the church could have done differently. He said something fascinating that I will never forget: "I never questioned my masculinity until I joined the church."

Tom was not very athletic, he loved music and art, and he didn't carry himself like most manly men in church. He didn't hunt, fish, watch football, and he didn't drive a muddy 4x4 truck. But Tom said that he never felt like less of a man until he became a member of a Christian church. "The church seemed to promote a particular view of masculinity that I didn't fit into. I came to believe that I must not be a real man. Perhaps I am gay."

I don't want to rehash the whole nature-versus-nurture debate; I am not saying that the church made Tom gay by promoting a cultural view of masculinity. I am only saying that the church sometimes makes it tough for people to fit in, only because they don't live up to an artificial standard of masculinity and femininity. Even if the church's view of masculinity had no influence on Tom's same-sex attraction, perhaps he could have worked through his same-sex attraction without feeling like he was too effeminate to be a Christian.

The church needs to promote biblical masculinity and femininity, and not American (or wherever you live) masculinity and femininity. When we try to cram people into synthetic gender roles that aren't mandated by the Bible, we inevitably force them to question their gender or feel like they don't belong in the church. Biblical men are those who resist retaliation, choose mercy over vengeance, and love their neighbors and their enemies. Whether you are an outdoorsman or an indoorsman, artsy or athletic, skinny or buff, a violinist or a quarterback, you are a real man if you love Jesus and are a humble servant to all. Biblical women display wisdom in their decisions, radiate modesty in this oversexualized culture, and manifest strength against the challenges life throws their way. Most of all, a biblical woman is not incomplete without a husband, but fully radiates the powerful image of God in her singleness, widowhood, or infertility. Whether you are a homeschool mom or the CEO of a construction company, if you love Jesus then you can live out your femininity to its fullest potential.

We need to realize how artificial standards of gender can make people feel like they don't belong.

6. WE ARE LIVING IN BABYLON

Many Christians in America view homosexuality through a political lens. They only think about gay people in terms of the gay lobby and the legalization of gay marriage. For years, such Christians placed a lot of time and energy in preventing the legalization of gay marriage, and they lived in fear that they might lose the culture war.

And in June 2015, they lost the culture war.

I'm referring, of course, to the Supreme Court decision to legalize gay marriage in all fifty states. Much of the Christian buzz that dominated the internet was driven by fear and anger—unbecoming traits for worshipers of a risen King. As I sat back and reflected on the ruling, three thoughts came to mind.

First, have no fear. Christianity was born in the midst of a secular Roman culture twenty times more immoral than America. And it thrived. Why? Because our Creator God is King and he has determined to establish an unstoppable, unshakable, global kingdom. Nations will act like nations, and empires will come and go. But God's countercultural, upside down kingdom will never end.

Second, stop fighting the culture war. If I can be completely honest, part of me was actually glad when I heard about the Supreme Court ruling on same-sex marriages. I obviously don't agree with the morality of their decision. But I'm sort of thankful that they made it because now the church can stop fighting the culture war and start asking more important pastoral questions about how we—the body of Jesus—can best love and minister to LGBT people. Now that the "war" is over, we can put down our guns and care for the wounded. And there have been many, many LGBT people who have been wounded, fatally in some cases, by the culture war that the church has been fighting.

Third, live as exiles in Babylon. This is our posture; this is our identity. We are living as strangers in a strange land, as exiles in the midst of a secular nation. We should not be surprised when a secular nation makes decisions that reflect secular thinking. We should not think the sky is falling when non-Christians embrace a non-Christian ethic. It's Babylon, and we are not Babylonians.

It's time for the church to stop treating LGBT people as some issue to debate and some lobby to vote against. It's time for the church to start treating them—who are us—as people to be loved.

7. REMEMBER—GOD IS HOLY

The church needs to realize that homosexuality is about people. We need to persistently humanize the topic and look into the faces of real people with real stories. But loving our neighbors can't be done without first loving God, so let us never forget that our God is holy.

We serve a Creator who is holy and just, transcendent and near, who touched Mount Sinai and set it ablaze, who spoke to Isaiah and crumpled him to his knees, who commissioned Satan to rip apart Job's life without telling him why. "This is the one to whom I will look," says our Lord: "He who is humble and contrite in spirit and trembles at my word" (Isa. 66:2). The psalmist declares: "Our God is in the heavens, and he does whatever he pleases" (Ps. 115:3). Our God is the sovereign king of the universe, and he creates, cultivates, and judges our morality.

And we serve a Savior who suffered —born in a feeding trough and nailed to a tree—and calls us to a life of joy and suffering. A life stitched together with the fabric of pain and pleasure, faith and fear, happiness and the horror of picking up our crosses and being nailed to them. "Whoever would save his life will lose it, but who-ever loses his life for my sake will save it" (Luke 9:24). God never promised to answer all our questions or make us happy on earth. Sometimes faithfulness leads to happiness; sometimes faithfulness leads to death. What God promised through it all is that when our earthly life whispers out of existence, we will all be raised anew with unbound joy in the new creation. And only then will God's Word match our experience, and all our suffering, pain, confusion, and doubt will fade into eternal bliss.

Until we acknowledge and delight in the holy otherness of God, we will always have a distorted view of homosexuality. And if the God of Isaiah and Job actually does prohibit homosexual relations, then it is neither wise nor safe to edit out those commands because they seem archaic, unloving, or at odds with our experience.

FIVE AFFIRMING INTERPRETATIONS OF ROMANS 1

There have been many different interpretations of Romans 1. In chapter 6, I addressed the most convincing one—the excessive lust view. However, there are several other interpretations that aren't as strong to my mind, but I want to briefly summarize and address the five most popular ones here.

1. HETEROSEXUALS HAVING HOMOSEXUAL SEX?

Some people have argued that Paul is only talking about heterosexuals having homosexual sex, and not gay people having homosexual sex. The implication, of course, is that Paul is not even talking about people who are born with a homosexual orientation. He is only talking about those born with a heterosexual orientation, who are acting contrary to their nature; that is, contrary to their orientation.[1]

I can see where they get this. Paul does say they "exchanged natural sexual relations for unnatural ones" (Rom. 1:26). But this interpretation has been largely abandoned, even by more recent affirming scholars. After all, ancient writers (including Paul) didn't think in terms of gay and straight people, but masculinity and femininity (see chapter 4). And even though some writers believed that same-sex desires were inborn, Paul doesn't seem to be talking about that here in Romans 1. The biggest problem with this view is that it interprets *para physin* to mean "against one's personal (sexual) nature," which isn't how the phrase is used by other writers, and it almost certainly does not mean that here in Romans 1. Plus, Paul's argument in Romans 1 is more of a corporate indictment of pagan society, not an evaluation of individual human beings based on their sexual orientation.[2]

For these historical and exegetical reasons, I seriously doubt that Paul was critiquing straight people having gay sex.

2. SAME-SEX RELATIONS WERE NOT SINFUL, ONLY IMPURE

Other scholars argue that Paul did not think that homoerotic behavior was inherently sinful.[3] Rather, Paul only assumed that it violated Jewish purity laws. After all, Paul uses the word "impurity" (*akatharsia*) in Romans 1:27 to describe same-sex eroticism. Therefore, homosexual sex may be impure by Jewish standards, but this doesn't mean it is sin by God's standards.

However, Paul uses the word "impurity" (*akatharsia*) elsewhere as a synonym for sinful behavior, not just behavior that violates certain Jewish purity laws.[4] As Bernadette Brooten points out: Paul uses the word impurity "twice in vice lists in conjunction with 'sexual immorality/fornication' and 'licentiousness' (Gal. 5:19; 2 Cor. 12:21)."[5] It's unlikely that Paul intends to distinguish between "impurity" and "sin" in Romans 1. Furthermore, Paul's use of *para physin* doesn't make sense of this view. Even other non-Christian Jews, such as Philo and Josephus, used this phrase to describe the immorality of same-sex practices and not just a violation of their Jewish purity laws. And the fact that Paul clearly talks about sins in Romans 1:18–25, and again in 1:29–32, makes it highly improbable that he took a quick break to talk about things he doesn't consider sin in 1:26–27—especially when every other Jew in Paul's time, and not a few Greco-Roman philosophers, considered same-sex relations to be immoral.

3. PAUL IS TALKING ABOUT PEDERASTY (SEX WITH BOYS) AND NOT ALL FORMS OF SAME-SEX RELATIONS

Robin Scroggs in his influential and well-reasoned book *Homosexuality in the New Testament* argues that Paul only knew of one form of homosexual practice: pederasty, or "the love of boys" (*paiderastia*).[6] Since this was the only (or the most dominate) form of homoerotic behavior known to Paul, this must be what he critiques in Romans 1.

If Scroggs is correct, then Romans 1 is irrelevant for our modern question of monogamous, consensual, same-sex marriages, since these didn't exist in Paul's world. Scroggs' thesis is well researched and carefully argued, but I don't think Romans 1 can be limited to a critique of pederasty.

Pederasty was not the only form of homoeroticism available to Paul, as we have seen. And again, if Paul had pederasty in view, why didn't he use one of the Greek words widely used to describe it, such as *paiderastes, paidophthoros,* or *paidophtoreo*? Moreover, there is nothing in his actual language in Romans 1 that offers a more narrow view of same-sex practice. Rather, he talks about women having sex with women, and men having sex with men. If he had a more specific form of homoerotic behavior in view, he certainly does not specify. Plus, if Paul was thinking of pederasty, I don't think Paul would blame *both* partners as he does in Romans 1:27 ("received in themselves the due penalty for their error"). Would Paul place equal blame on a boy who was mounted by a man?

The pederasty interpretation is not only an unlikely interpretation, but an impossible interpretation of Romans 1:26 where female homoeroticism is mentioned. Pederasty may have been common among men, but it didn't exist among women. Given the parallel between 1:26 and 1:27 (notice the term "likewise" at the beginning of 1:27), it wouldn't make sense to have two very different types of homosexual relations in view. That is, unless Paul made this clear. But he doesn't.

The pederasty interpretation raises more questions than it answers and is therefore not a convincing interpretation of Romans 1.

4. PAUL AGREES WITH HIS AUDIENCE IN ROMANS 1 SO THAT HE CAN REBUKE THEM IN ROMANS 2

Another view that has gained some traction is that Paul doesn't actually endorse what he says in Romans 1:18–32. Rather, he mimics a Jewish critique of Gentile pagans in 1:18–32 so that he can turn around and rebuke his Jewish audience in Romans 2. The "real Paul," then, comes out in Romans 2:1 when he turns his finger to the Jew who has been nodding his head in agreement: "You, therefore, have no excuse, you who pass judgment on someone else, for at whatever point you judge another, you are condemning yourself, because you who pass judgment do the same things."

Rhetorically, this view is accurate. Paul does stack the deck in Romans 1 so that he can blast his moral opponent in Romans 2. This is a solid reading of Paul's argument. But it's a false dichotomy. Paul's rhetorical twist does not mean that he is saying things he does not actually believe in Romans 1. Of course Paul believes that idolatry is wrong (1:21–23), that God should be honored (1:23), that God handed sinners over to their sin (1:24, 26, 28), that evil, covetousness, malice, envy, murder, strife, and deceit (1:29–30) are all still contrary to God's will. If so—and it can only be so—there is little reason to believe that Paul does not actually agree with what he said in Romans 1:26–27.

5. PAUL CONDEMNS ALL FORMS OF SAME-SEX RELATIONS

You may wonder how this could be an affirming interpretation. Let me complete the argument: Paul condemned all forms of same-sex relations, and that's why we need to move beyond Paul. There are several scholars and writers who take this view, although they each give different reasons for doing so.

Bernadette Brooten, for instance, spends three hundred pages giving some of the best historical and exegetical evidence for Paul's understanding of homosexual relations (focused on female same-sex relations), but then concludes: "I hope that churches today, being apprised of the history that I have presented, will no longer teach Romans 1:26f as authoritative."[7] Her main point is that Paul must have held a derogatory view of women; he didn't think that men should act like mere women by receiving sex from another man. But as we saw in chapter 7, I don't think there is solid evidence from Paul's letters that he had a low view of women.

Others take a similar approach, though they add their own twist.[8] All in all, the argument is the same: Paul condemned same-sex relations, but we moderns have more insight into same-sex relations than Paul did. So we should reevaluate Paul's words in light of modern knowledge.

This approach assumes a view of Scripture that I don't endorse. It would take a much longer discussion about biblical inspiration and the authority of Scripture, a discussion that we really don't have space for. And for what it's worth, I am writing this book for those who believe that the Bible *is* authoritative and should not be jettisoned in light of modern knowledge. In any case, I would only want to raise two questions.

First, if we should not follow Paul in what he says in Romans 1, then what other passages can we toss to the wind in light of modern knowledge? I do believe that modern knowledge can help with interpretation. But the view of Brooten and others doesn't say we

192 PEOPLE TO BE LOVED

should reinterpret Paul; they simply say that we should not believe what Paul says.

Second, how much do we actually know about same-sex orientation anyway? If you think that science has given us a clear, closed case, the-world-is-round-not-flat type of answer, then think again. Same-sex orientation is way too complicated and we have certainly not arrived at a bulletproof understanding of it. I get a little suspicious when modern scholars assume some sort of well-oiled conclusion about sexual orientation and homosexuality. According to everything I have read, we still have a ways to go. The discussion is complicated, as we have seen. So to stand on shaky ground (our understanding of sexual orientation) and critique Paul in light of it seems to be a bit ambitious—if not arrogant.

Call me old-fashioned but I do believe that Paul's words in Romans 1 *are* authoritative for Christians.

NOTES

CHAPTER 1: "MY NAME WAS FAGGOT"

1. Eric James Borges, "It Gets Better," YouTube: https://www.youtube.com/watch?v=InWhEIaCFkg (accessed November, 1, 2014).
2. You can read about many other similar stories in John Shore, *UNFAIR: Christians and the LGBT Question* (CreateSpace Independent Publishing, 2013). Or just talk to your LGBT friends who grew up in the church and ask them about their experience.
3. Gen. 19:1–10; Lev. 18:22; 20:13; Romans 1:26–27; 1 Corinthians 6:9; 1 Timothy 1:9–10. As we'll see, I don't think Genesis 19 is relevant for the discussion, so actually, there are only five.
4. Just to name a few, see Robin Scroggs, *The New Testament and Homosexuality: Contextual Background for Contemporary Debate* (Philadelphia: Fortress, 1983); William Countryman, *Dirt, Greed and Sex: Sexual Ethics in the New Testament and Their Implications for Today*, rev. ed. (Minneapolis: Fortress, 2007); Daniel Helminiak, *What the Bible Really Says about Homosexuality* (Estancia, NM: Alamo Square Press, 2000); Dale Martin, *Sex and the Single Savior: Gender and Sexuality in Biblical Interpretation* (Louisville: Westminster John Knox, 2006); James Brownson, *Bible, Gender, Sexuality: Reframing the Church's Debate on Same-Sex Relationships* (Grand Rapids: Eerdmans, 2013); Martti Nissinen, *Homoeroticism in the Biblical World: A Historical Perspective*, trans. Kirsi Stjerna (Minneapolis: Fortress, 1998).
5. See my book *Fight: A Christian Case for Nonviolence* (Colorado Springs: David C. Cook, 2013).
6. To be clear, I don't believe the Bible is our only authority, but our ultimate authority. I also believe human reason, experience, culture, and social situation influence one's interpretation of the Bible. The Bible is absolute truth, but human interpretation of that truth is fallible. Some people throw up their arms at this point and say that accessing absolute truth is therefore impossible. However, I believe

that a human interpretation, which is performed in community, in dialogue with tradition, and under the guidance of God's Spirit, can discover and understand absolute truth. For those who care about such categories, I am a critical realist (see, for example, N. T. Wright, *The New Testament and the People of God* [Minneapolis: Fortress: 1992], 50–64; compare this with Kevin J. Vanhoozer, *Is There Meaning in This Text? The Bible, the Reader, and the Morality of Literary Knowledge* [Grand Rapids: Zondervan, 2009]).

7. I love Roger Olson's articulation of this posture in his outstanding book *Reformed and Always Reforming: A Post-Conservative Approach to Evangelical Theology* (Grand Rapids: Baker, 2007).

8. Andrew Martin, *Love Is an Orientation: Elevating the Conversation with the Gay Community* (Downers Grove, IL: InterVarsity, 2009), 41.

9. Tim Otto, *Oriented to Faith: Transforming the Conflict over Gay Relationships* (Eugene: Cascade Books, 2014), 5.

10. Ibid., 6 emphasis mine.

11. Sadly, this is not in the book. Dumbledore says this to Harry at King's Cross station in *Harry Potter and the Deathly Hallows: Part 2*, film (2011).

12. However, my main focus is on LGB. The T portion (transgender) opens up a whole other set of questions and discussions, which we won't get into in this book. For a recent look at how to think Christianly about the transgender question, see Mark Yarhouse, *Understanding Gender Dysphoria: Navigating Transgender Issues in a Changing Culture* (Downers Grove, IL: IVP Academic, 2015).

CHAPTER 2: HOLY OTHERNESS

1. I am well aware of the massive debate about the relationship between sex and gender, and I am not going to get into it in this book. I will be using the term *sex* to emphasize the biological sex of a person assigned at birth and *gender* to describe someone's self-expression as a man or a woman, which is often, though not always, related in some way to one's biological sex.

2. Robert Gagnon uses this phrase throughout his book, *The Bible and Homosexual Practice: Texts and Hermeneutics* (Nashville: Abingdon, 2001).

3. I am following affirming scholar James Brownson, *Bible, Gender, Sexuality: Reframing the Church's Debate on Same-Sex Relationships* (Grand Rapids: Eerdmans, 2013), 85–109. But see also Gordon Wenham, a nonaffirming scholar, who says that the phrase *one flesh*

"does not denote merely the sexual union that follows marriage, or the children conceived in marriage, or even the spiritual and emotional relationship that it involves, though all are involved in becoming one flesh. Rather it affirms that just as blood relations are one's flesh and bone . . . so marriage creates a similar kinship relation between man and wife. They become related to each other as brother and sister are" (*Genesis 1–11* [Grand Rapids, MI: Zondervan, 1987], 71).

4. Psalm 121:1–2; Isa 30:5; Ezekiel 12:14; Hosea 13:9. God is called a "helper" in Exodus 18:4; Deuteronomy 33:7, 26, 29; cf. 1 Samuel 7:12; Ps. 33:20.

5. See Brownson, *Bible*, 29–30.

6. See, e.g., Exodus 19:2; Joshua 3:16; 6:5, 20; Isaiah 40:17.

7. Wenham, *Genesis 1–11*, 68. However, see John Walton's warning about being overly confident in translating *kenegdo* (*The NIV Application Commentary: Genesis* [Grand Rapids: Zondervan, 2001], 176).

8. James Brownson's book, which is probably the most thorough defense of the affirming view, never mentions *kenegdo* in Gen. 2.18, 20. It certainly works against his argument, but that's no reason to ignore the word altogether. Brownson does address the "otherness" argument made by nonaffirming writers, however. This argument says that human difference is necessary in marriage, and this difference is seen in sexual difference. Brownson argues that gay and lesbian relationships also exhibit difference and otherness, just not sexual difference (see his *Bible*, 264–65).

9. E.g., Mark 10:1–9; 1 Corinthians 6:16; Ephesians 5:22–33.

10. I agree with James Brownson, who argues against Robert Gagnon, that "the fact that male and female are both created in the divine image (Gen. 1:27) is intended to convey the value, dominion, and relationality shared by both men and women, but not the idea that the complementarity of the genders is somehow necessary to fully express or embody the divine image" (*Bible*, 31). Brownson is right: men don't need women, and women don't need men, to *fully express or embody the divine image.* I'm not sure if Brownson has correctly understood Gagnon. In any case, I agree with Brownson. Genesis 1–2 does not assume that "male and female must be present together in order to fully constitute the image of God" (*Bible*, 32).

11. We should note that even though Genesis showcases "minimalistic binaries," as my friend Roy Ciampa says, this doesn't rule out other combinations that don't fit these basic norms. For instance, God created land and sea—two binaries—but we know that he also

created lakes, rivers, ponds, and marshes. Likewise, the creation of male and female as binaries doesn't in itself rule out intersex and transgender people. But that's for another book.

12. I've received this sort of pushback when I blogged about Mark 10. See Preston Sprinkle, "David Gushee's Recent Shift on Homosexuality," *Theology in the Raw:* http://www.patheos.com/blogs/theology intheraw/2014/10/david-gushees-recent-shift-on-homosexuality/.

13. Sam Alberry makes the same point (*Is God Anti-Gay? Questions Christians Ask* [Surrey, U.K. The Good Book Company, 2013], 22–23).

14. See Matthew Mason, "Man and Woman He Created Them: Same-Sex Desires, Gender Trouble, and Gay Marriage in the Light of John Paul II's Theology of the Body," *Bulletin of Ecclesial Theology* 1.1 (2014): 35–52.

15. See e.g. Matthew Vines, *God and the Gay Christian: The Biblical Case in Support of Same-Sex Relationships* (New York: Convergent, 2014), 144–46.

16. The verb *submit* doesn't even occur in 5:22. The implied verb is carried over from 5:21, where mutual submission among the body is emphasized.

17. See, e.g., Aristotle, *Politics,* 1260a 9–14; Josephus, *Ag. Apion,* 2.199; Timothy Gombis, "A Radically Different New Humanity: The Function of the *Haustafel* in Ephesians," *JETS* 48 (2005): 317–30.

18. See for instance M. Sydney Park, *Submission within the Godhead and the Church in the Epistle to the Philippians: An Exegetical and Theological Examination of the Concept of Submission in Philippians 2 and 3* (LNTS 361; London: T & T Clark, 2007).

19. Throughout church history, sexual difference was not just assumed, but believed to be a necessary feature of marriage; see Christopher Roberts, *Creation and Covenant: The Significance of Sexual Difference in the Moral Theology of Marriage* (London: T & T Clark, 2007).

CHAPTER 3: FROM SEX IN THE CITY TO LAW & ORDER

1. As we'll see, the *act* of male same-sex intercourse is called an abomination (Lev. 18:22; 20:13), but the people committing the act are not.

2. John Boswell, *Christianity, Social Tolerance, and Homosexuality: Gay People in Western Europe from the Beginning of the Christian Era to the Fourteenth Century* (Chicago: University of Chicago Press, 1980), 93–94.

3. The best defense of the nonsexual view is by Scott Morschauser, "'Hospitality,' Hostiles and Hostages: On the Legal Background to Genesis 19.1–9," *JSOT* 27 (2003), 461–85. Morschauser makes a convincing case; however, I still think that the use of *know* in 19:8 informs its use in 19:5, lending support for the sexual interpretation. Moreover, the parallel story in Judges 19:22–26 is clearly sexual, thus strengthening a sexual interpretation of Genesis 19. In any case, if Morschauser is correct, then Genesis 19 is even more irrelevant for the question of homosexuality. (Thanks to Scott Hafemann for alerting me to this article.)

4. Actually, to be more precise, according to Genesis 18:20–21 (cf. 13:13) Sodom was condemned *before* the attempted gang rape in Genesis 19.

5. Isaiah 1:10–17; 3:9; Jeremiah 23:14; Matt. 10:5–10. Some ancient Jews interpreted Genesis 19 along the same lines without mentioning homosexual acts (for example, Wisdom of Solomon 19:13; Book of Jubilees 16:5–6; 20:5–6; Testament of Levi 14:6), while others believed that homosexual sex was part of the reason for destruction (Philo, *On Abraham* 133–41; *Questions and Answers on Genesis* 4.37; Josephus, *Antiquities of the Jews*. 1.194–95, 200–201). Some think that Jude 7, which mentions the men of Sodom going after "strange flesh" (*sarkos heteras*), supports the traditional interpretation. But in the context, "strange flesh" refers not to people of the same sex, but to angels—the ones whom the Sodomites were seeking to rape (see Richard Bauckham, *Jude, 2 Peter* [Grand Rapids: Zondervan, 1983], 54). The phrase *strange flesh* actually means "*other* flesh" and ironically contains the Greek word *heteras* from which we get *hetero*sexual. If *homo*sexual relations were what Jude meant, it would have made much more sense for him to say "same flesh" not "other flesh."

6. I disagree with Robert Gagnon, who argues that the use of the word *abomination* in Ezekiel 16:50 in reference to the sin of Sodom (16:49) refers to homosexual intercourse (*The Bible and Homosexual Practice: Texts and Hermeneutics* [Nashville: Abingdon, 2001], 80–84). Gagnon argues rightly that the use of *abomination* in the singular (rather than *abominations*) only occurs twice in Leviticus, 18:22 and 20:13: the only two passages where male same-sex intercourse is mentioned. The word, however, does not occur in Genesis 19. For Gagnon's argument to work, he needs Ezekiel to refract the word *abomination* through the lens of Leviticus 18:22 and 20:13 and back onto Genesis 19:1–9. This is certainly possible, but with no other references to homosexual behavior in Ezekiel,

with no occurrence of *abomination* in Genesis 19, and with no other passage in the Bible that makes such connection even when they are referencing Sodom, it seems like an interpretive stretch. The word *abomination* occurs many other times outside of Leviticus and in other passages in Ezekiel, but it never clearly refers to same-sex intercourse. Plus, the Sodomites never had sex in Genesis 19.

7. Everything I've said about Sodom also applies to the parallel incident in Judges 19:22–26. The crime committed in Gibeah was gang rape.

8. There are, as always, many other interpretations that have been offered. Saul Olyan says that Leviticus 18 and 20 only forbid male-male anal sex and only condemns the penetrator ("'And with a Male You Shall Not Lie the Lying Down of a Woman': On the Meaning and Significance of Leviticus 18.22 and 20.13," *Journal of the History of Sexuality*, 5.2 [1994]: 179–206). Certainly, the phrase "lie with" has anal penetration in mind, but I don't think this means that other forms of erotic activity are permissible. For instance, Leviticus 18:20 also says, "You shall not lie sexually with your neighbor's wife," which also has penetration in mind. But this does not mean that fondling your neighbor's breasts would be okay. Leviticus 18:23 says, "You shall not lie with any animal," but this does not therefore allow someone to get to second base with a sheep. Quite opposite from Olyan is Jerome T. Walsh who says it's not the penetrator who is guilty but the *penetrated* ("Lev. 18.22 and 20.13: Who Is Doing What to Whom?," *JBL* 120 [2001]: 201–9). This again seems very unlikely given the fact that Leviticus 20:13 condemns both partners in the act.

9. As Gagnon says, they are "unqualified and absolute" (*Homosexual Practice*, 115).

10. For instance, Deuteronomy 22:23–29 talks about the punishment for two people sleeping together. If it's mutual, then both are punished. But if "the man seizes her and lies with her, then only the man who lay with her shall die" (22:25).

11. The fifth-century Greek historian Herodotus refers to some sort of female cult prostitution in Babylon, and other ancient historians make similar, albeit vague, references (e.g., Strabo, Lucian). However, it's likely that Herodotus' statement is inaccurate and that other ancient authors simply draw from Herodotus. For an overview of ancient references, see Robert A. Oden, *The Bible without Theology* (Chicago: University of Illinois Press, 1987), 140–44.

12. (Cambridge: Cambridge University Press, 2010). Thanks to my brother-in-law Dr. Benjamin Foreman, an Old Testament scholar, for alerting me to the recent scholarship on temple cult prostitution.

13. See also Gen. 38:15, 21–22; Deuteronomy 23:18–19; 1 Kings 15:12; 22:47; 2 Kings 23:7; Job 36:14; cf. Jeremiah 5:7–8. In all of these references, however, there is no clear indication that the Hebrew term *qadeshim* should be translated as "male cult prostitutes." Similar words are used in cognate languages outside the Bible (e.g., Ugaritic, Akkadian) to refer to someone who serves at the temple; these words never suggest that sex or prostitution was involved in this temple service (see Mayer Gruber, "The *qadesh* and her Canaanite and Akkadian Cognates," *UF* 18 [1986]: 133–48. The only passage that *may* suggest otherwise is Genesis 38:15, 21–22. Here, Tamar is referred to as both a prostitute (v. 15) and a *qadeshah* (vv. 21–22). However, the context suggests that the two terms should *not* be equated (see Joan Goodnick Westenholz, "Tamar, *Qedesha*, *Qadishtu*, and Sacred Prostitution in Mesopotamia," *HTR* 82 [1989]: 245–65). Some people see the use of *qadesh* and *qadeshah* in Deuteronomy 23:18 as a clear reference to cult prostitution; however, this reading depends on v. 19 carrying on the same idea as v. 18, which mentions prostitution. If the verses are read separately, then there's no reason to connect *qadesh/qadeshah* with prostitution. In any case, when the Bible outlaws the qadeshim in Deuteronomy 23:18, it does so explicitly: "None of the sons of Israel shall be a *qadesh*." But Leviticus 18 and 20 don't mention the word qadesh.

14. *Torn: Rescuing the Gospel from the Gays-vs.-Christians Debate* (New York: Jericho Books, 2012), 174–78.

15. Ibid., 182.

16. Gagnon, *Homosexual Practice*, 100–10.

17. Martti Nissinen, *Homoeroticism in the Biblical World* (Minneapolis: Fortress Press, 2004), 42–44; Matthew Vines, *God and the Gay Christian: The Biblical Case in Support of Same-Sex Relationships* (Colorado Springs: Convergent: 2014), 79–96.

18. James Brownson uses the phrase "moral logic" throughout his book, *Bible, Gender, Sexuality.*

19. The Hebrew term for male is *zakar*, which highlights gender (it's not as broad as *adam*, which could mean "mankind"). The term for woman is *isshah* ("woman"), which isn't as gender specific as *neqevah*, which means "female" (see Gen. 1:27).

20. This, of course, is highly debated. For a good defense of my claim, see Paul Copan, *Is God a Moral Monster?* (Grand Rapids: Baker, 2011).

21. Proponents of the view that Leviticus 18 and 20 advocate a "low view of women," often point out that these texts never forbid lesbian sex. And this is true. The Old Testament never mentions or prohibits women from having sex with women. In fact, it's only mentioned once in the entire Bible: Romans 1:26. Those who say that Leviticus assumes a low view of women argue that same-sex female relations don't affect male honor, since no man is feminized in the act. And this is why women are never forbidden from having sex with each other. I'll admit that it does seem surprising that female same-sex eroticism is never mentioned in the Old Testament. As an honest interpreter, I want to be careful making an argument from silence and conclude that the Old Testament condemns female same-sex acts even though it never mentions them. If I were a lesbian (I think that's the first time I've ever said that ...), I'd certainly find such an argument rather biased and unconvincing. If the Bible doesn't say it, then who am I to make it say it? However, female same-sex eroticism is rarely (perhaps never) mentioned outside the Old Testament during this time either. The first clear reference we have of lesbian relations comes in the writings of the seventh/sixth-century BC poet Sappho. Even in cultures where some forms of male-male sex was discussed, female-female sex (or relations in general) was never mentioned. In other words, the Old Testament is not alone in its silence about female homoeroticism. Therefore, there are good grounds to conclude that romantic love between women either didn't exist in the Old Testament world, or if it did (more likely) it was kept secret. Either way, it would be unnecessary for Moses to prohibit something that wasn't being practiced or was simply unknown.

22. John Shore, "The Best Case for the Bible Not Condemning Homosexuality," *Huffington Post Religion:* http://www.huffington post.com/john-shore/the-best-case-for-the-bible-not-condemning-homosexuality_b_1396345.html (Accessed December 9, 2013).

23. Mark 7:19; Acts 15:22–35.

24. For example, Romans 14:5–6; Colossians 2:16.

CHAPTER 4: RATED R

1. See the *Middle Assyrian Laws* 18–20 and the discussion in Martti Nissinen, *Homoeroticism in the Biblical World: A Historical Perspective* (trans. Kirsi Stjerna; Minneapolis: Fortress, 1998), 24–28.

2. For homosexuality in the ancient Near East, see Donald J. Wold, *Out of Order: Homosexuality in the Bible and the Ancient Near East* (Grand Rapids: Baker, 1998); Nissinen, *Homoeroticism*, 19–36.

3. The famous *Epic of Gilgamesh* seems to display some consensual homoerotic elements, although it's disputed whether the relationship was perceived to be sexual or just deeply intimate (see Nissinen, *Homoeroticism*, 20–24). Also, there are a few stories from ancient Egypt about sexual relationships among men of equal standing, although these seem to be the exceptions to the norm (see Robert Gagnon, *The Bible and Homosexual Practice: Texts and Hermeneutics* [Nashville: Abingdon, 2001], 52).

4. The classic study on Greek homosexuality is by Kenneth J. Dover, *Greek Homosexuality* (Cambridge, Mass.: Harvard University Press, 1978). The best book on Roman homosexuality is by Craig Williams, *Roman Homosexuality* (2nd ed.; Oxford: Oxford University Press, 2010). Other helpful treatments of homosexuality in the Greco-Roman and Jewish world can be found in Nissinen, *Homoeroticism*, 57–102; Robin Scroggs, *The New Testament and Homosexuality: Contextual Background for Contemporary Debate* (Philadelphia: Fortress, 1983); Thomas K. Hubbard (ed.), *Homosexuality in Greece and Rome: A Sourcebook of Basic Documents* (Berkley: University of California Press, 2003), esp. 1–20. On female homoeroticism in the ancient world, see Bernadette Brooten, *Love Between Women: Early Christian Response to Female Homoeroticism* (Chicago: University of Chicago Press, 1996). Matthew Vines has a very good popular level summary of Greco-Roman material in his *God and the Gay Christian: The Biblical Case in Support of Same-Sex Relationships* (New York: Convergent, 2014), 33–44, 106–14.

5. *Bible, Gender, Sexuality*, 166, 170.

6. Vines, *God and the Gay Christian*, 106; cf. 23–44.

7. "Relations Natural and Unnatural: A Response to J. Boswell's Exegesis of Rom. 1," *Journal of Religious Ethics* 14 (1986):184–215 (200).

8. *Eth.*, 1148b.

9. Discussed in Nissinen, *Homoeroticism*, 81.

10. He says that semen is excreted into the anus, creating a need for friction (Pseudo-Aristotelian, *Problemata*, 4.26; cf. 879a36–880a5; 879b28–30).

11. I'm not, of course, saying that the desire to be penetrated is the same as same-sex orientation.

12. Soranus, *On Chronic Disorders*, 4.9.134. See the translation and notes in Hubbard, *Homosexuality*, 464.

13. *De morbis chronicis*, 4.131, 132, 134.

14. Maternus, *Matheseos libri viii*, 7.25.1. This work ("Eight Books of the *Mathesis*") dates to AD 334; see Bernadette J. Brooten, *Love Between Women: Early Christian Responses to Female Homoeroticism* (Chicago: University of Chicago Press, 1996), 132–37.

15. *Carmen Astrologicum*, (2.7.6) See Brooten, *Love Between Women*, 119–20. The text has been preserved in Arabic. The word *Lesbian* translates the Arabic *sahaqa*.

16. Ibid., 140.

17. See, among others, Amy Richlin, "Not before Homosexuality: The Materiality of the *Cinaedus* and the Roman Law against Love between Men," *Journal of the History of Sexuality* 3 (1993): 523–73; Rabun Taylor, "Two Pathic Subcultures in Ancient Rome, *Journal of the History of Sexuality* 7 (1997): 319–71. David Halperin has looked at many of these same texts and argued that it would be wrong to find in them some ancient form of sexual identity (see his *One Hundred Years of Homosexuality* [New York: Rutledge, 1990], 3–40). And Halperin is right: we can't use these texts to show that homosexuality as a sexual identity existed as such back then. The Greco-Roman world did not have the same category of what we call "homosexuality" or "gay/lesbian" as a sexual identity. Ancient writers thought in terms of *gender* identity and not *sexual* identity, and gender identity didn't depend on whom you liked to have sex with. However, this doesn't change the narrow point I'm making. I'm not saying that we should read into the ancient material some modern idea of "homosexuality" as a sexual identity. However, what I am saying is that ancient writers did speculate about inborn same-sex sexual desires. People who had these desires weren't called "gay"; such an identity didn't exist back then. But I don't think this really matters. What matters is that they believed in an ancient form of an inborn, and sometimes fixed, desire to have sex with people of the same gender.

18. For instance, many of my references above are not talking about a life-long, fixed, and exclusive same-sex orientation. Some of the references may explain why some men were bisexual—sexually attracted to women *as well as* men.

19. Brownson, *Bible, Sexuality, Gender*, 166, 170.

20. I'm embarrassed to say that I used to cite Nero as an example of consensual same-sex relations simply because it was a public marriage. This was a terribly inaccurate example, and I thank Roy Ciampa for pointing this out.

21. For a recent survey and analysis of texts, see Thomas K. Hubbard, "Peer Homosexuality," in *A Companion to Greek and Roman Sexualities* (ed. Thomas K. Hubbard; Chichester, U. K.: Blackwell Publishing, 2014) 128–49; Mark Smith, "Ancient Bisexuality and the Interpretation of Romans 1:26–27," *JAAR* 64 [1996]: 238–43. However, there are quite a few examples in Hubbard's article that can hardly be considered consensual or even between peers.

22. Various archaeological finds depict older men wooing and courting teenage boys to be their lovers. They bring them gifts and offer intellectual and moral training. Again, in no way am I trying to sugarcoat the atrocity. I'm only trying to show that pederasty was much more than a creepy outlet for sexual release.

23. Eva Cantarella defines pederasty as "a cultural, educational, and sexual practice, in which men courted, guided, taught, and had (either anal or intercrural) sex with male *paides*" (*Bisexuality in the Ancient World* [New Haven: Yale University Press, 1992], 136–42; cf. Smith, "Ancient Bisexuality, 229). Smith highlights the "cultural and political aspects" of pederasty and shows that the adult lover in pederastic relationships was "expected to train his beloved in the ways of Greek adult life, including social, political, and military expectations" (Ibid., 230); see too Scroggs, *Homosexuality*, 29–32.

24. Plato, *Symposium* 193B; cf. Aelian, *Varia historia* 2.21; Aristophanes, *Thesmophoria Women*, 1–276; See ibid. 142–43.

25. Gagnon wrongly says that Agathon was eighteen years old when their relationship first began, citing Plato, *Prot.* 315D-E, in support (see Gagnon, *Homosexual Practice*, 351). However, there's nothing in Plato here that indicates Agathon's age. The text only says that Agathon was "still quite young" when he was in relationship with Pausanias. And it doesn't state the age of Agathon when they *began* their relationship.

26. Plato, *Parmenides*, 127a; See the discussion in Hubbard, *Homosexuality* 6; cf. John Boswell, *Christianity, Social Tolerance, and Homosexuality: Gay People in Western Europe from the Beginning of the Christian Era to the Fourteenth Century* (Chicago: University of Chicago Press, 1980) *passim*.

27. Plato, *Symposium* 179E–180B; Aeschylus, *Myrmidons* frags. 135–37. Hubbard, "Peer Homosexuality," 142.

28. *Ephesian Tale*, 3.2.

29. *Leucippe and Clitophon* 1.7–8, 12–14; 2.33–38; see Scroggs, *Homosexuality*, 134. The relationship is still pederastic, but both lovers were roughly the same age.

30. Photios, *Bibliotheke* 94.77a-b; see Brooten, *Love Between Women*, 51.

31. *Dialogues of the Courtesans*, 5.1–3. This lesbian couple, however, ends up seducing a woman named Leaena into a sexual relationship.

32. *Paidagogos* 3.3.21.3.

33. *Tetrabiblos* 3.14 sect. 172; Brooten, *Love Between Women*, 332.

34. *Sifra Ahare* 9:8 forbids marriage between two men and marriage between two women, which would be superfluous if such marriages were unknown. Likewise, Sifra on Leviticus 18:3, which "does not prohibit female homoeroticism per se, but rather marriage between women" (Brooten, *Love Between Women*, 65, citing Michael Satlow in agreement. See his "'They Abused Him Like a Woman': Homoeroticism, Gender Blurring, and the Rabbis in Late Antiquity," *Journal of the History of Sexuality* 5 [1994] 16–17).

35. See Brooten, *Love Between Women*, 59–60.

36. It think it's a stretch to take Martial (1.24; 12.42) and Juvenal's (*Satire*, 2.120, 129) statements about men being given in marriage to other men as a description of historical reality. They are probably just mocking effeminate men.

37. See e.g. *Ant.* 1.200–201; *Ag. Apion* 2.273–75; Philo, *Laws* 3:37–42; *Contemplative Life*, 59–60. Josephus, *Ag. Apion* 2.215 probably has male-male rape in view.

38. *Ag. Apion* 2.199.

39. *Abr.* 135–37.

40. *Letter of Aristeas*, 152.

41. Greek: *mete gamoklopeein met arsena Kyprin orinein*, from *Ps. Phoc.* 3. "Cypris was the Aphrodite of the island of Cyprus" and rousing him means arousing an erotic passion for men (see Nissinen, *Homoeroticism*, 171 n. 32).

42. *Ps. Phoc.* 190–91. See also *Ps. Phoc.* 192, 213–14; *Sibylline Oracles* 3.184–87; 5.166.

43. *m. Sanhedrin* 7:4; t. *Abodah Zarah* 2:1; 3:2.

44. *b. Nid.* 13b says that the only type of homosexual acts condemned was anal penetration. *b. Yebam.* 76a and *Sabb.* 65a-b say that women who "rubbed" other women were not disqualified from marrying priests and that a woman hasn't committed adultery unless she was penetrated (vaginally or anally; cf. also y. *Gittin* 8:10, 49c). For a brief discussion, see Nissinen, *Homoeroticism*, 101.

45. Recall Josephus' prohibition of same-sex marriages cited above (*Apion* 2.199). *Letter of Aristeas* 152 and *Ps. Phoc.* 3 prohibit homosexual relations or passions without reference to age distinctions. In rabbinic literature, *b. Sanhedrin* 58a, *Sifra Ahare* 9:8, and Sifra on Leviticus 18:3 exclude marriages between two men or two women. See further, Nisinen, *Homoeroticism*, 99–101.

46. See Josephus, 2.199 and Philo, *Laws*, 3.32–42 among others.

47. Philo, *Laws*, 3.37–39 mentions all of these (and other!) reasons.

48. *Ps. Phoc.* 3.

CHAPTER 5: WHOM WOULD JESUS LOVE?

1. Matt. 15:19 (cf. Mark 7:21). As the argument goes, the Greek word *porneia* ("fornication") is a catch-all term for the sexual laws in Leviticus 18, which would include male same-sex intercourse. The main problem is that *porneia* isn't used in the Greek translation of Lev. 18, so how can we assume that it includes all of these laws? Maybe it does and maybe it doesn't (and if it does, it would therefore include sex during menstruation, but I don't see people arguing as passionately for this). I have a hard time saying *porneia* must include same-sex relations without concrete evidence. Plus, the word *porneia* is used with some flexibility in the first century. Sometimes it includes many different types of sexual sins, while other times it only includes adultery or other specific sins. I find it tough to say that *porneia* clearly includes same-sex relations when Jesus uses it in Matt. 15:19. See further Kyle Harper, "*Porneia*: The Making of a Christian Sexual Norm," *JBL* 131 (2011): 363–83.

2. Some say that Jesus spoke Aramaic and not Hebrew. However, there is good evidence for first-century Jews speaking Hebrew more than Aramaic, as seen from the many inscriptions and manuscripts from the first century that are written in Hebrew.

3. See chapter 4.

4. Matt 10:5–6; cf. 8:5–13; 15:21–39.

5. Cf. the debate about hand washing and the Corban law in Matt 15:1–9 (cf. Mark 7:1–23).

6. I've been in dialogue with my philosopher friend Jeff Cook about whether Jesus advocated a deontological or virtue ethic— a discussion that may have serious implications for the debate about homosexuality. Deontological ethics focus on obeying the rules, while virtue ethics focus on the moral character that is cultivated by certain actions. Put differently, deontological ethics focus on what we do, while virtue ethics look at who we become. I'm still working through this discussion, and probably will be for some time, but I do think that Jesus emphasized what we now call virtue ethics in his Sermon on the Mount.

7. With regard to the dietary laws, Jesus never clearly did away with them. In Mark 7, it was the author (Mark) and not Jesus who said, "In saying this, Jesus declared all foods clean" (Mark 7:19). It may be that Mark has drawn some implications from Jesus' words, but it's not clear that Jesus himself was ending the dietary code. Moreover, the phrase in the Greek translated "declared all foods clean" is difficult to translate and may carry no reference to the food laws. For a discussion, see Robert Geulich, *Mark 1:1–8:26* (WBC 34a; Grand Rapids: Zondervan, 1989), 737–38.

8. I have many scholarly friends who have helped me with this over the years. I want to thank Joel Willitts, Todd Wilson, Scott Hafemann, David Rudolph, Adam Finlay, and several others who have (re-) introduced me to the Jewishness of Jesus.

9. See *b.Gittin* 90a.

10. Matthew records Jesus' "exception clause" on two occasions ("anyone who divorces his wife, *except for sexual immorality*, makes her the victim of adultery," Matt 5:32; cf. 19:9) while Mark doesn't record Jesus' exception clause ("Anyone who divorces his wife and marries another woman commits adultery against her," Mark 10:11).

11. See my discussion in *Charis: God's Scandalous Grace for Us* (Colorado Springs: David C. Cook, 2014), 152–54.

12. This is my expanded translation. The Greek word *dei* translated "must" (NIV) refers to something or someone under divine compulsion (see e.g. Matt. 16:21). And the ancient practice of coming under someone's roof was a sign of peace and friendship, hence my translation "befriend" in the place of "stay at your house" (NIV).

13. Robert Gagnon disagrees with much of what I've said about Christ's "love without footnotes." Through several Facebook exchanges, Robert and I have gone back and forth over Jesus' mode of relating to sinners. Robert says that Jesus' love for sinners must be set in the general context of his message of repentance (e.g. Matt. 4:17). Therefore, Zacchaeus would have already known where Jesus stood on the issue of tax collecting and this knowledge is assumed in Luke 19. This is why Jesus never addressed Zacchaeus' sin. My response to Gagnon is twofold. First, it's clearly an assumption to say that Jesus never told Zacchaeus to repent since Zacchaeus was already aware of Jesus' message of repentance. Zacchaeus, of course, was living in Jericho and Jesus' primary preaching was carried out in Galilee. There is simply no good reason to assume that Zacchaeus had been in the Galilean crowds listening to Jesus' messages. Second, I do not disagree with Robert's general point, that Jesus preached about repentance and that repentance is necessary for salvation. Repentance is a major theme in Jesus' ministry, particularly in the Gospel of Luke (see especially F. Mendez-Moratalla, *The Paradigm of Conversion in Luke* [London, T & T Clark, 2004]; David Morlan, *Conversion in Luke and Paul: An Exegetical and Theological Exploration* [London: T & T Clark, 2013]). There's no denying this. My only caveat is that *to get that repentance*, Jesus fronted love.

14. I'm well aware that John 7:53–8:11 is not in some of the earliest manuscripts of John. However, it's very likely that this story actually happened and was later inserted into John's gospel, since the story is recorded in other historical sources outside of manuscripts of John's gospel (e.g., early manuscripts of Luke's gospel and in the writings of Papias).

15. David Kinnaman and Gabe Lyons, *UnChristian: What a New Generation Really Thinks about Christianity ... and Why It Matters* (Grand Rapids: Baker, 2007), 29.

16. John Burke, "When Two Lesbians Walk Into a Church Seeking Trouble," *CharismaNews:* http://www.charismanews.com/opinion/43109-when-two-lesbians-walk-into-a-church-seeking-trouble.

17. Ilan H. Meyer, Merilee Teylan, and Sharon Schwartz, "The Role of Help-Seeking in Preventing Suicide Attempts among Lesbians, Gay Men, and Bisexuals," *Suicide and Life Threatening Behavior* (2014).

18. My friend Bill Henson trains many churches and pastors in how to think through the question of homosexuality. Bill tells me that every

single church he has talked to says that young straight people are leaving the church based on how it treats the LGBT community.

19. John 14:15. John 15:10 seems to contradict this when it says, "If you keep my commandments, you will remain in my love." But this verse talks about *abiding in* not *initially receiving* Christ's love. Yes, Jesus demands obedience in response to his love, but such obedience doesn't earn Christ's love. For my understanding of grace and obedience, see *Charis*, 175–85.

CHAPTER 6: FALL SHORT OF GOD'S GLORY

1. It is important to note that Paul smuggles scenes from Jewish history into his critique of Gentile paganism in Romans 1:18–32. For instance, he alludes to the golden calf incident in Romans 1:23 (as viewed through the lens of Ps. 105:20 LXX). This means that Paul does not only have Gentiles in view in 1:18–32, but all people including Jews. Paul goes on to make this clear in 1:32 and 2:1–2.

2. The phrase "Christianity is one beggar telling another beggar where he found bread" is credited to D. T. Niles.

3. "Paul and Homosexual Practice: A Critical Evaluation of the Excessive-lust Interpretation of Romans 1:26–27," forthcoming.

4. See, for instance, Bernadette Brooten, *Love Between Women: Early Christian Response to Female Homoeroticism* (Chicago: University of Chicago Press, 1996), 59–60; Thomas K. Hubbard, "Peer Homosexuality," in *A Companion to Greek and Roman Sexualities* (ed. Thomas K. Hubbard; Chichester, U. K.: Blackwell Publishing, 2014), 128–49; Nancy Rabinowitz, "Excavating Women's Homoeroticism in Ancient Greece," in *Among Women: From the Homosocial to the Homoerotic in the Ancient World* (ed. Nancy Rabinowitz and Lisa Auanger; Austin: University of Texas Press, 2002), 106–66.

5. Karl A. Kuhn, an affirming scholar, makes the same point ("Natural and Unnatural Relations between Text and Context: A Canonical Reading of Romans 1:26–27," *Currents in Theology and Mission* 33 [2006]: 313–29 [315–16]).

6. For the following argument see Knut Holter-Stavanger, "A Note on the Old Testament Background of Romans 1,23–27," *BN* 69 (1993): 21–23; Ulrich Mauser, "Creation, Sexuality, and Homosexuality in the New Testament," in *Homosexuality and the Christian Community* (ed. Choon Leong Seow; Louisville: Westminster John Knox, 1996): 39–49; Robert Gagnon, *The Bible and Homosexual Practice: Texts*

and Hermeneutics (Nashville: Abingdon, 2001), 288–92; idem., "A comprehensive and Critical Review Essay of *Homosexuality, Science, and the 'Plain Sense' of Scripture*, Part 2," *HBT* 23 (2003): 206–39 (208–13). Others have argued against reading Romans 1 in light of Genesis 1–2; see Dale Martin, *Sex and the Single Savior: Gender and Sexuality in Biblical Interpretation* (Louisville: Westminster John Knox, 2006), 52–55; David Fredrickson, "Natural and Unnatural Use in Romans 1:24–27: Paul and the Philosophic Critique of Eros," in *Homosexuality, Science, and the 'Plain Sense' of Scripture* (ed. David Balch; Louisville: Westminster John Knox, 1999), 197–222 (222).

7. Although written in Hebrew, the Old Testament was translated into Greek around 150 BC. This "Septuagint" (or LXX), as it's called, became the standard version of the Old Testament for early Christians.

8. Matthew Vines agrees that Paul refers to creation here, but argues that "any lustful sex would violate God's intention at creation" (*God and the Gay Christian*, 114). Therefore, according to Vines, non-lustful same-sex unions are not in view in Romans 1. I will address this argument in more detail at the end of this chapter. For starters, Vines' reading goes against the grain of Paul's flow of logic. Paul talks about humans exchanging the Creator for creation (Rom. 1:23), which results in women exchanging men for women (1:26), and men exchanging women for men (1:27). Romans 1 doesn't talk about people exchanging non-lustful sex for lustful sex.

9. Romans 11 shows that *para physin* doesn't in itself mean that something is immoral. Context determines meaning. It is the context of Romans 1—and other writings where same-sex relations are critiqued—that shows that *para physin* is something that is immoral (See the discussion in Richard Hays, "Relations Natural and Unnatural: A Response to J. Boswell's Exegesis of Rom. 1," *Journal of Religious Ethics* 14 [1986]: 184–215 [198–99]).

10. According to James Brownson, "because same-sex relationships are nonprocreative, Paul regarded these relationships as selfish and socially irresponsible, neglecting the obligation of procreation" (*Bible*, 267, cf. pp. 244–45). This is rather odd for Brownson to argue since he previously says the exact opposite. Earlier, Brownson contended that according to Paul in 1 Corinthians 7 "Marriage . . . has as its purpose *not the bearing of children* but the exercise of mutual care and the avoidance of uncontrolled lust (1 Cor. 7:2–9)" (*Bible*, 117, emphasis mine). Again, he writes: "Marriage is still important, but the *purpose of procreation plays no role in Paul's discussion of marriage*"

(*Bible*, 117 emphasis mine). The same goes for the Pastoral Epistles, which he doesn't believe were written by Paul, and discussions about the household codes in Ephesians and Colossians (e.g., Eph. 5:21–33; Col. 3:18–4:1; Tit. 2:1–10). "[I]n all the instructions about the husband-wife relationship in these codes," Brownson says, "we never see any discussion of procreation at all" (*Bible*, 118).

11. Brownson, *Bible*, 245, cf. 237. Likewise, affirming scholar Daniel Helminiak says that "unnatural" does not mean that an act is wrong "according to the universal laws of nature"; rather, it simply means to act "unexpectedly" or "in an unusual way" (*What the Bible Really Says About Homosexuality* [San Francisco: Alamo Square, 1994], 79).

12. Josephus writes: "The woman, it [the Law] says, is in all things inferior to the man. Let her accordingly be obedient" to her husband (Ap. 2.24). Arius Didymus says that "the deliberative (reasoning) faculty in a woman is inferior, in children it does not yet exist, and in the case of slaves it is completely absent" Concerning Household Management, 148.14–18. Sirach, a Jewish author, believes: "Better is the wickedness of a man than a woman who does good" (Sir. 42:14).

13. E.g. Philo, *Abr.* 135–36.

14. Matthew Vines agrees that Paul does not have a low view of women. However, he still argues that a low view of women is inherent in Paul's phrase "against nature." Vines says that "demeaning views of women shaped the ancient categories of 'natural' and 'unnatural' sex that are used in Romans 1." "By the time he wrote Romans," says Vines, "Paul could invoke those terms ['against nature'] as shorthand reference due to their well-established usage" (*God and the Gay Christian*, 112–13). Vines argues, therefore, that the phrase "against nature" was pumped full of misogynist meaning, and Paul used it according to its established meaning, but Paul was not a misogynist. I'll let the reader evaluate the strength of this argument.

15. "[T]he sexual pleasure experienced by the female and male natures when they join together for the purpose of procreation seems to have been handed down in accordance with nature, whereas the pleasure enjoyed by males with males and females with females seems to be *against nature* (*para physin*), and the boldness of those who first engaged in this practice seems to have arisen out of an inability to control pleasure" (Plato, *Laws*, 636B-D).

16. For the use of *para* with *physin* meaning "*against* nature," see Hays, "Relations," 197–98; Brooten, *Love Between Women*, 241.

17. See Philo, *Post.* 180–81 (masturbation); Philo, *Spec. Leg.* 3.32 (sex during menstruation); Philo, *Spec. Leg.* 3.36 (sex with an infertile woman); Rufus, *On Sexual Matters*, 12 (sex for mere pleasure).
18. *On Sexual Matters,* 12 emphasis mine.
19. *On Sexual Matters*, 12.
20. The closest I've seen is in Philo, who talks about respecting "the law of nature" by not having sex with one's wife during menstruation (*Spec. Leg.* 3.32), and he even calls men who knowingly marry an infertile woman "enemies of nature." But the phrase *para physin* is reserved for same-sex relations. Herodotus refers to forms of intercourse that are not "according to law" (Herodotus 1.61), and Pseudo-Phoclydes talks about "shameful" acts of heterosexual intercourse, but neither uses the phrase *para physin* (see Brooten, *Love Between Women*, 248–49). The word *physis* is sometimes used to speak of all sorts of misguided behaviors, but *para physin* appears to be more of a technical phrase that describes same-sex relations *in contexts where sexual immorality is discussed.*
21. *On the Contemplative Life*, 59. Philo also labels pederasty as "an unnatural pleasure" (*Spec. Leg.* 3.39) and says that the Sodomites "threw off the laws of nature" (*Abr.* 133–41).
22. You can see the same thing in Aeschines, Against Timarchus, 185.
23. See further, Philo, *Spec. Leg.* 3.37–42; cf. *Abr. 133–41*; Josephus, *Against Apion*, 2.199; 2.273–75; Seneca, *Moral Epistles*, 122.7; Rufus, *On Sexual Matters*, 12; Plutarch, *Dialogue on Love*, 5; cf. Dionysius of Halicarnassus, *Ant. rom.* 16.4.3; Aeschines, *Tim.* 185; Athenaeus, *Deipn.* 13.84 (605d); Diodorus Siculus, *Hist.* 32.10.9.3.
24. "Relations Natural and Unnatural," 194.
25. Diodoros of Sicily uses the phrase "unnatural marriage" (32.10.9). Josephus describes same-sex relations as *para physin* in contrast to male-female marriages (*Ap.* 2.199).
26. Plutarch, *Dialogue on Love*, 5.
27. Philo *Spec. Leg.* 3.39; cf. *Abr.* 133–41.
28. Among others, see Soranus, *On Chronic Disorders*, 4.9; Dio Chrysostom, 7.149, 151–52.
29. Some scholars propose that Romans 1:26 is not even talking about female-female sex, but about non-procreative forms of heterosexual sex. See, for instance, J. Miller, "The Practices of Romans 1:26: Homosexual or Heterosexual?" *NovT* 37 (1995): 1–11, James Brownson, *Bible,* 244–46, and David Fredrickson, "Natural," 201.

This interpretation is unlikely for several reasons. First, the phrase *para physin* is never used in reference to non-procreative forms of heterosexual sex in ancient literature, but used on several occasions to describe lesbian sex. Second, the parallel between 1:26 and 1:27 (the latter clearly refers to male homosexual behavior) suggests that 1:26 refers to female homosexual sex. Third, if Paul wanted to critique men for having non-procreative sex with women, he probably would not have addressed women as the subject of the "exchange" in 1:26. That is, if non-procreative heterosexual sex were in view, Paul most likely would have said that "men exchanged the natural use of their women (i.e., coitus) for the unnatural (i.e., anal or oral sex)." But those who argue for heterosexual sex in Romans 1:26, force Paul to make an outrageous claim that would have been historically unparalleled: "women exchanged the natural use (i.e., coitus) of their husbands for the unnatural (i.e. anal and oral)." We have no evidence of women forcing their husbands into giving them anal sex. Finally, Paul's striking indifference to procreation in all of his discussions about marriage, sex, and gender, makes the heterosexual interpretation of Romans 1:26 nearly impossible.

30. The one reference that may go against this is Seneca, *Moral Epistles* 95.21, which condemns some women who indulge in drinking binges and "penetrate men" (figure that one out). In the context, though, Seneca critiques the women for acting like men. He never says that female homoerotic behavior is wrong because it is the product of excessive lust. Some Roman satirists also played on the manliness of some women, like Philaenis who "buggers boys," "bangs eleven girls a day," and lifts heavy weights "with an easy arm" (Martial 7.67). Not only is the historicity of such satirical pieces difficult to establish, the point again is that some women acted like men in the bed and in the gym.

31. See chapter 4.

32. Brownson, *Bible,* 164.

33. Ibid., 160, 161, 164, 166 emphases mine.

34. The phrase "passions of dishonor" in Romans 1:26 is tricky. I suggest that what makes the passions dishonorable is that they lead to unnatural actions, as the following "for" (*gar*) makes clear. Moreover, the "passions of dishonor" picks up on the previous phrase "to dishonor their bodies among them" in 1:24. Therefore, the "passions of dishonor" assumes the force of its prior verbal cognate in 1:24. It may be, then, that "passions of dishonor" should be rendered

"passions which bring dishonour" as C. E. B. Cranfield suggests
(*A Critical and Exegetical Commentary on the Epistle to the Romans*
[ICC vol. 1; Edinburgh: T & T Clark, 1975], 125).

35. In 1:24, the phrase "Therefore God gave them over to the desires
of their hearts" is followed by "to sexual impurity for the degrading
of their bodies with one another." Likewise in 1:26, "passions of
dishonor" (translation mine) is immediately followed by "*for* their
females exchanged the natural use for the unnatural" (translation
mine). It is the action that Paul prohibits.

36. Both words, in fact, can have either a neutral or positive sense. Paul
can "with great desire" (*epithumia*) long to see the Thessalonians
face to face (1 Thess. 2:17) and Jesus can "earnestly desire"
(*epithumia*) to eat the Passover meal with his disciples (Luke 22:15;
cf. Phil. 1:23). Both of these desires are good in light of the object of
the desire. But when men and women desire to have sex with people
of the same sex, and that desire leads to action—for it is the action
that Paul critiques in Romans 1:26–27—it then becomes clear why
epithumia and *pathos* are contrary to God's will here in this context.
The cognate Greek verb *epithumeo* is used in a positive or neutral
sense: Matt. 13:17; Luke 15:16; 17:22; 22:15; 1 Tim.3:1; Heb. 6:11;
and 1 Pet. 1:12.

37. Cf. Karl Kuhn: "For Paul, the unnatural actions and the unnatural
desire are one and the same" ("Natural and Unnatural," 318).
Likewise, the phrase "they burned with passion" (1:27) does refer
to overwhelming sexual desire, but sexual desire satisfied on people
of the same sex. Paul says something similar in 1 Corinthians 7:2–5
about getting married in order to satisfy one's sexual desires (1 Cor.
7:3–5, 8; cf. Gagnon, "Review," 221).

CHAPTER 7: LOST IN TRANSLATION

1. This story is recorded in Linda Belleville, "The Challenges of
Translating *Arsenokoitai* and *Malakoi* in 1 Corinthians 6:9: A
Reassessment in Light of Koine Greek and First-Century Cultural
Mores," *Bible Translator* 62 (2011): 22–29 (22).

2. Cited in Belleville, "The Challenges," 22.

3. There have been many scholarly discussions of these two words. The
ones I have found most helpful include John Boswell, *Homosexuality*,
341–53; David Wright, "Homosexuals or Prostitutes? The Meaning
of *Arsenokoitai* (1 Cor. 6:9; 1 Tim. 1:10)," *VC* 38 (1984): 125–53;
idem, "Translating *Arsenokoites* (1 Cor. 6:9; 1 Tim. 1:10," *VC* 41

(1987): 396–98; Dale Martin, *Sex and the Single Savior: Gender and Sexuality in Biblical Interpretation* (Louisville: Westminster John Knox, 2006), 37–50; Robert Gagnon, *The Bible and Homosexual Practice: Text and Hermeneutics* (Nashville: Abingdon, 2001), 303–36; Belleville, "The Challenges," 22–29; cf. Matthew Vines, *God and the Gay Christian: The Biblical Case in Support of Same-Sex Relationships* (New York: Convergent, 2014), 119–34.

4. Daniel Helminiak, *What the Bible Really Says about Homosexuality* (New Mexico: Alamo Square Press, 2000), 107.

5. *Sex and the Single Savior*, 43.

6. *Sex and the Single Savior*, 43 emphasis original.

7. *Malakos* corresponds to the Latin *mollus*, which Jerome used to translate *malakos* in the Vulgate (see Martti Nissinen, *Homoerotism in the Biblical World: A Historical Perspective* [Minneapolis: fortress, 1998], 117).

8. That is, by ancient Roman standards. What it means to confuse gender distinctions will look different for different cultures. Some men in ancient Rome could be accused of being *malakos* ("soft") if they were known as a ladies' man or displayed too much PDA with their wife. According to Roman culture, such behavior showed lack of discipline, and since women were believed (by men) to lack discipline, then men who lacked discipline toward *women* were considered to be *womanly*, or *malakos*. The term *malakos* therefore cannot be reduced to the modern concept of homosexuality, and some *malakoi* would certainly not be considered gay today.

9. *Spec. Laws* 3.37–41; cf. *Abr.* 135–37.

10. Lucan, 10.133–34 emphasis mine; cf. Williams, *Roman Homosexuality*, 140.

11. Phaedrus, *Fable*, 4.16.

12. For instance, Plutarch describes men who were overly desirous of *women* as "soft" (*On Moral Virtue* 447B; *Amatorius* 750B). Aristotle described men who lacked self-control as *malakos* (*Nic. Eth.* 7.4.2). See further David Fredrickson, "Natural and Unnatural Use in Romans 1:24–27," in *Homosexuality, Science, and the "Plain Sense" of Scripture* (ed. David Balch; Grand Rapids: Eerdmans, 2000), 197–222 (219–20).

13. Mart. 2.62; cf. Ovid, *Ars* 1.505–24 and the discussion in Williams, *Roman Homosexuality*, 142. Playing the passive sexual role with other men does not mean that such a man would not also engage in sex with women or even shave other parts of his body in order to attract women.

14. Or more bluntly, men were the penetrators while women were the penetrated. If a man was effeminate, there is a good chance he took the passive role in sexual intercourse with men, though not necessarily to the exclusion of having sex with women.

15. On the lexical meaning of this word in light of its individual components, see Scroggs, *Homosexuality*, 106–7; Wright, "Homosexuals or Prostitutes?" 129–32.

16. David Wright shows that the verbal force of *arsenokoites* cannot be flipped around to mean "men who sleep around." Wright shows through many other parallels that the first part (*arsen*) is the *object* while the second part (*koite*) carries the verbal force acting upon the object. So, "one (presumably a man) who sleeps with men;" see Wright, "Homosexuals or Prostitutes?" 129–32.

17. Martin, *Sex and the Single Savior*, 39.

18. Boswell, *Homosexuality*, 338–54.

19. *Bible, Gender, Sexuality*, 271. Justin Lee pretty much says the same thing: "some scholars ... speculate that Paul could have coined the term [*arsenokoites*] in reference to" Leviticus 18 and 20. But then he goes on to argue, like Brownson, that Leviticus is talking about cult prostitution (*Torn*, 185).

20. See also Numbers 31:17–18; Judges 21:11–12.

21. *God and the Gay Christian*, 126.

22. Scroggs, *Homosexuality*, 83, 108.

23. *Syb. Or.* 2.73.

24. As Wright points out, *Syb. Or.* 2.71–73 is almost certainly not a Christian interpolation (Wright, "Homosexuals," 137–38).

25. *b. Sanh.* 54a (the focus here is on pederasty, but the passage goes on to apply Lev 20:13 to sexual relations between a man and another male "whether an adult or a minor"); see also *b. Shabb.* 17b; *b. Sukkah* 29a; *y. Ber.* 9.50.13c; *b. Niddah* 13b; Scroggs, *Homosexuality*, 83, 108. Nissinen rejects this evidence since "the Rabbinic sources in which *mishkab zakur* appears are considerably later than Paul" (*Homoeroticism*, 116). While it's true that Talmudic literature is far removed from the time of the New Testament, it often records traditions and conversations that happened many years earlier— sometimes hundreds of years earlier. So the use of *mishkab zakur* in later Jewish literature may capture earlier uses of the Hebrew equivalent to the Greek word *arsenokoites*. In any case, Jewish writers unambiguously used *mishkab zakur* to refer to and condemn same-sex relations.

26. According to *TLG*, it is used 73 times in Greek literature between Paul and AD 1500.

27. Both Dale Martin and Robert Gagnon try to support their very different understandings of *arsenokoites* by looking at later vice lists where they occur.

28. *Refutation of All Heresies* 5.26.22–23; quoted in Gagnon, *Homosexual Practice*, 318.

29. Eusebius, *Preparation for the Gospel*, 6.1.

30. E.g. *Comm. Matt.* 14:10; *Fr. 1 Cor.* 27; *r. Exod.*, on Exodus 12:15.

31. *Expositions on Proverbs* 7.74 from J. P. Migne (ed.), *Patrologiae Cursus Completus* (Patrologiae Graecae Tomus XVII, Origenes, 1857), p. 181–82, cited from *GayChristian101:* http://www.gaychristian101.com/Define-Arsenokoites.html.

32. The email was read on Oct. 23, 2014. The Syriac version referred to by Simon is the Bohairic version.

33. Scroggs, *Homosexuality*, 108; Helminiak, *What the Bible Really Says*, 110.

34. Roy Ciampa is probably correct that it's unlikely that Paul would have said *paiderastes* since this term was often used positively ("Flee Sexual Immorality: Sex in the City of Corinth," in *The Wisdom of the Cross: Exploring 1 Corinthians* [ed. Brian Rosner; Downers Grove, IL: IVP Academic, 2011], 113). However, the other two terms *paidophthoros* ("corruptor of boys") and *paidophtoreo* ("seducer of boys") were widely used negatively by Jews; if Paul had pederasty in mind, it's probable that he would have used one of these terms.

35. Roy Ciampa does not find the absence of these words significant (Ciampa, "Flee Sexual Immorality," 113). In other words, *arsenokoites* could very well refer to pederasty, even though Paul doesn't use one of the typical words for pederasty. While I agree with Ciampa that the absence of pederastic terms is not decisive, I still think it is one among many reasons why Paul's terms *malokos* and *arsenokoites* shouldn't be limited to pederasty (see Belleville, "The Challenges").

36. This pattern is noted by both affirming (Nissinen, *Homoeroticism*, 114) and nonaffirming scholars (Gagnon, *Homosexual Practice*, 334–35; Mounce, *Pastoral Epistles*, 30–31).

37. *Ps. Phoc.* 3–8; cf. *Did.* 2:2–3; *Barn.* 19:4; see Gagnon, *Homosexual Practice*, 335–36. Philo for instance stuffed all sorts of sexual sins under the larger umbrella of the seventh commandment, including incest, bestiality, prostitution, sex during menstruation, and sex with boys (*Spec. Laws* 3.1–82). Gagnon also notes that Philo also placed

kidnapping under the umbrella of the eighth commandment against stealing (*Spec. Laws* 4.13–19; Gagnon, *Homosexual Practice*, 335).

CHAPTER INTERLUDE: A SUMMARY

1. See Christopher Roberts, *Creation and Covenant: The Significance of Sexual Difference in the Moral Theology of Marriage* (London: T & T Clark, 2007).

CHAPTER 8: "BORN THIS WAY"

1. "Sexual Orientation & Homosexuality," *American Psychological Association:* http://www.apa.org/topics/lgbt/orientation.aspx.
2. For a good discussion with a thorough bibliography of studies, see Mark A. Yarhouse, *Homosexuality and the Christian: A Guide for Parents, Pastors, and Friends* (Minneapolis: Bethany House, 2010), 57–80. See also Stanton L. Jones and Mark A. Yarhouse, *Homosexuality: The Use of Scientific Research in the Church's Moral Debate* (Downers Grove, IL: InterVarsity Press, 2000).
3. Cited in Jennell Paris, *The End of Sexual Identity: Why Sex Is too Important to Define Who We Are* (Downers Grove, IL.: InterVarsity Press, 2011), 61.
4. This was the summary given by my friend Dr. Sam Roberto through an email exchange in September 2013. For medical research on the plasticity of the brain, see Pascual-Leone, A., Freitas, C., Oberman, L., Horvath, J. C., Halko, M., Eldaief, M. et al., "Characterizing Brain Cortical Plasticity and Network Dynamics Cross the Age-span in Health and Disease with TMS-EEG and TMS-fMRI," *Brain Topography* 24 (2011): 302–15.
5. See for instance, Fiona Macrae, "Compulsive pornography users shows [*sic*] the same brain activity as alcoholics and drug addicts," *Daily Mail:* http://www.dailymail.co.uk/news/article-2428861/Porn-addicts-brain-activity-alcoholics-drug-addicts.html.
6. Justin Lee, *Torn: Rescuing the Gospel from the Gays-Vs.-Christians Debate* (New York: Jericho, 2012), 62.
7. John Corvino, "Nature? Nurture? It Doesn't Matter," *John Corvino:* http://johncorvino.com/2004/08/nature-nurture-it-doesnt-matter/.
8. See Yarhouse, *Homosexuality*, 41–43; Paris, *The End of Sexual Identity*, 55–76.
9. "Sexual Orientation & Homosexuality," *American Psychological Association:* http://www.apa.org/topics/lgbt/orientation.aspx.

10. Yarhouse, *Homosexuality*, 42.

11. Lesli got this advice from her friend (who is now my friend) Bill Henson, who runs a great ministry called *Lead Them Home* (www.leadthemhome.org).

12. For an excellent discussion on how to respond to loved ones who come out as gay, see Yarhouse, *Homosexuality*, 99–153.

CHAPTER 9: GAY AND CHRISTIAN

1. Denny Burk, "Is Temptation a Sin?" *Denny Burk's blog:* http://www.dennyburk.com/is-temptation-a-sin/. See also Denny Burk, "Is Homosexual Orientation Sinful?" *Canon & Culture:* http://www.canonandculture.com/is-homosexual-orientation-sinful/.

2. Burk, "Is Temptation a Sin?"

3. Denny just co-wrote a book on sexual orientation: Denny Burk and Heath Lambert, *Transforming Homosexuality: How to Live Faithfully with Same-Sex Attraction* (Phillipsburg, NJ: P&R, 2015). Unfortunately it was published after I turned in my manuscript for this book so I wasn't able to interact with it. My summary of Burk's view is based on his blogs and our personal interactions.

4. "[T]hey burned with passion" (*exekauthesan en te orexei*, 1:27). Cf. Wis. 14:2; 15:5; Sir. 18:30; 23:6 where similar wording is used.

5. According to the APA. (See "Sexual Orientation & Homosexuality," *American Psychological Association:* http://www.apa.org/topics/lgbt/orientation.aspx.)

6. "The soul of Jonathan was knit to the soul of David, and Jonathan loved him as his own soul" (1 Sam. 18:1; cf. 20:17). Jonathan also "delighted very much" in David and "took great pleasure" in him (1 Sam. 19:1). David and Jonathan "kissed one another and wept with one another," since they would not see each other again (1 Sam. 20:41). Hebrew verb "to kiss" occurs twenty-seven times in the Old Testament, but refers to erotic kissing only three times in the OT. That means in twenty-four of the twenty-seven uses of the verb "to kiss," it's used in a non-erotic context. Finally, when David gets news about Jonathan's death, he cries out: "very pleasant have you been to me; your love to me was extraordinary, surpassing the love of women" (2 Sam. 1:26).

7. Julie Rodgers, "Can the Gay Be a Good?" *Spiritual Friendship:* http://spiritualfriendship.org/2014/10/23/can-the-gay-be-a-good/.

8. Ibid.

9. I have many SSA/Gay Christian friends who have reiterated over and over the same thing that Julie Rodgers has pointed out.

10. In fact, it's likely that the "passions of dishonor" in 1:26 collects both the desire and act from 1:24 and applies it to female homoeroticism in 1:26. Notice the parallel:

> "*desires* of their hearts . . . to *dishonor* their bodies" (1:24)
> "*passions of dishonor* . . . for their women exchanged . . ." (1:26)

Inherent in the phrase "passions of dishonor" are both the desire and action from 1:24. This means that "passions of dishonor" assumes that one is acting on those desires, which is why Paul continues by talking about a sinful act ("for [*gar*] even their women exchanged . . .").

11. The main word for desire (*epithumia*) can be used to describe a positive desire, a neutral desire, or a negative desire. Burk says: "Whether the desire is good (as in Matt. 13:17) or evil (as in Matt. 5:28) depends entirely on what it is a person desires." And he is correct except for the word "entirely." I don't think that a desire for something good is always good. Such desire could become lust—an unhealthy fixation on something that is in itself good. Take wine, for instance. Wine is good (well, some wine anyway), and it is good to want a glass of it. But a person's desire could become unhealthy and "not the way it's supposed to be" (as Neal Plantinga says) if it becomes overwhelming and controlling. The same goes for food, wealth, and a whole host of other creational goods. Likewise, someone could have an idle attraction toward something that is not good—a neighbor's wife, etc.—that isn't itself wrong until it springs into active desire, or lust, which is when sin is born (James 1:14).

12. I don't understand how Burk can read James 1:13–14 and conclude: "the desires themselves are sinful," when James clearly says that desires *give birth to sin*, thereby distinguishing desire from sin.

13. I refuse to put scare quotes around the term Christian when referring to those who hold to an affirming view. I call them Christian to refer to their confession of faith and not a person's actual redemptive state. Scare quotes would imply that I doubt the genuineness of their faith. But since we're talking about a massive group of people, and not a single individual, it's impossible to know the redemptive condition of every single person who has ever claimed to be an affirming Christian—unless you're God. Last time I checked, it was pretty clear that I'm not.

14. Two recent books that treat homosexuality as a secondary issue are Tim Otto, *Oriented to Faith: Transforming the Conflict over Gay Relations* (Eugene, OR: Cascade, 2014) and Ken Wilson, *A Letter to My Congregation: An Evangelical Pastor's Path to Embracing People Who Are Gay, Lesbian, and Transgender into the Company of Jesus* (Canton, MI: Read the Spirit Books, 2014).

15. Justin Lee, *Torn: Rescuing the Gospel from the Gays-Vs.-Christians Debate* (New York: Jericho, 2012), 169.

CHAPTER 10: ON THE SIDE OF THE ANGELS

1. There will always be rare exceptions to the following three, like my friends Lindsay and Sarah, who are celibate lesbian partners. They are in a committed, life-long relationship (they don't call it marriage), but remain celibate since they don't believe the Bible sanctions homosexual sex. You can read more about their perspective at www.aqueercalling.com.

2. Alan Chambers said recently that 99.9% didn't experience change, and this has been quoted by some people as proof that reparative therapy is a complete sham. However, Alan told me that what he meant is that 99.9% of people who sought change still battled same-sex attraction to some degree. As we'll see below, this does not mean that people never experienced any change, only that hardly anyone changes from totally gay to totally straight.

3. See for instance Jamie Scot, "Shock the Gay Away: Secrets of Early Gay Aversion Therapy Revealed," *Huffington Post:* http://www.huffingtonpost.com/jamie-scot/shock-the-gay-away-secrets-of-early-gay-aversion-therapy-revealed_b_3497435.html.

4. See Eve Tushnet, *Gay and Catholic: Accepting My Sexuality, Finding Community, Living My Faith* (Notre Dame: Ave Maria Press, 2014), 63–65; Tim Otto, *Oriented to Faith: Transforming the Conflict over Gay Relationships* (Eugene, OR: Cascade, 2014), 9.

5. *Ex-Gays? A Longitudinal Study of Religiously Mediated Change in Sexual Orientation* (Downers Grove, IL: IVP Academic, 2007).

6. According to the Jones-Yarhouse study, 15% of the people tested experience a significant degree of change, which included a reduction of same-sex attraction and an increase of opposite-sex attraction, and another 23% experienced a noticeable reduction of same-sex attraction (cited in Yarhouse, *Homosexuality*, 88).

7. I interviewed both Nathan and Sara and Brain and Monica on my blog; see Preston Sprinkle, "What Is a Mixed Orientation

Marriage?" *Theology in the Raw:* http://www.patheos.com/blogs/theologyintheraw/2014/11/what-is-a-mixed-orientation-marriage/#ixzz3KqXY9XN5.

8. Matthew Vines, *God and the Gay Christian: The Biblical Case in Support of Same-Sex Relationships* (New York: Convergent, 2014), 50.

9. Ibid., 19.

10. From the transcript of Matthew Vines' YouTube video: "The Gay Debate: The Bible and Homosexuality," *YouTube:* https://www.youtube.com/watch?v=ezQjNJUSraY.

11. Vines, *God and the Gay Christian*, 163.

12. Ibid., 166.

13. Dan Mattson, "No One's 'Doomed' to Celibacy," *Letters to Christopher:* http://letterstochristopher.wordpress.com/2013/08/17/no-ones-doomed-to-celibacy/.

14. Ron Belgau, "No One's 'Doomed' to Celibacy," *Spiritual Friendship:* http://spiritualfriendship.org/2013/08/18/no-one-is-doomed-to-celibacy/.

15. See Christopher Ash, *Marriage: Sex in the Service of God* (Vancouver: Regent College Publishing; Leicester, IVP, 2003).

16. Ron Belgau, "Christian Post Responses to Matthew Vines," *Spiritual Friendship:* http://spiritualfriendship.org/2012/10/03/christian-post-responses-to-matthew-vines/.

17. Preston Sprinkle, "Celibate Gay Christians," *Theology for Real Life:* http://facultyblog.eternitybiblecollege.com/2013/10/celibate-gay-christians/#.VJIpJyffc78.

18. *Oriented to Faith*, 23.

19. As stated by my friend Julie Rodgers.

20. Matt shared his story in my class on homosexuality and also through several Facebook conversations.

21. Barry Danylak, *Redeeming Singleness: How the Storyline of Scripture Affirms the Single Life* (Wheaton: Crossway, 2010), 19 (citing statistics by Barna).

22. The verb *kaleo* ("to call") is used in reference to salvation in Matt 9:13; 1 Corinthians 1:9; 7:18, 22; Galatians 1:6, 15; 1 Thessalonians 2:12; 1 Timothy 6:12; 2 Timothy 1:9. The adjective klesis occurs ten times in the New Testament. Nine of these refer to being called to salvation (Matt. 22:14; Rom. 1:1, 6, 7; 8:28; 1 Cor. 1:2, 24; Jude 1:1; Rev. 17:14) and one time it refers to Paul being called as an apostle (1 Corinthians 1:1).

23. Rom. 1:1; 1 Cor. 15:9; Gal. 1:16.

24. "A spiritual gift is not a talent or bestowment for one's personal benefit but a divine enablement given for the mutual benefit of strengthening the substance and mission of the church" (Danylak, *Redeeming Singleness*, 199).

25. In Danylak's words: "The charisma of singleness is a Spirit-enabled freedom to serve the King and the kingdom wholeheartedly, without undue distraction for the longings of sexual intimacy, marriage, and family" (*Redeeming Singleness*, 200).

26. *Redeeming Singleness*, 200.

27. Oddly enough, I got this quote from some notes that Lance scribbled in the margins of my copy of Otto's book *Oriented to Faith*, which I loaned him. I don't think I have ever quoted someone's marginal notes before.

28. My friend Matt Anderson used the phrase "on the side of the angels" in his blog "Can Christians Be Gay? An Inquiry," *Mere Orthodoxy*: http://mereorthodoxy.com/can-christians-gay-inquiry/.

AFTERWORD: THE CHALLENGE

1. This line is a riff from a Tweet by Lore Ferguson (@loreferguson) on 10/29/14. Lore was paraphrasing J. D. Greear, but I haven't been able to locate the exact quote from Greear.

APPENDIX: FIVE AFFIRMING INTERPRETATIONS OF ROMANS 1

1. See, e.g. John Boswell, *Christianity, Social Tolerance, and Homosexuality: Gay People in Western Europe from the Beginning of the Christian Era to the Fourteenth Century* (Chicago: University of Chicago Press, 1980).

2. See Richard Hays, "Relations Natural and Unnatural: A Response to J. Boswell's Exegesis of Rom. 1," *Journal of Religious Ethics* 14 (1986): 184–215 (200).

3. William Countryman, *Dirt, Greed, and Sex: Sexual Ethics in the New Testament and Their Implications for Today* (rev. ed.; Minneapolis: Fortress, 2007); Daniel Helminiak, *What the Bible Really Says about Homosexuality* (New Mexico: Alamo Square Press, 2000).

4. Rom. 6:19; 2 Cor. 12:21; Gal. 5:19; 1 Thess. 2:3; 4:7.

5. *Love Between Women: Early Christian Response to Female Homoeroticism* (Chicago: University of Chicago Press, 1996), 289.

6. *The New Testament and Homosexuality: Contextual Background for Contemporary Debate* (Philadelphia: Fortress Press, 1983).
7. *Love Between Women*, 302.
8. Dan O. Via, "The Bible, the Church, and Homosexuality," in *Homosexuality and the Bible: Two Views* (Minneapolis: Fortress, 2003), 1–39; William Schoedel, "Same-Sex Eros: Paul and the Greco-Roman Tradition," in *Homosexuality, Science, and the "Plain Sense" of Scripture*, ed. David L. Balch (Grand Rapids: Eerdmans, 2000), 43–72.